Polarized America

The Walras-Pareto Lectures, at the École des Hautes Études Commerciales, Université de Lausanne

Mathias Dewatripont and Jean Tirole, *The Prudential Regulation of Banks*, 1994

David M. Newbery, *Privatization, Restructuring, and Regulation of Network Utilities*, 2000

Stephen L. Parente and Edward C. Prescott, *Barriers to Riches*, 2000

Joseph P. Newhouse, *Pricing the Priceless: A Health Care Conundrum*, 2002

Nolan McCarty, Keith T. Poole, and Howard Rosenthal, *Polarized America: The Dance of Ideology and Unequal Riches*, 2006

Andrei Shleifer, *The Failure of Judges and the Rise of Regulators*, 2012

Nolan McCarty, Keith T. Poole, and Howard Rosenthal, *Polarized America: The Dance of Ideology and Unequal Riches, second edition*, 2016

Polarized America

The Dance of Ideology and Unequal Riches

second edition

Nolan McCarty, Keith T. Poole, and Howard Rosenthal

The MIT Press
Cambridge, Massachusetts
London, England

This book was set in Palatino by Toppan Best-set Premedia Limited. Printed and bound in the United States of America.

Library of Congress Cataloging-in-Publication Data

Names: McCarty, Nolan M., author. | Poole, Keith T., author. | Rosenthal, Howard, 1939- author.
Title: Polarized America : the dance of ideology and unequal riches / Nolan McCarty, Keith T. Poole, and Howard Rosenthal.
Description: second edition. | Cambridge, MA : MIT Press, 2016. | Series: Walras-Pareto lectures | Includes bibliographical references and index.
Identifiers: LCCN 2015038321 | ISBN 9780262528627 (pbk. : alk. paper)
Subjects: LCSH: Equality–United States. | Polarization (Social sciences)–United States. | Income distribution–United States. | United States–Politics and government–1989-
Classification: LCC HN90.S6 M37 2016 | DDC 305.50973–dc23 LC record available at http://lccn.loc.gov/2015038321

10   9   8   7   6   5   4   3   2   1

From NMc to Janis, Lachlan, and Delaney
From KP to Janice
From HR to Illia, Manu, and Gil

Contents

Preface to the Second Edition

Both political polarization and economic inequality have accelerated into record territory since the publication of *Polarized America* in 2006. Money has poured into campaign finance at unprecedented levels. Immigration has turned into a hot button issue; noncitizens continue to represent a substantial fraction of the adult population. Government policy, impeded by polarization and gridlock, has left income and estate taxes at relatively low levels. The intent of the Affordable Care Act to reduce health care inequality for the poor has been blunted by the refusal of most red states to expand their Medicaid programs.

In the first edition of this book, our data series stopped in 2002 or 2004. Here we document and interpret the trends of the past ten years using data that run through 2012 or 2014. All the figures, tables, and statistical analyses have been updated. (The sole exception is the technical appendix to chapter 3.) The text has been modified or added to reflect the latest evidence.

The most important changes are in chapter 5, which deals with campaign finance. In the first edition, we estimated the ideological position of a campaign contributor by simply taking the money-weighted average of the ideological positions of incumbents who received money from the contributor. Our colleague Adam Bonica has more recently elaborated and extended that method to jointly estimate the positions of contributors and candidates, including the losers of primary or general elections. He has joined us, as a full partner, in writing the current version of chapter 5.

In large part, America today is what it was a decade ago, only worse. The relationship of voting to county median income is stronger than ever. The economic position of the median *voter*, for years maintained by the arrival of noncitizens at the bottom of the income distribution and by the low participation of poor citizens, has eroded. On the other hand, by comparison to first edition results, the last two elections, those of 2012 and 2014, show a weakened connection of income to voter behavior and to congressional representation. These changes could conceivably be short term, with low-income Republican voting by poor whites and higher participation by nonwhites both being a response to an African American president. Or they could be long term, with politics being permanently distorted by the campaign contributions of the plutocracy.

Acknowledgments

Work on this book officially started almost a decade ago when Howard Rosenthal gave the Walras-Pareto Lectures, based in part on our joint work, at the University of Lausanne. He is very grateful for the warm reception from his hosts, particularly Alberto Holly, Damien Neven, and Elu von Thadden, and for Alberto's persistence in insisting that the book be finished.

The intellectual origins of the book are even older. Our central obligation is to the analytical approach to politics that developed in the 1960s and 1970s at four universities, Carnegie Mellon, the University of Rochester, Washington University in St. Louis, and the California Institute of Technology. Rosenthal owes much to the stimulus of his early colleagues at Carnegie Tech—Otto Davis, Melvin Hinich, James Laing, and Peter Ordeshook—and to his later collaborators, Thomas Romer, Thomas Palfrey, and Alberto Alesina.

Keith Poole was the most influenced by the Rochester school, as he was trained by the two central figures in the development of the analytical approach, William Riker and Richard McKelvey. McKelvey stopped at Carnegie Mellon on his way to Caltech. Most unfortunately, we have lost both Bill and Dick. We hope they are looking and reading from above.

Nolan McCarty began his research career as a graduate student in the Graduate School of Industrial Administration (GSIA) at Carnegie, his dissertation being supervised by Poole and Rosenthal. His interest in American politics was in no small part kindled by Larry Rothenberg, a visitor from Rochester. McCarty's early papers with Poole and with Rothenberg are the origins of the campaign contributions analysis in chapter 5, which also continues work that Poole and Rosenthal conducted with Romer.

Shortly after Poole and Rosenthal began their collaboration, Rosenthal spent a year as a Fairchild Scholar at Caltech. During this stay Poole and Rosenthal wrote their 1984 *Journal of Politics* article "The Polarization of American Politics," the protoplasm of this book.

Poole's first gig at Carnegie was as one of the two inaugural fellows of the postdoctoral program in political economy at GSIA. This program and some of the research reflected in this book found financial support thanks to the efforts of Allan Meltzer. Many of the other postdoctoral fellows, especially Zeev Maoz, David Austen-Smith, Randy Calvert, Fritz Schneider, Guido Tabellini, Peter Van Doren, Alesina, Jim Snyder, and Rothenberg, were an integral part of our research environment.

As our joint work progressed, we benefited from a lot of release time and research assistance provided by think tanks. McCarty and Rosenthal were both National Fellows at the Hoover Institution. All three of us have been fellows at Stanford University's Center for Advanced Study in the Behavioral Sciences (CASBS). If this book conveys a message successfully, the kudos go to Kathleen Much, the center's editor par excellence (a.k.a. the "book doctor"). Rosenthal was also a visiting scholar at the Russell Sage Foundation, where sitting next to Frank Bean would lead to valuable contributions to chapter 4. He and McCarty also participated in the RSF-sponsored Princeton working group on inequality. The other members of that working group—Larry Bartels, Paul Dimaggio, Leslie McCall, and Bruce Western—have provided lots of feedback on much of this manuscript. The RSF support is reflected in the work reported in chapter 6. The broader inequality project of the RSF also led to Rosenthal's collaboration with Christine Eibner, which is reflected in chapter 4.

Poole and Rosenthal have also benefited from multiple NSF grants from the Political Science program and the supercomputer program. Indeed, this project is very much technology-driven. The NSF supercomputer project gave us the capacity—today available in high-end PCs—for a dynamic analysis of the 11 million individual roll call votes that took place between 1789 and 1986. Without this support, chapter 2 of this book would not have been imaginable, and the rest of the book would not have followed.

Special thanks are owed to Robert Erikson and David Rhode, two superb editors of the *American Journal of Political Science* who encouraged this research at a time when the *APSR* had its head and somewhat more of its anatomy buried in the tar pits of traditional congressional scholarship.

Research on this project was both facilitated and hindered by the fact that the three of us accumulated eleven institutional affiliations, as visitors and regular faculty, during the gestation of this project: Brown University, CASBS, Carnegie Mellon, Columbia University, the Free University of Brussels, the University of Houston, the Hoover Institution, New York University, Princeton University, the University of Southern California, and the University of California–San Diego. Our colleagues at these institutions provided insight and advice on this project that more than compensated for the productivity lost in moving around so much.

Rosenthal would especially like to thank his colleagues from ECARES at the Free University of Brussels—Erik Berglof, Patrick Bolton, Mathias Dewatripont, and Gerard Roland—for the insights that came from eating lots of baguette sandwiches in the Canadian ambassador's residence. He also thanks his fellow MIT alums Sam Popkin and Susan Shirk. McCarty extends a special thanks to Doug Arnold, Larry Bartels, Chuck Cameron, Tom Gilligan, John Huber, Ira Katznelson, Keith Krehbiel, John Matsusaka, Bob Shapiro, and Greg Wawro, both for advice on this project and for support early in his career. He'd also like to thank his junior colleagues Josh Clinton, David Lewis, Adam Meirowitz, and Markus Prior for helping to keep his mental faculties perking during our daily Starbucks run. Poole would like to thank his former colleagues at the University of Houston—Ray Duch, Harrell Rogers, Bob Lineberry, Kent Tedin, Ernesto Calvo, Noah Kaplan, and Tim Nokken—who gave valuable feedback on portions of this book while he was the Kenneth L. Lay Professor of Political Science. Poole would also like to thank Gary Cox and Mat McCubbins for convincing him to live by the sea and the palm trees.

This book reflects a steady development of our research in the near-decade since the Walras-Pareto Lectures. The lectures covered the topics found in chapters 2 and 5, but both of these chapters reflect substantial additional research. Much of the material in chapter 2 and a wisp of chapter 3 appeared in our AEI monograph, *Income Redistribution and the Realignment of American Politics*. Chapter 2, however, reports substantial additional findings on the evaluation of competing hypotheses about polarization. Chapters 3, 4, and 5 reflect entirely unpublished material. Chapters 1 and 6 draw heavily on Rosenthal's essay in the Russell Sage Foundation volume *Social Inequality*, gracefully edited by Kathy Neckerman, and an essay McCarty wrote for a volume edited by Paul Pierson and Theda Skocpol.

Last but not least, we are very grateful to Jim Alt, who organized a presentation of the first draft at the Eric Mindich Encounter with Authors at Harvard in January 2005. We would like to thank all the participants for their very useful comments, with special thanks to Mo Fiorina, who got stuck in one more East Coast blizzard. We thank the participants, too numerous to cite individually, who participated in the many seminars we have presented on the topics in this book, as well as our editor, John Covell, and the four anonymous reviewers, who provided excellent feedback on earlier versions of the manuscript.

Work on the second edition was facilitated by McCarty's stay at the School of Social Science at the Institute for Advanced Study and Rosenthal's at the Center on Global Economic Governance at Columbia University. In the ten years since the first edition, the University of Georgia and New York University have been added to our institutional affiliations. Poole and Rosenthal thank their most recent colleagues for valuable interaction.

1   The Choreography of American Politics

We dance round in a ring and suppose,
But the Secret sits in the middle and knows.

—Robert Frost, "The Secret Sits"

Rarely these days does a news cycle pass without new stories of political dysfunction. Legislative stalemate, "fiscal cliffs," and failed "grand bargains" have become the norm in Washington. At the same time, we are routinely governed by "continuing resolutions" as appropriation bills go unpassed, while presidential nominees cool their heels for months waiting for Senate confirmation. In such a setting, it is little wonder that important long-term problems such as immigration, climate change, and entitlement reform go unaddressed.

Our political leaders themselves are often the most vocal in the lament that Washington does not work as well as it did two generations ago. Recently, the *New York Times* published an article featuring four departing members of Congress with a combined 120 years of experience. While the profiled lawmakers were two staunch liberals, Tom Harkin of Iowa and Henry Waxman of California, and two reliable conservatives, Saxby Chambliss and Jack Kinston, both of Georgia, all four decried how polarization and partisanship had destroyed Congress's ability to meet the country's needs.[1] Each fondly recalled a bygone era of bipartisan compromises that Congress now seems unable to deliver. Perhaps the most notable thing about the article is how unremarkable it is. Even congressional obituaries contain an obligatory paean to the way Washington once was. On the death of former senator Edward Brooke, the *New York Times* described him as a "skilled coalition builder at a time when Congress was less ideologically divided than today."[2]

Voters and citizens have begun to take note of Washington's failures. Incessant conflict and failures to deliver have begun to erode the public's confidence in the ability of our representative institutions to govern effectively. In February 2015, only one American in five approved of the way Congress was handling its job. Sadly, that level of support was double the level in late 2013, when a fifteen-day government shutdown drove congressional approval below 10 percent.[3]

As we argue throughout the book, the nostalgia of the retiring legislators and the obituary writers is not entirely misplaced. In the middle of the twentieth century, the Democrats and the Republicans did dance almost cheek to cheek in a courtship of the political middle. But over the past forty years, the parties have deserted the center of the dance floor in favor of the wings. What many public commentators miss, however, is that polarization was not a soloist but part of an ensemble, partnered with many other fundamental changes in the American society and economy. Most important, just as American politics became increasingly divisive, economic fortunes diverged. Middle- and high-income Americans have continued to benefit from the massive economic growth experienced since World War II. But material well-being for the lower-income classes has stagnated. For each story about successful people like Mark Zuckerberg and Sam Walton, there are contrasting stories about low-wage, no-benefit workers.

The Wal-Mart story underscores how unequally America's economic growth has been allocated. Wal-Mart has brought efficiency to low-cost retail distribution to the mass public, and the returns for Wal-Mart capital have been substantial. According to *Forbes*, Sam Walton's heirs have a net worth of $132 billion and are four of the ten richest Americans. More broadly, in 1970 a household in the 95th percentile of the income distribution had about five times the income of a household in the 25th percentile. By 2006 the disparity had increased to eight times.[4]

It is important to note that inequality rose in a period of increasing prosperity, with the added riches going much more to the haves than to the have-nots. Households with an annual income of over $100,000 (in year 2000 dollars) increased from under 3 percent in 1967 to over 12 percent in 2000. Even the middle of the income distribution was more prosperous. In year 2012 dollars, median income increased from $43,600 in 1967 to $56,895 in 1999. Inequality took a real (versus perceived) bite out of consumption only at the very bottom of the income distribution during this time period. From 1999 until 2013, the median income of American households was essentially flat. In 2013 the median income was $51,939. This unequal increase in riches is likely, as we explain in chapters 2, 3, and 4, to have contributed to polarization.

Economists, sociologists, and others have identified a number of factors behind the shift to greater inequality. Returns on education have increased, labor union coverage has declined, trade exposure has increased, corporate executives have benefited from sharp increases in compensation and stock options, and family structure has changed through high rates of divorce, late marriage, assortative mating, and two-income households. An additional factor helping tie our ensemble together is the massive wave of immigration, legal and illegal, since the 1960s.

The new immigrants are predominantly unskilled. They have contributed greatly to the economy by providing low-wage labor, especially in jobs that American citizens no longer find desirable. They also provide the domestic services that facilitate labor market participation by highly skilled people. On the other hand, immigrants have also increased inequality both directly, by occupying the lowest rungs of the economic ladder, and indirectly, through competing with citizens for low-wage jobs. Yet as noncitizens they lack the civic opportunities to secure the protections of the welfare state. Because these poor people cannot vote, there is less political support for policies that would lower inequality by redistribution.

In this book, we trace out how these major economic and social changes are related to the increased polarization of the U.S. party system. We characterize the relationships as a "dance"—that is, relationships with give-and-take and back-and-forth, where causality runs both ways. On the one hand, economic inequality feeds directly into political polarization. People at the top devote time and resources to supporting a political party strongly opposed to redistribution. People at the bottom would have an opposite response. Polarized parties, on the other hand, might generate policies that increase inequality through at least two channels. If the Republicans move sharply to the right, they can use their majority (as has been argued for the tax bills of the first administrations of Ronald Reagan and George W. Bush) to reduce redistribution. If they are not the majority, they can use the power of the minority in American politics to block changes to the status quo. In other words, polarization in the context of American political institutions now means that the political process cannot be used to redress inequality that may arise from nonpolitical changes in technology, lifestyle, and compensation practices.

Measuring Political Polarization

Before laying the groundwork for our argument that political polarization is related to economic inequality, we need to discuss how we conceptualize and measure political polarization. What do we mean by "polarization"? Briefly, polarization refers to a separation of politics into liberal and conservative camps. We all recognize that members of Congress can be thought of as occupying a position on a liberal-conservative spectrum. Elizabeth Warren is a liberal, Dianne Feinstein a more moderate Democrat, Claire McCaskill even more so; Susan Collins is a moderate Republican and Ted Cruz is a conservative Republican. The perception of conservativeness is commonly shared. There is a common perception because a politician's behavior is predictable. If we know that Susan Collins will fight a large tax cut, we can be fairly certain that all or almost all the Democrats will support her position.

There are two complementary facets to the polarization story. First, at the level of individual members of Congress, moderates are vanishing. Second, the two parties have pulled apart. *Conservative* and *liberal* have become almost perfect synonyms for *Republican* and *Democrat*.

Because we are social scientists and not journalists or politicians, we need to nail these shared impressions with precise operational definitions. When two of us (the two not in high school at the time) published "The Polarization of American Politics" in 1984, we measured polarization with interest group ratings. Each year, a number of interest groups publish ratings of members of Congress. Among the many groups are the United Auto Workers (UAW), the Americans for Democratic Action (ADA), the National Taxpayers Union (NTU), the American Conservative Union (ACU), and the League of Conservation Voters (LCV). Each interest group selects a fairly small number of roll call votes, typically twenty to forty, from the hundreds taken each year. A senator or representative who always votes to support the interest group's position is rewarded with a score of 100. Those always on the "wrong" side get a score of 0. Those who support the group half the time get a score of 50, and so on.

To see that moderates had vanished by 2003, consider the ratings of the ADA for that year. The possible ADA ratings rose in five-point steps from 0 to 100. Of the twenty-one possible ratings, nine were in the range of 30 through 70. Yet only eleven of the hundred senators (McCain, AZ; Campbell, CO; Lieberman, CT; Breaux, LA; Landrieu, LA; Collins, ME; Snowe, ME; Nelson, NE; Reid, NV; Edwards, NC; and Chafee, RI) fell in one of the nine middle categories. In contrast, ten Democrats got high marks of 95 or 100 and fourteen Republicans got 5 or 0. That is, more than twice as many senators (twenty-four) fell in the four very extreme categories as fell in the nine middle categories (eleven). By 2013 there was modest improvement, with fifteen senators falling in the middle categories.[5]

Our 1984 article documented two findings about the scores of the ADA and other interest groups. First, the interest groups gave out basically the same set of ratings or the mirror image of that set. If a general-purpose liberal interest group like the ADA gave a rating of 100 to a representative, the representative would nearly always get a very high rating from another liberal interest group, such as the LCV, even when the interest group focused on a single policy area, such as the environment. Similarly, a 100 ADA rating made a very low rating from a conservative group such as ACU or NTU a foregone conclusion. This agreement across interest groups meant that interest groups were evaluating members of Congress along a single, liberal-conservative dimension. Individual issue areas, such as race, no longer had a distinctive existence. Second, the interest groups were giving out fewer and fewer moderate ratings in the 40s, 50s, and 60s. Moderates were giving way to more extreme liberals and conservatives. Put simply, as polarization developed, the interest groups had little difficulty placing Ted Kennedy and Jesse Helms as ideological opposites, and they were finding fewer and fewer Jacob Javitses and Sam Nunns to put in the middle. The change we noted occurred in the last half of the 1970s; indeed, our data went only through 1980.

We summarized our findings by combining all the ratings to give a single liberal-conservative score to each member.[6] We then measured polarization in a variety of technical ways, which we explain more fully in chapter 2. One measure was simply how much the scores for members of the two political parties overlapped. If moderates were abundant in both parties, there would be substantial overlap, or low polarization. If the Democrats had only liberals and the Republicans only conservatives, there would be no overlap, or high polarization. We found that the overlap had shrunk.

Using only interest group ratings, however, has two limitations. First, interest groups select only a small number of roll call votes. The ADA, for example, uses just twenty per year. The more moderate scores we found for 2013 as against 2003 may not reflect true moderation but the ADA changing the goal posts set by the small number of roll calls the organization selects.

As each house of Congress conducts hundreds of roll calls each year, ADA's selections might be a biased sample of this richer universe.[7] Second, interest group ratings became common only in the second half of the twentieth century. We cannot do a long-run study of polarization, inequality, and immigration just on the basis of interest group ratings. So we developed NOMINATE, a quantitative procedure that would score politicians directly from their roll call voting records, using all of the recorded votes. To locate the politicians' positions, these techniques use information on who votes with whom and how often. For example, Max Baucus (D-MT), Elizabeth Warren (D-MA), and Ted Cruz (R-TX) served in the Senate together in 2013. If Baucus voted with both Warren and Cruz much more frequently than Warren and Cruz voted together, then these techniques would position Baucus as moderate, in between the two more extreme senators. Using this algorithm over millions of individual choices made by thousands of legislators on tens of thousands of roll calls allowed us to develop quite precise measures of each member's position on the liberal-conservative spectrum. In chapter 2, we go into much more detail about how these measures are calculated. We also discuss the various ways we measure polarization from these scales. In the remainder of this chapter, we measure polarization by the average difference between Democratic and Republican legislators on the DW-NOMINATE scale. The acronym DW-NOMINATE denotes Dynamic Weighted Nominal Three-step Estimation. The procedure is described in McCarty, Poole, and Rosenthal (1997). Hereafter in this book we abbreviate it to NOMINATE. NOMINATE is based on all recorded roll call votes in American history and permits us to look at long-run changes in polarization.

The Common Trajectory of Polarization and Inequality

Our measure of political polarization closely parallels measures of economic inequality and of immigration for much of the twentieth century. We show this correlation with three plots of time series.

One measure of income inequality is the Gini index of family income calculated by the U.S. Bureau of the Census. The Gini index shows how the entire distribution of income deviates from equality. When every family has the same income, the Gini index is zero. When one family has all the income, the Gini index is one. In figure 1.1, we show the Gini index and polarization in the post–World War II period.[8] Income inequality falls from 1947 through 1957 and then bounces up and down until 1969. After 1969, income inequality increases every two years, with a couple of slight interruptions. Polarization remains at a low level until 1977, and thereafter follows an unbroken upward trajectory.

We stress an important aspect of the timing of the reversal in inequality and polarization. In some circles, both these phenomena are viewed

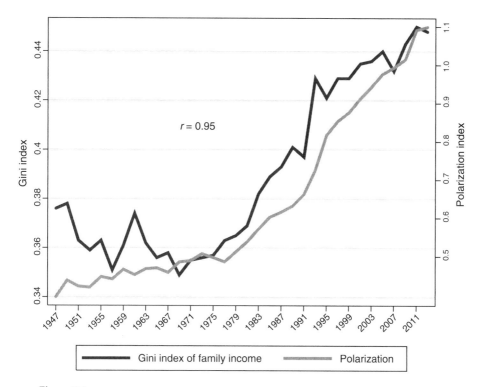

Figure 1.1
Income inequality and House polarization, 1947–2012. *Note:* Polarization is measured as the difference between the Democratic and Republican Party mean NOMINATE scores in the U.S. House. The Gini index and polarization measures correspond to the first year of each biennial congressional term. *Source:* Gini index data from the U.S. Census Bureau (2014).

as the consequence of Ronald Reagan's victory in the 1980 elections. Both reversals, however, clearly predate Reagan and Reaganomics. Reagan conservatism was a product sitting on a shelf in the political supermarket well before 1980. When customers switched brands on Reagan's election, it was arguably the result, rather than the cause, of a preference shift marked by rising inequality and party polarization.[9]

When we relate polarization to citizen political preferences in chapter 3, we can look only at the period from the 1950s to the present. Our principal data source for the chapter, the National Election Study, first polled in 1952. When we look at citizenship and campaign contributions in chapters 4 and 5, we are further restricted to starting in the 1970s. The Census Bureau began asking questions on both citizenship and voter turnout in 1972, and the Federal Election Commission kept campaign finance data starting in 1974. Despite these data limitations, we should emphasize that polarization underwent a long decline in the first two-thirds of the twentieth century. We cannot relate the decline in polarization to the Gini index or other Census Bureau measures of inequality, but we can see the larger picture thanks to an innovative study by Thomas Piketty and Emmanuel Saez (2003), which has been updated to 2012.[10]

Piketty and Saez used income tax returns to compute the percentage share of income going to the richest of the rich. In figure 1.2, we plot the share going to the top 1 percent of the income distribution. This longer series matches up nicely with our polarization measure over the entire twentieth century.[11]

The decline in polarization throughout the first seventy years of the twentieth century is echoed by much of the literature written toward the end of the decline or just after. During this period, Americans were seen as having grown closer together politically. In 1960, the sociologist Daniel Bell published *The End of Ideology: On the Exhaustion of Political Ideas in the Fifties*. A year later, the political scientist Robert Dahl pointed to a nation moving from oligarchy to pluralism (Dahl 1961). Similarly, the new "rational choice" school in political science emphasized Tweedledee/Tweedledum parties focused on the median voter (Downs 1957), members of Congress largely concerned with constituency service (Fiorina 1978), and universalism in pork-barrel politics (Weingast, Shepsle, and Johnsen 1981). What these authors were pointing to was echoed in analyses of roll call voting patterns in the House and Senate. Put simply, the fraction of moderates grew and

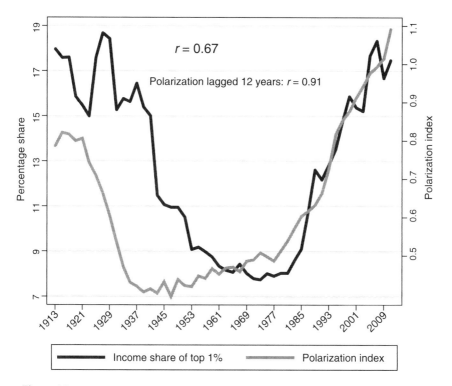

Figure 1.2
Top 1 percent income share and House polarization, 1913–2012. *Source:* Alvaredo et al. (2015).

the fraction of extreme liberals and extreme conservatives fell from 1900 to about 1975 (McCarty, Poole, and Rosenthal 1997; Poole and Rosenthal 1997). By the beginning of the twenty-first century, the extremes had come back.

The corresponding story for immigration is told by figure 1.3. Immigration is captured by looking at the percentage of the population that is foreign-born. (This is the only measure available before the Census Bureau began biennial collection of data on citizenship in 1972. From 1972 on, we will look, in chapter 4, at the percentage of the population represented by those who claim to be noncitizens.) For comparison, we have taken the polarization period back to 1880, the first census after the modern Democrat-Republican two-party system formed at the end of Reconstruction following the elections of 1876.

Until World War I, the percentage of foreign-born persons living in the United States was very high, hovering in the 13–15 percent range.

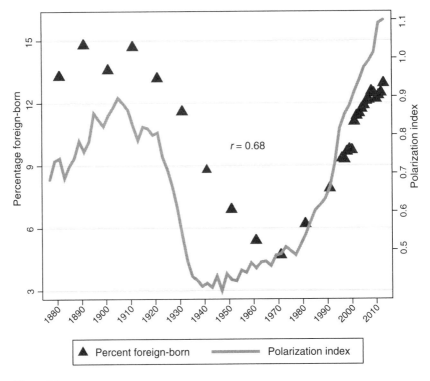

Figure 1.3
Percent foreign-born and House polarization, 1880–2012. *Note:* Each observation of foreign-born population corresponds to a U.S. decennial census or an annual observation from the Census Bureau's Current Population Survey.

With the curtailing of immigration, first by the war and then by the restrictive immigration acts of the 1920s, the percentage of foreign-born fell continuously until the 1970 census, just after immigration was liberalized by the 1965 reforms. The percentage of foreign-born thereafter increased sharply, exceeding 12 percent in the census of 2010. In 1970, a majority of the foreign-born had become naturalized citizens. By 2012, a substantial majority of the foreign-born was formed by noncitizens. Parallel to the track of immigration, polarization hovers at a high level until 1912 and then declines and stabilizes until 1977. The immigration series, like the income series, largely parallels our polarization measure.[12]

When we ourselves first saw figures 1.1, 1.2, and 1.3, we realized that major indicators of the politics, the economics, and the demographics of the United States had followed very similar trajectories over many decades. We decided to investigate the political and economic mechanisms linking these three trajectories. This book reports the outcome of our investigation.

A Focus on Income

Throughout the book, we look at income and other components of economic well-being as important variables in defining political ideology and voter preferences. We do not, however, discount the importance of such other factors as race and "moral values." We chose to emphasize economics partly because we seek to redress an imbalance in political science: income has been largely ignored, and race or ethnicity and class (as measured by occupation rather than income) receive more attention. We chose economics also because many public policies are defined largely in terms of income. Access to Medicaid under the Affordable Care Act is income based, as are, for those not qualifying for Medicaid, subsidies to buy coverage on the health care exchanges. The Affordable Care Act also increased the tax burden on high-income earners. With respect to taxation, the tax bills of 1993, 2001, and 2003 were among the most important domestic policy changes of the Clinton and George W. Bush administrations. Indeed, the overwhelming majority of congressional roll calls are over taxes, budgets, and economic policies, especially after the issue of de jure political rights for African Americans left the congressional agenda at the end of the 1960s. Most important, income is closely related to how people vote, to whether they participate in politics by either voting or making campaign contributions, and to whether they are eligible to vote as U.S. citizens.

Race is related to the current absence of redistribution in the United States (Alesina and Glaeser 2004) and to the absence of public spending in local communities (Alesina, Baqir, and Easterly 1999; Alesina and La Ferrara 2000, 2002). The claim that welfare expenditures in the United States are low because of race has been made by many authors, including Myrdal (1960), Quadagno (1994), and Gilens (1999). The basic claim of this literature is that the correlation with poverty lowers the willingness of voters to favor public spending for redistribution. But it is hard to see racism as hardening in the last quarter of the twentieth century when inequality was increasing. Racism and racial tension seem to have been rife when inequality and polarization were falling; we recall here the lynchings and race riots in the first half of the twentieth century and the urban riots of the 1960s. (Similarly, with regard to occupation or class, unionization has been declining since the 1950s.) We do explicitly consider race when treating ideological polarization in Congress and income polarization in the mass public, but it does, in historical perspective, appear appropriate to make income and economics our primary focus.

The Dance Card

In our second chapter we document the polarization of politicians. Most of our evidence concerns the two houses of Congress; we also include brief discussions of the presidency and a number of state legislatures. Polarization has increased for two reasons. First, Republicans in the North and South have moved sharply to the right. Second, moderate Democrats in the South have been replaced by Republicans. The remaining, largely northern, Democrats are somewhat more liberal than the Democratic Party of the 1960s.

The movements we observe tell us only about the relative positioning of politicians. We say that Republicans have moved to the right because newly elected Republicans have, on the whole, voted in a more conservative manner than the Republicans who remain in Congress. Northern Democrats, in contrast, don't look sharply different from the Democrats of old.

At the same time, however, how policy issues map onto liberal-conservative preferences may have changed. The Republicans have moved sharply away from redistributive policies that would reduce economic inequality. The Democrats, as analyzed by John Gerring (1998), have moved their platforms away from general welfare issues to issues based on social identity (race, gender, and sexual orientation) of individuals. For example, figure 1.4, drawn from Gerring, shows that the Democrats increased emphasis on general welfare through the 1960s but then deemphasized it in the 1970s. The turn in platforms thus matches the reversals in economic inequality and polarization. In parallel with Gerring's findings, we show that race as an issue has been absorbed into the main redistributive dimension of liberal-conservative politics. Taxes, minimum wages, and other traditional redistributive policy areas continue to be liberal-conservative issues; they have been joined by issues related to social identity.

What explains the changes in polarization and the accompanying rhetoric? The changes, we argue, have no simple institutional explana-

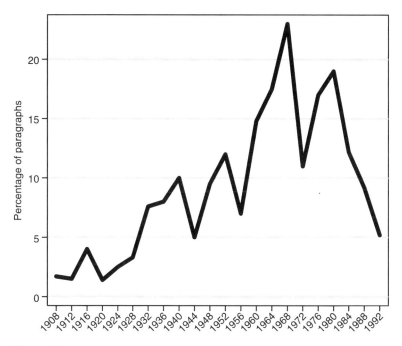

Figure 1.4
Attention to social welfare in the Democratic Party platform as indicated by percentage of paragraphs in platform devoted to social welfare policies, 1908–1992. *Source:* Author calculations based on Gerring (1998), figure 14. Used by permission.

tions, such as primaries, reapportionment after censuses, and gerry-mandering. We thus open the door for inequality and immigration to be the dance partners of polarization.

We proceed, in chapter 3, from politicians to the mass electorate. We use survey data to argue that both partisan identification (Democrat, Independent, or Republican) and presidential vote choice are increasingly linked to income. The relatively poor are increasingly Democratic and the rich Republican. We show that income is important in subgroups of the population that are frequently treated as homogeneous voting blocs based on racial conservatism or moral values. Indeed, the income effect is now stronger in the South than in the North and stronger among white "born-agains" or evangelicals than among other whites. We reconcile our findings with the observation that high per capita income states are now blue (Democratic) and low per capita income states are red (Republican). We also observe that real per capita income, equity ownership, and home ownership for average Americans have dramatically increased as polarization has increased. These increases, we argue, are largely consistent with the hypothesis that the main cause of polarization has been a move to the right by Republicans.

In chapter 4 we show that movement to the right, away from redistribution, has been facilitated by immigration. Over the past forty years, noncitizens have become not only a far larger share of the population but also disproportionately poorer. Because noncitizens are ineligible to vote, less pressure to redistribute comes from the bottom of the income distribution. For example, the Council on Medical Service of the American Medical Association reports that in 1999, immigrants represented about 10 percent of the overall population but 22 percent of those without health insurance.[13] The Migration Policy Institute reports that 43 percent of noncitizens had no health insurance in 2002.[14] In a UCLA Health Policy Research Center study, Wallace et al. (2012) estimated that 51 percent of undocumented immigrants were without health insurance in 2009. The association of voting rights with citizenship thus diminishes support for federal health insurance. Indeed, Congress in recent years has restricted access to Medicaid for immigrants.[15] President Obama's recent executive order limiting deportations for some immigrants explicitly denies health insurance benefits to this group.

In chapter 5 we argue that polarization in Congress is echoed by patterns of campaign contributions. Contributions are increasingly concentrated on ideological extremes. The strongest evidence that campaign contributions have had a polarizing effect comes not from money that is contributed to candidates but from money contributed to political parties and from unlimited contributions to 527 and 503(c) organizations. We show that contributors with extreme liberal and extreme conservative preferences gave a disproportionately large share of this money. This polarized giving has reinforced the ideological extremism of political parties and elected officials.

We use chapter 6 to study the impact of polarization on public policy. We show that changes in such policies as taxes and minimum wages have mirrored the historical trends we found in polarization. As polarization has increased in the past forty years, real minimum wages have fallen; top marginal tax rates and estate tax rates have been reduced. In addition, we discuss how, in the American system of checks and balances, polarization reduces the possibilities for policy changes that would reduce inequality.

Because legislation in the United States cannot be produced by a simple parliamentary majority, a minority of liberals or a minority of conservatives is frequently able to block policy change.[16] The veto powers of political minorities are particularly important when status quo policies are not indexed for inflation. Federal minimum wages are fixed in nominal dollars. A conservative minority has been able to block substantial increases in the minimum wage, even when the Democrats had unified control of Congress under Jimmy Carter and in the early years of both the Clinton and Obama administrations. Therefore, the real minimum wage has fallen. The economist David Lee (1999) has argued that failures to increase the minimum wage are responsible for about half the increase in the disparity between the wages of the median worker (50th percentile) and those of the worker in the 10th percentile of the wage distribution. Lee's work ties the absence of policy change to increased inequality. We, in turn, argue that polarization favors the policy status quo.

Immigration policy aptly illustrates how sticky status quos can affect inequality. Goldin (1994) documents how presidential vetoes withheld restrictive immigration legislation until the 1920s even though congressional majorities had favored it for several decades. During the period before World War I, polarization rose and income inequality was extremely high. The logjam was finally broken by the restrictive immigration laws of the 1920s. The new status quo also proved to be sticky. Reform came only after forty years, with legislation in 1965. As long as the status quo of the 1920s held, immigration, inequality, and polarization fell and remained at low levels. Subsequent to 1965, the new policy has prevailed despite an increase in popular support for restricting immigration.

Before we can analyze the policy consequences of polarization, we need to establish when and how polarization occurred. We now turn to that task.

2 Polarized Politicians

Pennsylvania Extreme 2000s

The fundamental transformation of American politics can be summed up by the recent history of Pennsylvania's two Senate seats. In 1991, Pennsylvania's three-term senator John Heinz was killed in a plane accident. A Republican, Heinz had compiled a moderate record as his party's leading supporter of environmental and labor union causes. In the special election that followed, the Republicans ran another relatively moderate candidate, Richard Thornburgh, a former governor and U.S. attorney general, against Harris Wofford, the interim senator. Wofford, who began his career as the first associate director of the Peace Corps, was significantly more liberal than Heinz. In a campaign orchestrated by James Carville, Wofford ran on a platform of fundamental reform of the health care system in the United States. Thornburgh was beaten easily, and health care became the "hot" issue going into the 1992 presidential elections.

The 1990 election produced another upset in Pennsylvania. Newcomer Rick Santorum defeated eight-term congressman Doug Walgren, a liberal Democrat from the Pittsburgh area. In the House, Santorum compiled a conservative voting record, placing himself well to the right of Heinz and the majority of Pennsylvania House Republicans. In spite of his conservatism, Santorum was able to move up to the Senate by defeating Wofford in 1994. So, in a period of three years, this Senate seat was held by one of the most moderate members of the U.S. Senate, then by one of the most liberal Democrats, then by one of the most conservative Republicans. The Heinz-Wofford-Santorum transition from moderation to the extremes has been repeated over and over again for the past thirty-five years. After the first edition of this book was published, Santorum lost his seat, in the Democratic landslide of 2006, to Robert Casey, who, despite his pro-life stands, has an overall voting record almost as liberal as that of Senate majority leader Harry Reid.

The transition from moderation to extremity continued in Pennsylvania's other Senate seat. The quintessential moderate, Arlen Specter, was replaced, in the 2010 election, by Pat Toomey, whose voting record is far more extreme than even Santorum's. This process of extremists replacing moderates has increasingly polarized American politics.

To show that the dynamics of the Pennsylvania Senate seats are far from atypical, in this chapter we provide systematic evidence from the historical roll call voting record to demonstrate that the members of Congress have in fact become highly polarized along a liberal-conservative ideological dimension. This surge reversed a long secular decline in polarization that started early in the twentieth century and resulted in low levels of polarization that persisted until the late 1960s. Many in the Republican Party led by President Eisenhower had accepted much of the New Deal welfare state, and both Democrats and Republicans were solidly behind the foreign policies of anticommunism and containment.[1] John F. Kennedy campaigned to increase defense spending and cut tax rates. This consensus led to record levels of bipartisanship and cooperation in Congress. But that consensus was short-lived. By the mid-1970s, the Vietnam War had signaled the end of bipartisan foreign policy, while sluggish economic performance had led to serious consideration of alternatives to Keynesianism and the welfare state.

Two of us, Poole and Rosenthal (1984), documented the dramatic turnaround of the 1970s in "The Polarization of American Politics." We found that beginning in the mid-1970s, American politics at the congressional level became much more divisive.[2] More Democrats staked out consistently liberal positions and more Republicans supported wholly conservative ones. The primary evidence in that study, which focused exclusively on the Senate, was the ratings issued by interest groups such as the Americans for Democratic Action (ADA), the League of Conservation Voters (LCV), and the U.S. Chamber of Commerce. In *Congress: A Political-Economic History of Roll Call Voting*, we (Poole and Rosenthal 1997) validated our earlier analysis, using evidence from roll call votes rather than from interest group ratings. We further found that the polarization surge had continued unabated through the 100th Congress (1987–1988). As we document below, polarization accelerated through 2014, the last year for which we analyze data. Our data also confirm the more casual observations of polarization in the conflict over aid to the Contras in Nicaragua, the confirmation hearings and votes after the nominations of Robert Bork and Clarence Thomas to the Supreme Court, the rhetoric of Newt Gingrich's "Contract with America," the budget showdown between Speaker Gingrich and President Clinton in 1995, the impeachment process in 1998–1999, the partisan rancor over the Iraq War, and the nearly solid Republican opposition to the stimulus package (part of the American Recovery and Reinvestment Act) and the Affordable Care Act in 2009 and to the Dodd-Frank financial regulation bill in 2010.

Measuring Ideology and Polarization: A Primer

How do we know that polarization has occurred? Every aficionado of American political history would know that Ted Kennedy (D-MA) and Barbara Boxer (D-CA) were liberals, Sam Nunn (D-GA) and Jacob Javits (R-NY) were moderates, and Tom DeLay (R-TX) and Jesse Helms (R-NC) were conservatives. But how does one demonstrate that Jesse Helms was more conservative than Rick Santorum? And how do we know that Santorum is more conservative than Heinz was, as the two men obviously never served in the Senate together? How do we locate Boxer relative to someone even more remote, say, William Jennings Bryan, who denounced Republicans for "crucifying mankind on a cross of gold"?

Most political scientists traditionally have measured liberal-conservative positions by using the interest group ratings we used to announce the "Polarization of American Politics." Groups construct ratings by choosing the roll call votes that are important to their legislative agendas and determining whether a yea or nay vote indicates support for the group's goals. Indices are then constructed from the proportion of votes a member casts in favor of the group. These indices are highly similar across groups (Poole and Rosenthal 1997, chap. 8). The similarity reflects the fact that the interest groups themselves are polarized along the same liberal-conservative lines. Almost any two liberal groups, such as the ADA or LCV, have ratings that are highly correlated, and their ratings are mirror images of those of any conservative group such as the Chamber of Commerce.

One important limitation of these interest group scores is that they are designed primarily to assess differences among the legislators in a single Congress. Therefore, they do not provide any direct information about the differences between legislators serving at different times, or even the behavior of the same legislator over the course of her career. To illustrate this problem, consider the following example. In 1998, both Helms and Santorum received perfect conservative scores of 0 from the ADA. Paul Wellstone (D-MN) received a perfect liberal score of 100. Kennedy, clocking in at 95, did almost as well. In 1980, the ADA rated Helms at 11 and Heinz at a moderate score of 50. So if we believe the annual ADA measures capture member ideology, we could use the "glue" provided by Helms to conclude that Santorum was more conservative than Heinz. This use of overlapping cohorts of legislators is also the basis of the methods developed by Poole (1998, 2005) and Groseclose, Levitt, and Snyder (1999).

But there are additional problems with using interest group ratings. First, group ratings are based on small, selective samples of roll calls that tend in particular to clump lots of legislators at the extreme scores of 0 or 100. This clumping tends to obscure real differences among legislators, as we saw with the 0 ADA ratings of Helms and Santorum in 1998. (In 1997, Helms was again a 0, but Santorum was a 15, more in line with "inside the Beltway common knowledge.") In fact, there is evidence that groups may choose votes strategically in order to divide the legislative world into friends and foes (Fowler 1982; Snyder 1992). This tactic creates an artificially large number of 0s and 100s. Second, because the ratings go from 0 to 100 every year, the range of positions is invariant across time. Not surprisingly, Barry Goldwater (R-AZ) had a 0 rating in 1980. Was he as conservative as Helms and Santorum were in 1998?[3]

Given these problems, we can get much better measures of ideology from *scaling* methods that use all the roll call votes. These methods all assume that legislators make their choices in accordance with the spatial model of voting. In a spatial model, each legislator is assumed to have a position on the liberal-conservative dimension. This position is termed the ideal point. The ideal point is directly analogous to a rating if the interest group is more liberal or conservative than all of the legislators (Poole and Daniels 1985; Poole and Rosenthal 1997).[4]

Just as the 435 representatives and 100 senators have ideal points, we allow each roll call to be represented by Yea and Nay positions on the liberal-conservative scale. The underlying assumption of the spatial model is that each legislator votes Yea or Nay depending on which outcome location is closer to his or her ideal point. Of course, the legislator may make "mistakes" and depart from what would usually be expected, as a result of pressures from campaign contributors, constituents, convictions, or just plain randomness. Using our assumptions of spatial voting with error, we can estimate the ideal points of the members of Congress directly from the hundreds or thousands of roll call choices made by each legislator.

To understand better how the spatial positions of legislators can be recovered from roll call votes, let's consider the following three-senator example. Suppose we observed only the following roll call voting patterns from Senators Warren (D-MA), Collins (R-ME), and Cruz (R-TX):

Roll call	Warren	Collins	Cruz
1	Yea	Nay	Nay
2	Yea	Yea	Nay
3	Nay	Yea	Yea
4	Nay	Nay	Yea
5	Yea	Yea	Yea
6	Nay	Nay	Nay

All of these votes can be explained by a simple model in which all senators are assigned an "ideal point" on a left-right scale and every roll call is given a "cutpoint" that divides the senators who vote Yea from those who vote Nay. For example, if we assign ideal points ordered Warren < Collins < Cruz, we can perfectly explain the first vote with a cutpoint between Warren and Collins, and the second vote by a cutpoint between Collins and Cruz. In fact, all six votes can be explained in this way. Note that a scale with Cruz < Collins < Warren works just as well. But a single cutpoint cannot explain votes 1 through 4 if the ideal points are ordered Collins < Warren < Cruz, Collins < Cruz < Warren, Cruz < Warren < Collins, or Warren < Cruz < Collins. Therefore none of these orderings is consistent with a one-dimensional spatial model.

As two orderings of ideal points work equally well, which one should we choose? Given that Warren espouses liberal (left-wing) views and Cruz is known for his conservative (rightist) ones, Warren < Collins < Cruz seems like a logical choice. The real world, however, is rarely so well behaved as to generate the nice patterns of the first six votes. What if we observed that Cruz and Warren occasionally vote together against Collins, as in votes 7 and 8 below? Such votes cannot be explained by the ordering of Warren < Collins < Cruz:

Roll call	Warren	Collins	Cruz
7	Yea	Nay	Yea
8	Nay	Yea	Nay

If few votes like 7 and 8 are infrequent relative to votes 1 through 6, it's reasonable to conclude that they were generated by more or less random factors outside the model. If there are many more votes like 1 through 6 than there are deviant votes, any of the common scaling procedures will still generate the ordinal ranking Warren < Collins < Cruz.[5] In our scaling procedure, NOMINATE, the frequency of the deviant votes provides additional information about the nominal values of the ideal points. For example, if there are few votes pitting Cruz and Warren against Collins, we place Cruz and Warren far apart. When Cruz and Warren are far apart, their ideological (spatial) differences are strong, so random events will rarely lead them to vote together. Alternatively, if the Cruz-Warren coalition occurred more frequently, we would place them closer together, consistent with the idea that small random events can lead to such a pattern.

It is easy to measure the success of the one-dimensional spatial model. In our example, the "classification success" is simply the proportion of explained votes (that is, types 1 through 6) of the total number of votes. Notice, however, that classification success will be inflated if there are a lot of unanimous votes, as in 5 and 6, because any ranking of the senators can explain them. Therefore, it is often useful to assess the spatial model against a null model in which all senators are assumed to vote with the majority position. A sensible measure of the improvement of the spatial model over this "majority" model is *proportional reduction in error* (PRE). The PRE is defined as

$$\frac{\text{Majority errors} - \text{Spatial errors}}{\text{Majority errors}}.$$

Going back to our three-senator example, we discard the two unanimous votes 5 and 6. There is a single majority error on votes 1 through 4 and 7 through 8 since all six votes have 2–1 majorities. There is one spatial error on votes 7 and 8. The PRE for each of votes 1 through 4 is one since there are no spatial errors. The PRE for votes 7 and 8 is zero since there are as many majority errors as spatial errors. The average PRE is 2/3 since overall there are only two spatial errors as against six majority errors ($(6 - 2)/6 = 2/3$).

Sometimes there are so many votes like 7 and 8 that it becomes unreasonable to maintain that they are simply random. An alternative is to assume that a Cruz-Warren coalition forms because there is some other policy dimension on which they are closer together than they are to Collins. We can accommodate such behavior by estimating ideal points on a second dimension. In this example, a second dimension in which Cruz and Warren share a position distinct from Collins's will explain votes 7 and 8. Both dimensions combined will explain all of the votes. Obviously, in a richer example with a hundred rather than three senators, two dimensions will not explain all the votes, but the second dimension will typically add explanatory power.[6] In our discussions below, we will evaluate the importance of higher dimensions by measuring their incremental ability to predict roll call votes correctly.

A cottage industry of specific techniques for recovering ideal points has emerged in recent years. These variations differ not so much in spirit as in their technical assumptions.[7] In fact, the patterns of polarization that we discuss below are robust as to how legislator positions are measured. Nevertheless, we rely on NOMINATE (Poole 2005) because it is the only methodology that allows both comparison of the dispersion of positions across time and intertemporal change in the positions of individual legislators. That is, NOMINATE solves the problem of the comparability of Santorum and Goldwater. It also captures some major changes in position, such as the conservative-to-liberal journey of Senator Wayne Morse of Oregon.

To capture shifts like Morse's, the NOMINATE scores allow a linear change in position throughout a legislator's career. One can change from liberal to conservative—but not back again. Although restrictive, this assumption is not particularly important. As a matter of fact, for the period covered by this book, there are only very small changes in legislator positions (Poole and Rosenthal 1997, 73–74). Large changes occur only for those legislators who switch parties (McCarty, Poole, and Rosenthal 2001). To account for these jumps, we estimate two separate ideological paths for these "party-switchers."

To match the common-language designation of liberals with the left and conservatives with the right, we adjust the NOMINATE scores so that each member's *average* score lies between −1 and +1, with −1 being the most liberal position and +1 the most conservative. For the example that introduced this chapter, Heinz ended his career at +0.03, Wofford ended at a liberal −0.35, and his replacement, Santorum, ended at a conservative +0.42.

As the comparison of Wofford and Santorum shows, party, at least as much as constituency, has a strong influence on ideal points (McCarty, Poole, and Rosenthal 2001). The biggest changes are indeed associated with legislators who change party during their careers. Morse, for example, moved from −0.22 to −1.01. Each legislator adjusts his position, to some degree, as a function of party affiliation. Heinz may well have had a more liberal voting record had he been a Democrat. On the other hand, party is a much coarser measure than a NOMINATE score. There is always substantial diversity of NOMINATE positions within each party and, at times, ideological overlap between the parties.

Although we computed the NOMINATE scores using all the roll calls in the history of the U.S. Congress, in this chapter we start all time series with the 46th Congress, which was elected in 1878. This was the first congress elected after the presidential election of 1876, which ended Reconstruction and marked the restoration of a competitive, national two-party system. A second reason for beginning our analysis here is that the election of 1876 initiated the most bipolar period after the Civil War in American political history. As documented by C. Vann Woodward in *Reunion and Reaction* (1951), Samuel Tilden undoubtedly won the 1876 presidential election, but a coalition of Republicans and southern Democrats in Congress threw the election to Rutherford B. Hayes by awarding Hayes *all* of the contested electoral votes. The southerners were rewarded with the withdrawal of federal troops from the secessionist states. This event essentially ended the reign of the pro–civil rights forces in the Republican Party. The post-Reconstruction Democrat-Republican party system emerged. The ensuing congresses near the end of the nineteenth century were the most polarized since the end of the Civil War. They provide us with a benchmark to assess polarization in our own times. During most of the period treated in this book, a single liberal-conservative dimension does an excellent job of accounting for how members vote, be it on minimum wages, gun control, or the shopping list of issues represented by the Contract with America or by a presidential State of the Union address. One way of directly measuring the predictive power of the liberal-conservative dimension is to compute the percentage of votes on which a legislator actually votes for the roll call alternative that is closest to her on the dimension. This "classification" success exceeds 84 percent across all congresses since 1877.

One issue area, however, clearly did not fit the standard liberal-conservative pattern—civil rights for African Americans. For much of the post–World War II era, the voting coalitions on racial issues were distinct from those on other issues. This issue is represented in our spatial model by a second dimension, with southern Democrats at one end and eastern liberal Republicans, such as Jacob Javits of New York, at the other. We find that it is important to allow for these two political dimensions in the middle of the twentieth century. Consequently, we present results for the two-dimensional NOMINATE estimations. Just as one-dimensional scores run from −1 to +1, in two dimensions a legislator's career average scores must lie in a circle with a radius of 1.

The Decline and Surge of Polarization

From our estimates of legislator preferences and the corresponding measurement of polarization, we can identify five distinct yet complementary trends that add up to a fundamental transformation of American politics.

1. Almost all political conflict in Congress is expressed in the liberal-conservative terms of the first dimension. Consequently, most roll call votes can be interpreted as splits on the basic liberal-conservative dimension. Other dimensions, such as a civil rights dimension, have largely vanished, as the coalitions on those issues have increasingly begun to match those of the liberal-conservative dimension.

2. The dispersion of positions of members on the liberal-conservative dimension has increased. Compared to the 1960s, extreme conservative as well as extreme liberal positions are more likely to be represented in Congress.

3. The ideological composition of the Democratic Party has become more homogeneous. Intraparty regional differences, between northern and southern Democrats, have abated. As extreme conservatives have entered the Republican congressional party over the past forty years, moderates have exited, holding the homogeneity of the party almost constant.

4. The positions of the average Democrat and average Republican member of Congress have become more widely separated. That is, the difference in the party means has increased over time.

5. There is less overlap in the positions of the parties. There are no longer any liberal Republicans or conservative Democrats in Congress. The moderates are vanishing.

As we have indicated, the surge in polarization began in the 1970s. The decline in polarization that took place in the second quarter of the twentieth century just reverses the pattern for the surge: a decline in classification, less dispersion, more intraparty heterogeneity, a decrease in difference in party means, more overlap of positions. We now turn to documenting these points.

Roll call votes can be interpreted as splits on a basic liberal-conservative dimension. Other dimensions have vanished.

Figure 2.1 shows that in both chambers, the two-dimensional spatial model accounts for most individual voting decisions throughout this

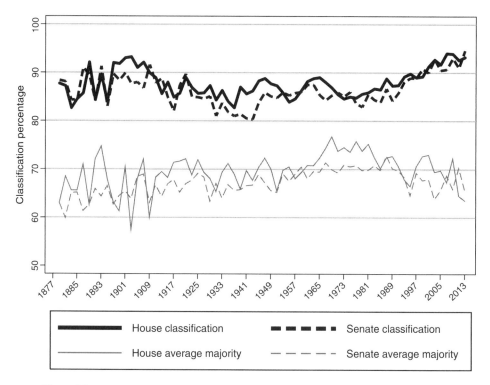

Figure 2.1
Classification of roll call votes, 1879–2014. *Source:* Computed from the two-dimensional NOMINATE model. Only roll calls with at least 2.5 percent in the minority are included.

period. Classifications peaked at the turn of the twentieth century, exceeding 90 percent in the House and reaching nearly 90 percent in the Senate. In both chambers, classifications in the twenty-first century once again exceed 90 percent. Over the past decade, classification is higher than at any time since Reconstruction.

The very high rates of classification success we observe do not happen simply because most votes in Congress are lopsided votes where members say "Hurrah." On the contrary, as the figure indicates, Congress has had mostly divisive votes, with average winning majorities between 60 and 70 percent. Importantly, the size of winning margins has declined since the 1980s just as the classification of the two-dimensional model has improved.

The high rate of classification success also does not result from an important second dimension. An important second dimension was present in both chambers at midcentury, as shown in figure 2.2. From

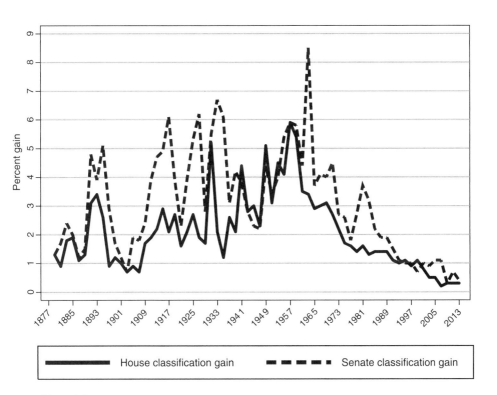

Figure 2.2
Classification gain of second dimension, 1879–2014. *Source:* Computed from the two-dimensional NOMINATE model.

the late 1960s onward, however, the second dimension has abruptly declined in importance. From Bill Clinton's presidency onward, it improves classification by only about 1 percent.[8] Clearly, most roll call votes in the twenty-first century are splits on a single dimension. This dimension corresponds to the popular conception of liberals versus conservatives.

The positions of the average Democratic and average Republican member of Congress have become more widely separated.

Figures 2.3 and 2.4 show the means of the political parties on the first dimension for the post-Reconstruction period for the House and Senate, respectively.

In both chambers, the Republicans became more moderate until the 1960s.[9] The Republican mean bottomed out in the 1960s and then moved in a sharply conservative direction in the 1970s. The pattern for

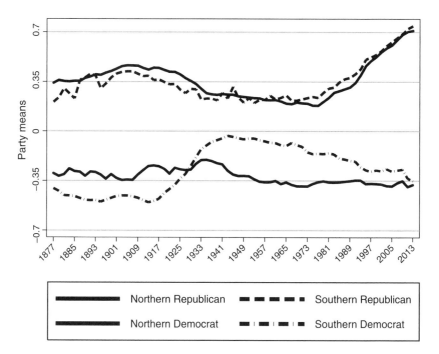

Figure 2.3
Party means in the U.S. House by region, 1879–2014. *Note:* The range of NOMINATE scores is approximately −1.0 to +1.0. The South is defined as the eleven states of the Confederacy plus Kentucky and Oklahoma. *Source:* Computed from NOMINATE scores, available at PooleandRosenthal.com.

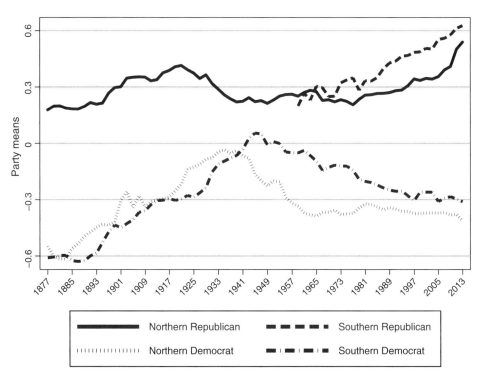

Figure 2.4
Party means in the U.S. Senate by region, 1879–2014. *Note:* The range of NOMINATE scores is approximately –1.0 to +1.0. The South is defined as the eleven states of the Confederacy plus Kentucky and Oklahoma. Because of small numbers, the southern Republican mean is computed only after 1956. *Source:* Computed from NOMINATE scores, available at PooleandRosenthal.com.

the Democrats is almost exactly the opposite. Consequently, the two party means moved closer together during the twentieth century until the 1970s and then moved apart.

On the second dimension, this pattern reverses. As figure 2.2 shows, the second dimension's importance to classification peaks during the period when the civil rights issue was active, from the 1930s through the 1960s. In contrast to the story for the first dimension, the Democratic Party separated on the second dimension during this period because southern Democrats had a conservative position on race. But the lack of polarization on the first dimension in the civil rights period is not simply the consequence of the relevance of a second dimension. First-dimension polarization started its decline well before the civil rights issue arose. Moreover, as we explain later in the chapter, the decline and surge of polarization are found in the North even when we completely ignore the roll call votes of southerners.

The dispersion of positions of members on the first dimension has increased; the ideological composition of the Democratic Party has become more homogeneous. Intraparty regional differences between northern and southern Democrats have abated. As extreme conservatives have entered the Republican congressional party over the past forty years, moderates have exited, holding the homogeneity of the party almost constant.

Since the mid-1970s, the dispersion of members of Congress has systematically increased in both chambers. The pattern is disclosed by figures 2.5 and 2.6. Dispersion is shown by the standard deviation for all members on the first dimension. The increasing standard deviation shows that members are tending to appear more at either the

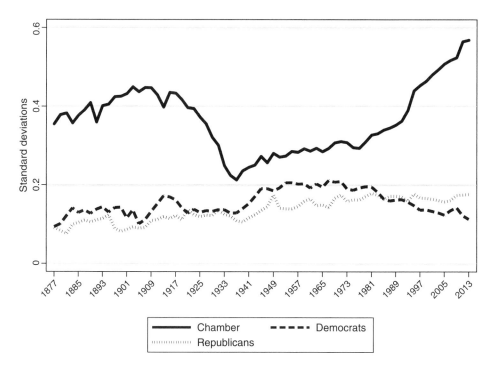

Figure 2.5
Standard deviations of House NOMINATE positions, 1879–2014. *Note:* The range of NOMINATE scores is approximately −1.0 to +1.0. *Source:* Computed from NOMINATE scores, available at PooleandRosenthal.com.

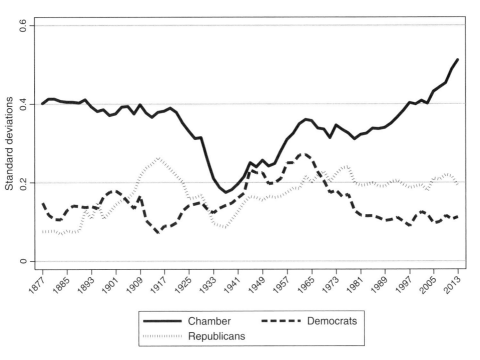

Figure 2.6
Standard deviations of Senate NOMINATE positions, 1879–2014. *Note:* The range of
NOMINATE scores is approximately −1.0 to +1.0. *Source:* Computed from NOMINATE
scores, available at PooleandRosenthal.com.

conservative end or the liberal end of the dimension. Moderates are
vanishing. Polarization along the dimension has reached the levels
present during the intense conflicts over regulatory policy and monetary policy at the end of the nineteenth century.

The figures also show that, at the same time, the Democratic Party
is becoming more homogeneous. The standard deviation for the
Democrats has fallen in the past thirty years as the party's moderate
southern wing has almost vanished. In contrast, the standard deviation
for the Republicans has been almost constant in both houses. Its
moderates have also vanished, but they have been replaced by extreme
conservatives. The effect of the two changes has been to hold homogeneity constant as the party has shifted to the right. What has happened
within both parties is unlikely to reflect increased party discipline
within Congress but a more fundamental change in the ideology

of who is elected to Congress. The upshot is that the parties now represent polarized blocs; voting coalitions that cut across the blocs are infrequent.

The results we have presented for standard deviations on the first dimension are validated by an approach that considers both dimensions simultaneously. For each pair of members of a chamber, one can compute the two-dimensional distance between the pair. For each party, we average these distances for all pairs in the party to get within-party distances. We also average the distances for all pairs of one Republican and one Democrat to get between-party distances. Like the overall standard deviation, between-party distances have increased since the 1970s (see figures 2.7 and 2.8). The within-party distances fell for the Democrats, although not as precipitously as the standard deviations. These results demonstrate that the pattern of a surge and decline in polarization persists, even when the civil rights dimension is explicitly taken into account.

The moderates are vanishing from Congress.

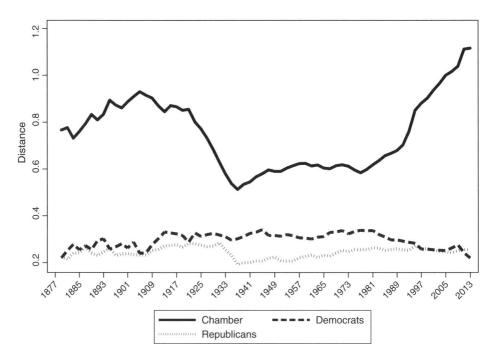

Figure 2.7
Average two-dimensional distances in the House, 1879–2014.

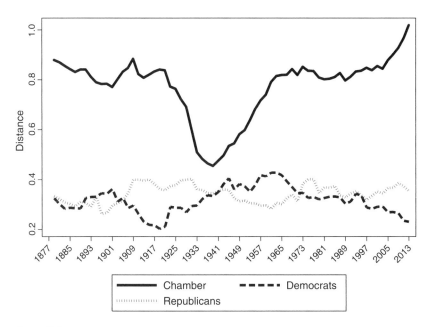

Figure 2.8
Average two-dimensional distances in the Senate, 1879–2014.

In fact, the disappearance of moderates is synonymous with polarization. We quantify the disappearance by calculating the percentage of the total membership that have ideal points closer to the mean of the other party than to the mean of their own party. Figure 2.9 discloses a clean pattern for the House: almost no overlap until the late 1950s, a sharp increase in the 1960s, and a drop back to no overlap by the end of the 1990s.[10] The Senate story is the same, with an important exception. Overlap there also increased in the 1920s and 1930s. Progressive Republican senators from farm belt states frequently voted with the Democrats. There is a much smaller uptick in the House because the farm belt states have relatively few members of the House. The farm belt story also relates to House-Senate differences in the earlier figures in this chapter.

Another way of looking at vanishing moderates is to note how many Democrats have ideal points to the right of the leftmost Republican. Over the past twenty years, only one senator, Zell Miller of Georgia, fell into this category, and he left Congress in 2005. As the histogram in figure 2.10 shows, the two parties in the 113th House (2013–2014) are completely separated.[11]

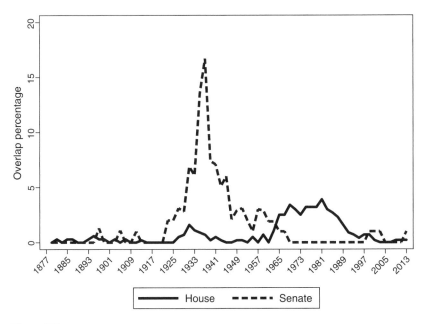

Figure 2.9
Percent party overlap in Congress, 1879–2014.

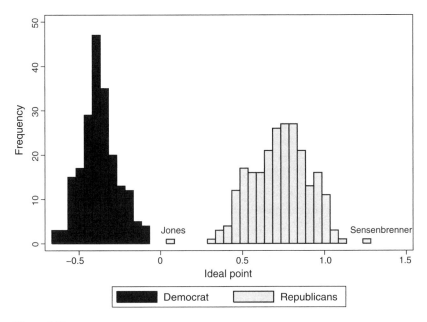

Figure 2.10
Distribution of ideal points in the 113th House (2013–2014).

We have documented the surge and decline in polarization. What brought this pattern about? In the remainder of this chapter, we examine a number of distinct hypotheses about what caused the surge in polarization. In the next section, we explore the extent to which the link between constituency interests and congressional voting has changed during the surge. It is important, given our arguments, that the congruence between constituency income and congressional voting has increased substantially. But the increased link to constituency interest is only part of the story. The surge in polarization cannot be explained solely by constituency characteristics. We find that for a given constituency, the difference between Democratic and Republican representatives has grown. We then consider many other hypotheses that others have proffered to explain polarization, including those related to the southern realignment, enhanced capacities for party leadership, congressional apportionment, and primary elections. These alternative explanations are never lead dancers and rarely get picked for the chorus line.

Polarization and Representation

Political scientists and economists have often tackled the question of representation and accountability by examining how well characteristics of a given electoral constituency explain the behavior of their representatives. Essentially adopting the "delegate" position, in Burke's famous dichotomy, these scholars have defined good representation as what occurs when a representative's behavior is strongly associated with measures of her constituency's preferences and interests.[12]

Studies of roll call voting in the House have shown that the behavior of representatives deviates in large and systematic ways from the preferences of the average or median constituent. This finding persists even when the mismeasurement of constituency interests is not at issue.

For example, senators from the same state do not vote identically. Our comparison of Bob Casey and Pat Toomey illustrated the obvious: senators from the same state but different parties pursue very different policy goals. The difference is picked up in their polarized NOMINATE scores. If the two senators are from the same party, they are, of course, more similar. Even here, however, there are differences. These differences occur even when the senators have similar NOMINATE scores, as in the case of John Heinz and Arlen Specter, and not just when they differ sharply, as in the case of Specter and Rick Santorum. The ideological model in fact outperforms a model that scores a prediction failure only when two senators are from the same state and party but vote differently (Poole and Rosenthal 1997). In addition, Poole and Rosenthal developed a version of NOMINATE whereby they could study those aspects of roll call voting that were not explained by ideological position. How the two senators from the same state deviated from ideology was correlated, but the correlations were not particularly strong, even if the two senators were from the same party.

Congressional districts, being single-member, do not allow the same natural experiment that is possible for the Senate. It is possible, however, to compare the voting behavior of a member with that of her successor. Poole and Romer (1993) found that same-party replacements of House members had NOMINATE scores that could be very different from those of their predecessors. True, a relatively liberal Democrat was likely to be replaced by another liberal Democrat. Nonetheless, the within-district variation of same-party replacements was about half the total variation of positions in the party. A representative has a great deal of latitude in building a coalition of supporters and in expressing his or her personal ideology.

Because constituency interest fails to explain all, or even very much, of the variation in roll call voting behavior, scholars have focused on the importance of party and ideology. These factors play little role in a world of Burkean delegates or Downsian competition, but empirical studies have routinely verified their importance as determinants of legislative behavior. While scholars generally agree that no one factor can explain legislative behavior, there is an ongoing debate about the relative importance of ideology, constituency, and party as considerations in casting roll call votes.

Our analysis reveals several important clues about polarization. The first and most important is that the contributions of party, constituency, and ideology in explaining roll call behavior have changed dramatically over the past thirty years. Not surprisingly, given our results about polarization, political party is a much more consequential factor in explaining NOMINATE scores of representatives in 2014 than it was in the 1970s. As we will see, this is not because constituency factors are less important. In fact, if we measure constituency representation as the multiple correlation between constituency interests and a representative's behavior, representation has improved substantially. In other words, a set of simple constituency demographics better explains NOMINATE scores now than it did forty years ago.

At first blush, the simultaneous increase in the importance of party and constituency seems counterintuitive. But it is entirely consistent with polarization. Because most voters in congressional elections are poorly informed about the specifics of the respective member's voting record, they often vote on the basis of partisan cues and reputations. As the parties polarized, these cues became much more informative, leading to the election of members with records more reflective of their districts.

The personal ideologies of members of Congress are not waning as a component of roll call voting. It is often hard to measure the ideological component directly or to distinguish it from mismeasured constituency characteristics.[13] Therefore, we use the racial, ethnic, and gender identity of the representative as a proxy. We find that, even controlling for party and the ethnic and racial composition of the district, these factors are significant predictors of roll call voting behavior. This finding suggests that accounts of polarization that focus primarily on increased partisan homogeneity (Bishop 2004) are incomplete. If the voters in a congressional district were completely homogeneous in their preferences, switching the representative from male to female or from black to white shouldn't make a difference. It does.

Constituency, Party, and Ideology

To provide evidence for our claims, we estimate econometric models of the following form:

$\text{NOMINATE}_i = \alpha + \beta R_i + \gamma C_i + \delta P_i + \varepsilon_i,$

where

NOMINATE_i is the NOMINATE score of the representative of district i,

$R_i = 1$ if the representative of district i is a Republican and 0 otherwise,

C_i is a vector of constituency characteristics of district i,

P_i is a vector of personal characteristics of the representative from district i,

ε_i is the error term, and

α, β, γ, and δ are the corresponding coefficients.

Before we turn to the results, it is useful to discuss the interpretation of the basic equation and several restricted versions. First, note that if we restrict both γ and δ to zero, then our estimate of β would reflect polarization as measured by the difference in party means. In the restricted model with just $\delta = 0$, however, β can be interpreted as the polarization of the parties within a given district.[14] Thus, focusing on β in the restricted model helps to distinguish between two distinct hypotheses about polarization.

The first hypothesis is that polarization has arisen because of better matching between representatives and districts. In other words, conservative districts are more likely to elect Republicans and liberal districts are more likely to elect Democrats. In such a situation, we could observe an increase in polarization even if there were not more divergence in the candidates running in each individual district. Under this hypothesis, β with $\delta = 0$ would not increase over time. The second hypothesis is that polarization has arisen because of greater divergence between the parties at the district level. Thus, for a given type of district, the Republican representatives are more conservative and the Democratic representatives are more liberal. This hypothesis predicts that β with $\delta = 0$ should increase over time.

Now consider the effect of constituency characteristics, C. It is useful to distinguish between direct and indirect constituency effects. The direct effects represent the impact of those characteristics when the party of the member and the member's personal or ideological characteristics are controlled for. They are estimated as γ. But C has an indirect effect on the legislator's ideal point through its effects on the party and other characteristics of the representative. These indirect effects can be captured by comparing the direct effects and the estimates of γ with both $\beta = 0$ and $\delta = 0$ that capture the total effects.

The distinction between total, direct, and indirect effects is also crucial in distinguishing among several arguments about the representational consequences of polarization. If polarization is simply the result of parties fleeing the voters, we would expect to see a decline in the explanatory power of constituency variables. Alternatively, if politicians are responding to more extreme voter preferences, the direct effect of constituency would go up. An additional possibility is a mixture of these two extremes. Polarization may provide voters with clear choices, enhancing the correlation between the representative's party and the set of constituency variables, C. In such a scenario, polarization would increase the indirect effect but not necessarily the direct effect.

The Data

Below we present the results of the model for five different terms of the U.S. House of Representatives: the 93rd (1973–1974), the 98th (1983–1984), the 103rd (1993–1994), the 108th (2003–2004), and the 113th (2013–2014). These terms were chosen to represent each of the past five decades.[15]

The dependent variable for this analysis is each House member's first-dimension NOMINATE score. We include the scores for all members who voted a sufficient number of times to obtain a score. Some districts have multiple observations because of deaths and resignations.[16] Because Speakers of the House rarely cast roll call votes, there are only 434 observations for the 93rd and 98th Houses. Vermont independent Bernie Sanders caucused with the Democrats, so we treat him as one.

We use congressional district characteristics that are compiled by the decennial census. The measures were chosen on the basis of previous studies and consistency of measurement over time. The first characteristic, median family income, plays an important role in many of our arguments. For comparability purposes, we measure income in tens of thousands of dollars, adjusted to the price level of 2014 using the Labor Department's CPI-U series. For measures of the education level of the district, we compute both the percentage of the district residents twenty-five years old or older who have college degrees and the percentage who graduated from high school and attended some college. We also capture the ethnic and racial composition of the district by measuring the percentage of constituents who identify as African American and the percentage who identify as Hispanic.[17] We control for America's historical regional cleavage with an indicator variable for districts in the South.[18] To capture ideological effects, we indicate a representative's membership in racial, ethnic, and gender groups.

Results: The Importance of District Income

In tables 2.A1 to 2.A5 (in appendix 2.1), we present the results of the full specification of the model along with two restricted versions. In each table, model A includes only constituency characteristics. The coefficients from model A reflect the total effects of these factors. In model B, we add the indicator variable for the member's party. As we discussed above, we can interpret the coefficient on party as the average within-district polarization. Model C includes the full specification. Here we interpret the coefficients on personal characteristics as ideological effects and the coefficients on constituency characteristics as direct constituency effects.

We begin with the most recent congress, the 113th House, in table 2.A1. Most of the constituency variables in model A are statistically significant. A southern location and college *attendance* of constituents are correlated with more conservative scores, whereas having African American and Hispanic constituents and constituents with college *degrees* each lead to more liberal scores.[19] Even though model A is relatively sparse, it captures more than 42 percent of the variation in NOMINATE scores. This is relatively strong explanatory power insofar as Poole and Romer's results about replacement suggest a low upper bound to the explanatory power of constituency.[20] The statistical insignificance of income represents a significant departure from our findings in the first edition. We will return to this issue below.

Moving to model B, we get an estimate of within-district polarization of 1.050. The total difference in party means is 1.099. Consequently, we find that differences in constituencies account for less than 5 percent of the total party polarization.

In model C, we examine the role of personal characteristics. The results show that African American and female members have more liberal voting records, but the effect for African American members is significant only at the 10 percent level and the effect for females is insignificant. Controlling for Hispanic population, Hispanic members are estimated to position themselves slightly to the right, though that effect is not significant. These results are surprising perhaps only to hardcore Downsians, but even more interesting is the large mitigation in the constituency effects when the individual characteristics and party are included. For example, the coefficient on the percentage of African Americans in the district vanishes when party and individual characteristics are included. In fact, in the full model, the effect of African American constituents is statistically zero.[21] This result suggests that the representation of African Americans comes almost entirely indirectly through the choice of party and through the ability to elect African American members of Congress. A similar story holds for Hispanic representatives. The effects of income, education, and region are also primarily indirect. Using the baseline of the most recent Congress, we can conduct similar analyses of earlier terms to gather clues about polarization and the changing nature of congressional representation. We first note the increasing explanatory power of party, constituency, and individual characteristics. Figure 2.11 plots the explanatory power as measured by R^2 for each of the models for each congressional term.

In the constituency-only model (A), the explanatory power rises from 19 to 42 percent. Polarization does not seem to have made members' voting records less representative of their districts. It is important to note that this increase in explanatory power is not simply a product of the southern realignment. When we run the model on northern and southern districts separately, we obtain similar increases in R^2 from 1973 to 2013 for both regions. In the North, the R^2 increased from 0.19 to 0.31, while the South witnessed an increase from 0.21 to

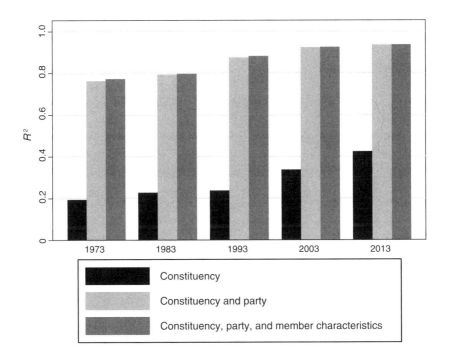

Figure 2.11
Explanatory power of the models.

0.56. The models that include party and member characteristics also show substantial gains in explanatory power.

Our estimates of the relationship of district income to congressional voting confirm our arguments about the increasing political salience of income. Figure 2.12 plots the estimated difference in NOMINATE score of the member representing the highest-income district and the one representing the lowest-income district (holding all other district characteristics constant).

We will consider first the results of the constituency-only model (the first bar of each triple). Clearly, the effect of family income rose substantially through the mid-2000s before reverting. In the 1973–1974 and the 1983–1984 Houses, the effect of income was negative and not statistically significant. But in 1993, the income effect was positive and significant, and it grew larger in 2003. The income effect in 2003–2004 was substantively large. An increase in family income of two standard deviations is associated with a 0.225 shift to the right, larger than the

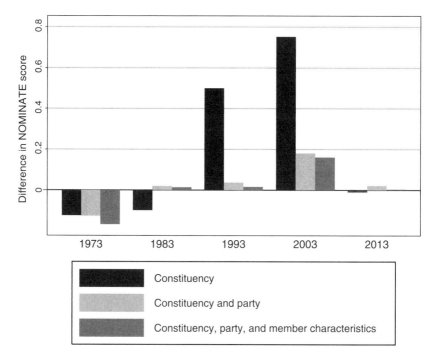

Figure 2.12
Effect of district income on left-right position. *Note:* Estimated difference between richest and poorest district is provided for each model.

shift associated with reducing the percentage of African Americans by the same two standard deviations. The second and third bars in figure 2.12 represent the estimated income effects from models B and C, which control for party and member characteristics. The estimated effects are much smaller when we control for party, suggesting that most of the increased relationship between district income and congressional voting originates in the increased propensity of Republicans to win election in high-income districts. Nevertheless, the results from the 2003–2004 House suggest that there was then a significant effect of income that was independent of its effect on the selection of representatives.

The increased magnitude of the income effects represented by figure 2.12 through 2003 is attributable to two distinct factors. The first is the increased size of the coefficient on income. The second is that increasing income inequality has increased the gap between the richest and poorest districts. This income gap grew (in year 2013 dollars) from $75,742 in 1973 to $96,378 by 2003. Almost all of this increase is attributable to increasing incomes in the highest-income districts. This increase in interdistrict inequality accounts for about 20 percent of the current difference in NOMINATE scores between high-income and low-income districts.

But, as we noted before, there is no statistically significant relationship between a member's NOMINATE score and the median income of her district in 2013–2014. So what happened?

The answer appears to lie in the outcomes of the 2006 and 2010 landslide congressional elections. To illustrate this point, table 2.1 presents the Republican vote seat shares over the past decade for two sets of districts: the 125 poorest and the 125 wealthiest.

First, we note that the Republicans took a big hit in the wealthy districts in the 2006 elections for the 110th Congress as a result of dissatisfaction with the Iraq War and the mishandling of the response to Hurricane Katrina. The Republicans took an additional but smaller hit in wealthy areas in 2008 during the financial crisis. But the Republican share in well-to-do districts has recovered substantially.

Perhaps the more interesting story concerns the trajectories of the poorest districts. The Republicans were stuck in the mid-30s before dipping in the 2008 election. But the Tea Party election of 2010 resulted in a seventeen-point jump in the Republican share of poor districts.

When we estimate model A for each congressional term from 2006 to 2013, we find that the income coefficient is relatively constant until

Table 2.1
Republican vote share in the poorest and richest congressional districts

House (years)	Vote share (%)
	Poorest 125 districts
108 (2003–2004)	35.2
109 (2005–2006)	35.2
110 (2007–2008)	34.8
111(2009–2010)	27.2
112 (2011–2012)	44.0
113 (2013–2014)	43.2
	Richest 125 districts
108 (2003–2004)	59.2
109 (2005–2006)	56.8
110 (2007–2008)	46.8
111(2009–2010)	42.0
112 (2011–2012)	52.8
113 (2013–2014)	49.6

2011 (following the 2010 elections) and then drops by half, but remains significant. Only in 2013 does the null result on income obtain. The null result appears to be the consequence of recent Republican success in relatively poor congressional districts. We address this topic in our concluding chapter.

The results from model B suggest that polarization is not simply the result of better sorting of representatives to districts. Figure 2.13 illustrates the growth in the estimates of the effects of member partisanship, once we control for constituency characteristics.

Our estimate of within-district polarization from model B has risen from 0.59 in 1973 and 1974 to 0.80 in 2003 and 2004. Over the same period, constituency sorting has also increased. In the 1973–1974 House, the unconditional difference in party means was essentially the same as our estimate of within-district polarization. This result holds because the constituency characteristics were much more weakly related to the party of their representative in the 1970s than they are today. Partisan sorting has increased and is partly responsible for the increase in the total effects of the constituency variables. But the increased sorting is dwarfed by the increase in within-district polarization.

When viewed over time, the results on member characteristics tell a mixed story.[22] Clearly, Hispanic and female members generated more

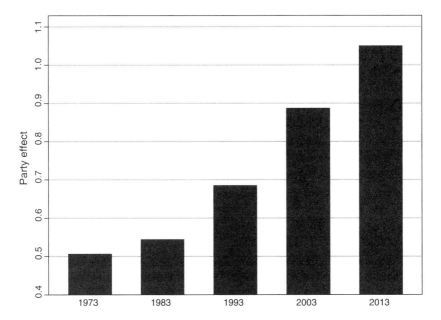

Figure 2.13
Partisan difference on left-right scale. *Note:* Estimates of party coefficient in model B are provided.

distinctive voting records. Neither the Hispanic nor the female coefficients are significant in the 1970s and 1980s, but both have become so more recently. Surprisingly, however, African American representatives have become less distinctive, if we control for party and constituency.[23] As we do not find a similar change for females and Hispanics, it would be hard to argue that this finding is the result of greater Democratic Party pressure for African American representatives to conform. Much of the effect is the consequence of the departure of white southern Democrats, which means that the entire Democratic Caucus votes more like the Congressional Black Caucus. But it is also a reflection of the recent success of some African American candidates such as Sanford Bishop (GA), Andre Carson (IN), and Steven Horsford (NV) in nonmajority districts.[24]

Summary

Polarization may be elite-driven, as we argue in parts of this book, but our results here suggest that it does have some basis in the preferences of voters. Polarization has been associated not with a decline but rather with a strengthening of the association between the demographic characteristics of House districts and the voting behavior of their members. This finding is the "choice, not an echo" benefit of polarization.

Also crucial to the dance between ideology and unequal riches is our finding that polarization has been associated with a strengthening of the relationship between the economic well-being of a district and the representative's ideal point. A nonfactor in 1973, district income became a direct and an indirect effect on the conservatism of the district's House member now, although that effect has attenuated over the past five years as a result of the increasing importance of identity politics and ascriptive issues (see chapter 7).

Alternative Explanations

Although this book focuses on the links between political polarization and the unequal economic performance of the past forty years, a number of other plausible arguments have been put forward to explain congressional polarization.

The Southern Realignment
When V. O. Key (1949) penned his classic *Southern Politics in State and Nation*, the Democratic Party was monolithic in its control of southern local politics and was the only relevant intermediary between southerners and national politics. The southern Republican Party was, ironically, a more liberal alternative, but one available only to voters in the mountainous, impoverished regions of Virginia, Kentucky, and Tennessee. The Democratic dominance of the South, combined with the congressional seniority system and the party's presidential nomination rule requiring a two-thirds majority (until 1936), guaranteed that the Democrats would do the South's bidding in national politics.

With the possible exception of partisan polarization, no other change to the American polity is as important as the transformation of the southern United States from the core of the Democratic Party to the reddest of Republican strongholds. The trajectory of these changes is revealed in figures 2.14 to 2.17.

The transition began with a shift in presidential voting, starting with the Goldwater candidacy in 1964. By 1972 the South was solidly

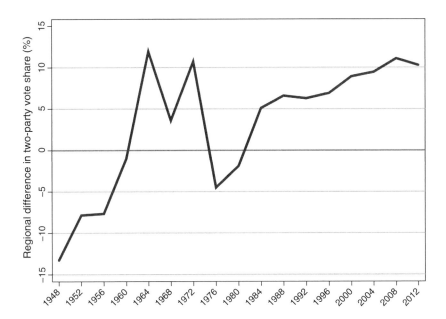

Figure 2.14
Difference in Republican share of two-party presidential vote between South and North, 1948–2012. *Note:* The South is defined as the eleven states of the Confederacy plus Kentucky and Oklahoma.

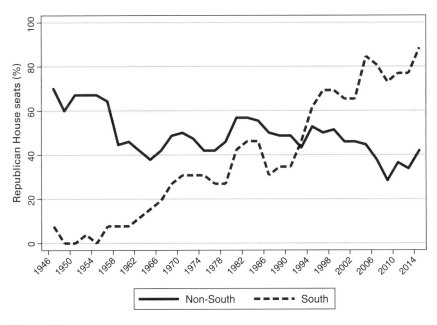

Figure 2.15
Republican percentage of seats in U.S. Senate, 1948–2014. *Note:* The South is defined as the eleven states of the Confederacy plus Kentucky and Oklahoma.

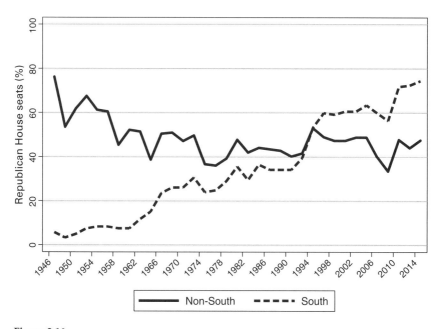

Figure 2.16
Republican percentage of seats in U.S. House, 1948–2014. *Note:* The South is defined as the eleven states of the Confederacy plus Kentucky and Oklahoma.

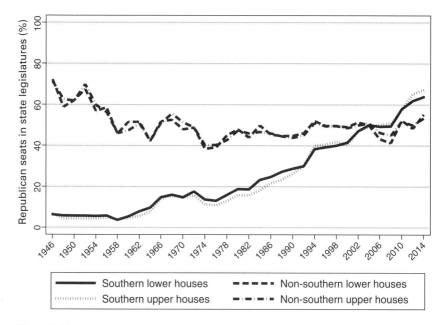

Figure 2.17
Republican percentage of seats in state legislatures, 1948–2014. *Note:* The South is defined as the eleven states of the Confederacy plus Kentucky and Oklahoma.

Republican. The only time after 1964 that a Democratic presidential candidate performed better in the South than in the North was 1976, when Jimmy Carter, a governor from the deep South, defeated Gerald Ford. Bill Clinton, another southern governor, did relatively well in the South, but he won his two elections on the basis of northern votes. By 2000, Al Gore, another southern Democratic presidential nominee, lost even his home state.

The realignment moved slowly down the ballot. Southern Republicans gradually increased their numbers in Congress, but they did not obtain a majority of southern seats in both the House and Senate until the 1994 elections. State and local politics long seemed immune to the Republican advance. Nevertheless, the once formidable Democratic advantage in the thirteen southern state legislatures had been reduced by 2014 to majority control of only the lower chamber in Kentucky— just one in twenty-six chambers.

The conventional view is that the southern Republican Party was built on a foundation of racial conservatism following the Democratic Party's success in passing the 1964 Civil Rights Act, the 1965 Voting Rights Act, and the 1968 Open Housing Act. Without denying the importance of race in the realignment, we present evidence in the next chapter suggesting that the standard view may need to be altered in important ways. As we show, the changes in the South do not contradict but rather complement our basic story.

It is important to keep in mind that many of the nation's economic and demographic changes were magnified in the South. Economic growth in that region has been torrid for the past forty years. Real per capita income grew an average of 200 percent in southern states between 1959 and 1999, compared to 140 percent for the country as a whole. The eight fastest-growing states in the nation were all former members of the Confederacy. The gains were as unequally distributed as elsewhere.

A cause and consequence of this growth was the large migration to the South of middle- and upper-class whites who lacked the old southern enmity toward the GOP. The migrants included both George H. W. Bush and Newt Gingrich. And, with the exception of Texas and Florida, the South is only now beginning to feel the effects of the new waves of immigration. Even without the additional factor of race, the conditions were ripe for southern politics to reflect the same types of political alignment found in the rest of the country.

In table 2.2, we present evidence to suggest that the southern realignment was related to economics. By the early 1970s, the southern districts represented by Republicans were considerably well-heeled than those represented by Democrats. Inflation-adjusted median family income was about $6,000 greater in Republican districts than in Democratic ones. By 2004, the gap had grown to $11,400. Republican gains appear to reflect primarily the consolidation of control of high-income districts rather than the capture of middle- and lower-income districts.[25] We do, however, see the gap drop somewhat between 2005 and 2013. Again, this is the result of the Republican Party's recent success in the poorer white districts of the South.

Whatever the cause of the southern realignment, a major consequence was that many of the moderate and conservative southern Democrats in Congress were replaced by conservative Republicans. Clearly, this shift contributed to the establishment of the Republicans as the conservative party. But the realignment-induced replacement effect cannot be the whole story. In figure 2.18, we show the polarization measure for the entire House from the NOMINATE scaling used throughout this book. We also show the result from a separate scaling for the House minus its southern members. The two series are very highly correlated and follow the same U-shaped trajectory. The figure suggests that polarization among non-southern legislators is the driving force in recent years.

A "southern" theory of polarization (at least the simple version) flounders on its inability to explain an equally prominent feature of the past forty years: the disappearance of liberal Republicans outside

Table 2.2
Partisan control of southern House seats by income

Southern House seats	Median family income (2013$)
Republican seats, 93rd House	$52,698 ($n = 37$)
Democratic seats, 93rd House	$46,526 ($n = 83$)
Difference	$6,172 ($t = 3.18$)
Republican seats, 108th House	$67,331 ($n = 84$)
Democratic seats, 108th House	$55,901 ($n = 56$)
Difference	$11,430 ($t = 4.67$)
Republican seats, 113th House	$61,876 ($n = 108$)
Democratic seats, 113th House	$52,081 ($n = 41$)
Difference	$9,795 ($t = 3.19$)

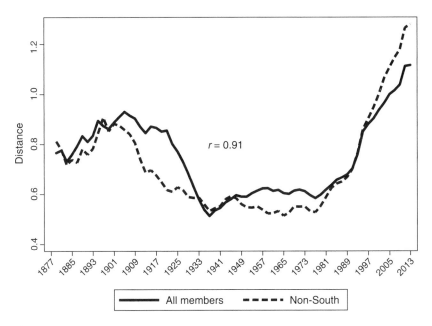

Figure 2.18
Southern effect on polarization in U.S. House, 1879–2014. *Note:* Measures of distance between two parties (differences in mean NOMINATE scores) with and without southern members.

the South. In 1973, the Senate had three Republicans positioned near the median Democrat: Clifford Case (NJ), Ed Brooke (MA), and Jacob Javits (NY). In 2014, their seats were held by Corey Booker, Edward Markey, and Charles Schumer, all from the liberal wing of the Democratic Party. Other liberal Republican seats from 1973 have shifted to the Republican right. Hugh Scott's (PA) seat wound up in the hands of Rick Santorum. Even in Kansas, which has not elected a Democrat to the Senate since 1932, the relatively moderate Jim Pearson and Bob Dole have given way to the conservatives Pat Roberts and Jerry Moran.

A second hypothesis about the link between realignment and polarization centers on how the southern stampede to the Republican Party altered the basic dimensions of political conflict. During the post-Reconstruction period, two spatial dimensions accounted for between 85 and 90 percent of roll call voting decisions. The primary dimension divides the two major parties, and the second dimension picks up regional divisions within the two major parties. As we have discussed, the first dimension is picking up, roughly speaking, the conflict between rich and poor. In contrast, during the civil rights conflicts of the mid-twentieth century, the second dimension was based on race— North versus South. Since the early 1970s, however, the importance of the second dimension has steadily declined, and congressional voting has become increasingly unidimensional. Racial issues formerly divided both parties internally but have now ceased to do so. To demonstrate this point, we have compared the fit of the one-dimensional NOMINATE model to the two-dimensional fit for votes on legislation related to civil rights. Figure 2.19a shows the aggregate proportional reduction in error (APRE)[26] for the one-dimensional model and the incremental improvement of the two-dimensional model for votes on race and civil rights.

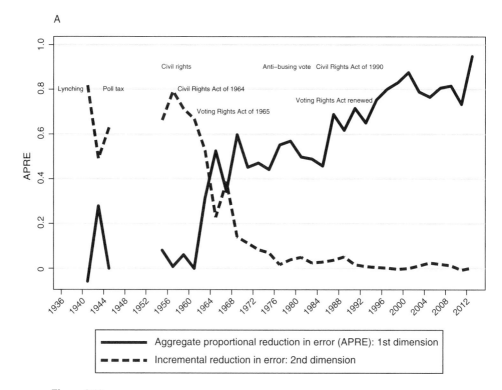

Figure 2.19a
Civil rights votes, 1937–2012. *Note:* Congresses with fewer than two votes were not included in the calculations.

During the post-Reconstruction period, voting on civil rights for African Americans was effectively kept off the congressional agenda except for a scattering of votes on lynching. The elections of 1936 produced a majority of northern Democrats in both houses of Congress. Consequently, votes on civil rights for African Americans became more numerous, including antilynching laws, voting rights in the armed forces during World War II, and then basic civil rights laws.

Figure 2.19a shows that when race reappeared on the agenda of Congress in the late 1930s, the votes are largely explained by a second dimension separating northern and southern representatives, regardless of party. Beginning in the late 1950s, the second dimension began to disappear. The movement of this issue to the first dimension sped up dramatically after the passage of the landmark 1964 Civil Rights Act and the election of a northern Democratic majority in the 1964 elections.

The timing of this transition roughly corresponds to that documented by Carmines and Stimson (1989), who stress the effects of the 1958 congressional elections and 1960s civil rights legislation on the polarization of American politics resulting from the issue of race. Although we concur on the timing, we disagree about the nature of the transformation. For Carmines and Stimson, American politics has become the politics of race. We suggest instead that racial politics has become more like the rest of American politics.

To demonstrate this point, figures 2.19b–c plot the fit of the first dimension and the incremental fit of the second dimension for two canonical sets of economic left-right issues. The first consists of votes on labor regulation and the minimum wage. Except for a brief period in the late 1930s, voting on these issues has largely been explained by the first ideological dimension. Figure 2.19c extends the analysis to a broad category of "government management" votes from the classification scheme developed by Clausen (1973). Clearly, these issues have anchored the first dimension for the past seventy years, and the power of the first dimension to explain these votes rose during the period of polarization. Therefore, it seems far more likely that the voting cleavages over race are converging to the preexisting economic cleavages rather than the other way around.

The trend toward increasing unidimensionality that began in the early 1970s in both the House and the Senate cannot be adequately

B

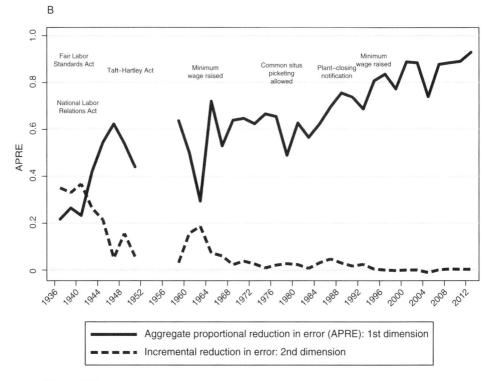

Figure 2.19b
Labor and minimum wage votes, 1937–2012. *Note:* Congresses with fewer than two votes were not included in the calculations.

explained in terms of partisan control of Congress, changes in congressional rules, or agenda selection effects. Rather, it is clear that it must reflect a long-term change in the substance of party conflict. These trends closely track the exodus of the South from the national Democratic Party coalition. The southern realignment clearly changed the dimensionality of political conflict, but it is not at all clear how the change in dimensionality generated greater polarization.

Even though the replacement and dimensionality stories are incomplete, the South is certainly an important part of the story. First, Perlstein (2001) identifies the South as an important organizational nucleus for the conservative movement that has come to dominate Republican Party politics in the years since Goldwater's defeat in 1964. In the 1960s, southern Republican congressmen were centrists, typified by George H. W. Bush (TX) and Howard Baker (TN).

C

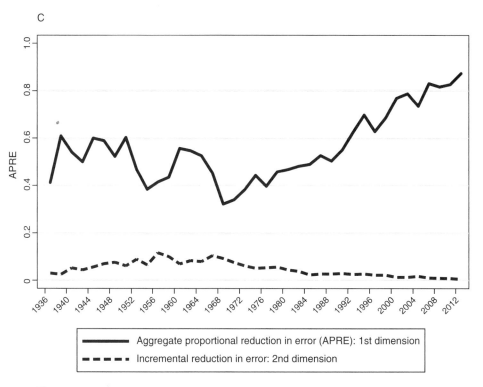

Figure 2.19c
Government management votes, 1937–2012.

But many, if not all, of the southern Republican legislators elected to Congress in the 1970s and 1980s were conservatives who got their start in politics during Goldwater's campaign. The South provided fertile soil for a movement that eventually spread to the rest of the country.

Second, had the Democratic Party retained the allegiance of southern voters, the Republicans would have been denied an electoral majority for their low-tax and antiregulation platform. The electoral cushion provided by southern votes allowed the Republicans to pursue noncentrist policies and win elections. As we document in the next chapter, southerners do not uniformly vote against their economic interests. On the contrary, like other Americans, southerners split along income lines. The richer the southerner, the more likely he or she is to vote Republican.

Partisan Reforms in Congress

Another proposed explanation for polarization lies in the series of reforms undertaken in the House since the 1970s (see Rohde 1991). According to such accounts, power in Congress was decentralized among its committees until a series of post-Watergate reforms strengthened the majority-party caucus at the expense of committees.[27] Party power was further centralized in 1995 when Newt Gingrich and the Republican Conference exercised enormous discretion in the selection of committee chairs and imposed term limits on them.

The centralization of party power may affect polarization measured by NOMINATE scores in two ways. First, it may generate "artificial extremism" (Snyder 1992) if party leaders use their agenda control to select issues on which to divide their partisans from the other side. In the extreme, if every vote is on an issue that divides Democrats and Republicans, the voting patterns may look extremely polarized even if the parties are not very far apart. Polarization would be a statistical artifact. Second, increased party leadership might also exacerbate polarization if leaders were better able to force their moderate wings to vote with the party majority.

These claims fail to have face validity. First, the explanations are very House-centered, so that explaining the polarization of the Senate and various state legislatures becomes a tortuous exercise. It is probably true that partisan leadership has become more prominent in the Senate, but reform there has been less ambitious than in the House. The Senate's supermajority requirement embedded in its cloture rule (partially modified in 2014) also makes it extraordinarily difficult to pursue the partisan strategies that would create artificial extremism. Second, partisanship within Congress as an explanation is at odds with the increase in constituency representation that we documented earlier. Nevertheless, it is worthwhile examining these hypotheses in some detail.

Because no one wants to read a book, much less write one, based on a statistical artifact, we begin with "artificial extremism." The concept was first applied to the use of interest group ratings. Snyder (1992) shows that if the votes chosen by a group produce a distribution of cutting lines with a variance less than the distribution of legislator ideal points, the distribution of ratings will be artificially bimodal. Fortunately, we can be confident that this is not a large problem for NOMINATE. First, unlike interest group ratings, NOMINATE uses almost all the votes in a given term to estimate each ideal point.

Interest groups can select only those votes that divide friend from foe, but no such selection bias exists when all votes are used. Thus, despite any increase in partisan control over the agenda, there is a wide variety of roll call cutpoints each term. Second, there is a critical difference between interest group ratings and NOMINATE scalings. In an interest group rating, the distance between two legislators is directly proportional to the number of roll call cutpoints that separate them. This is generally not the case for NOMINATE because it relies on maximum likelihood estimation. So as long as the distribution of cutpoints is sufficiently wide, an increase in the density of cutting lines between the two parties will not automatically produce an increase in polarization.

To assuage any remaining concerns, we conducted an experiment. We reran NOMINATE for the 1st through the 113th Congresses *constraining each House to have the same distribution of roll call margins*.[28] The average distribution of margins for all 113 Houses was used as the common margin and the number of roll calls for each House was set at 400. The distribution is shown in table 2.3.

To construct the artificial data for each House, we sampled each margin category *with replacement* to get the required number. For example, if for some Houses there were 75 roll calls with margins in the range of 66 to 70, then 44 roll calls from those 75 were drawn with replacement. If there were no roll calls in the range, no roll calls could be included. But this caveat cannot affect our basic results about contemporary polarization, as no House since the 78th (1943–1944) had a missing margin.

Table 2.3
Roll call weights

Majority size	Frequency	Relative frequency
50–55	92	0.23
56–60	80	0.20
61–65	60	0.15
66–70	44	0.11
71–75	32	0.08
76–80	24	0.06
81–85	20	0.05
86–90	16	0.04
91–95	20	0.05
96–97.5	12	0.03

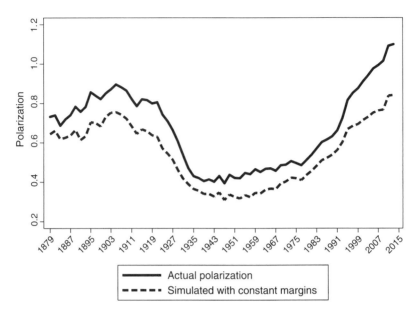

Figure 2.20
Polarization when roll call margins are held constant.

Figure 2.20 shows that the pattern of polarization from the margins experiment is essentially the same as the actual polarization. The pattern of polarization would be essentially the same even if the agenda were held constant. Of course, this experiment does not prove that the *level* of polarization is not inflated by artificial extremism, but it casts grave doubts on the role of artificial extremism in the *increase* in polarization.

We now ask whether increased polarization is a reflection of the enhanced ability of party leaders to discipline party members. This question has bedeviled the recent literature on legislative behavior because increased party pressure is, in general, observationally equivalent to better matching of legislator preferences and party. In the previous section, we provided evidence that polarization was a combination of increased sorting and increased party effects. But the analysis cannot distinguish between pressures internal to the legislature, such as those from leaders and caucus majorities, and those that are external, emanating from primary electorates, partisan constituents, and contributors.

One approach to distinguishing between internal and external pressure is to look for "selective" party pressures on close or important votes. Essentially, this approach seeks to determine the extent to which certain roll calls are more partisan than others and postulates that the variation results from the activity of party leaders and whips. A version of the approach was first developed by Snyder and Groseclose (2000). Because, as they argue, rational leaders would expend little effort whipping on lopsided votes, those votes can be used to estimate measures of preferences uncontaminated by party effects. Therefore, after estimating legislator preferences using 65–35 divisions or greater, they regressed each vote on the measure of preferences and a party dummy variable. They found that the party variable is statistically significant on a large percentage of the close roll calls but, as expected, on few lopsided ones.

In "The Hunt for Party Discipline in Congress" (McCarty, Poole, and Rosenthal 2001), we criticized the Snyder-Groseclose approach on several methodological grounds and proposed a different technique for uncovering selective party pressure. We assumed that each roll call has a separate cutting line for each party. If there is no party effect, the two cutting lines will be identical, just as in the standard spatial model. If party discipline is applied, however, some Republicans to the left of the common cutpoint will vote with their party and some Democrats to the right will vote with theirs. The result is a separate cutpoint for each party. Because party discipline generally involves getting moderates to vote with extremists, the cutpoint for the Democrats should be to the right of the cutpoint for Republicans.

For a more concrete example, consider the one-dimensional spatial configuration illustrated in figure 2.21. If the cutpoint is constrained to be the same for both parties, this produces the standard spatial model.

Figure 2.21
Cut-point models.

For the example of figure 2.21, with a common cutpoint, there are three classification errors, legislators 3, 11, and 15. When each party can have its own cutpoint, this produces a model that allows for party discipline. Moderate Democrats to the right of some Republicans can vote with the majority of their party. Moderate Republicans to the left of some Democrats can vote with the majority of their party. The best cutpoint for the Republicans in figure 2.21 remains the common cutpoint. Legislator 15 is the only R classification error. But the best cutpoint for the Democrats is to the right of the common cutpoint. The D cutpoint leaves only legislator 3 as a classification error for this party. Rather than estimate either the one-cut-point model or the two-cut-point model via a metric technique, such as NOMINATE, one can simply find the joint rank order of legislators and cutpoints that minimizes classification error. Poole (2000) presents an efficient algorithm that closely approximates the global maximum in correct classification.[29]

To assess the importance of selective party pressure, we simply compare the predictive success of the two-cut-point model to that of a one-cut-point model. When party pressure is important, the two-cut-point model should perform much better. The upshot of our results, reproduced in figure 2.22, is that the correct classification gains of the two-cut-point model are modest and that there is no evidence that selective party pressures have increased.[30]

Of course, it's entirely possible that even if the ability to apply selective pressures has not increased, general party pressure (which would be reflected in each member's ideal point) has increased. But, as we have already noted, it is impossible at this point to distinguish between general party effects that are internal to the legislature and those that are external. We can only hope to convince the reader that the preponderance of the evidence presented throughout the book speaks in favor of our externalist account.

Apportionment and Redistricting

Following the 2000 census reapportionment, congressional incumbents were all but invincible in the 2002 elections. Incumbents were also safe in 2004. Almost all the incumbents who lost in that year were beaten by other incumbents in contests engineered by the controversial Tom DeLay–inspired mid-decade redistricting in Texas. The effects of the 2010 census reapportionment were very similar. The 2012 elections

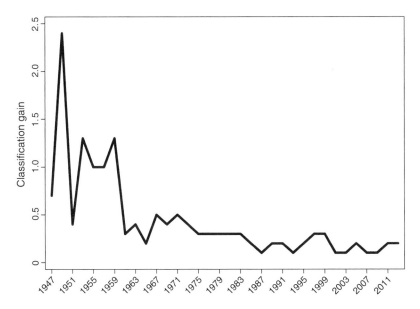

Figure 2.22
Classification gain, one cutpoint versus two cutpoints. *Note:* The classification gains are
for a one-dimensional voting model. All representatives were scaled together, and a
separate cutpoint was then estimated for each party. The classification gains are similar
to those scalings in which each party has an independent rank order of ideal points as
well as a separate cutpoint.

differed from the 2002 elections because President Obama was running
for reelection and turnout was higher than in 2002. The Republicans
lost sixteen seats, but only six of these losses were incumbents'. The
remaining ten were open seat losses. The events of 2002 and 2012 have
brought the politics of congressional districting under the punditry
microscope.

As important as these controversies surrounding apportionment
and redistricting are, it is not obvious that they are much more than a
symptom of our political maladies rather than their cause. As polarization and partisanship have increased in the electorate, it would be
surprising if congressional incumbents were not more secure, independent of how their districts are drawn. And clearly, norms against
redrawing the boundaries at mid-decade are hard to sustain when
partisan balance is so even and the ideological stakes are so high. The
strongest argument against overemphasizing the politics of apportionment is the fact that the U.S. Senate (which of course is never

redistricted) has endured an almost identical history of polarization. Second, the elections following redistricting are not especially notable for a subsequent increase in polarization. If all eighteen of the congressional terms since 1978 were ranked by the term-over-term increase in polarization, the four that follow post-redistricting elections (1982, 1992, 2002, and 2012) would rank seventh, third, ninth, and eighteenth, respectively—hardly impressive evidence of an effect. It would be premature, however, to dismiss a link between districting and polarization out of hand, as three of the last four post-apportionment elections (1982, 1992, and 2002) have led to above-average increases in the polarization in the House. It behooves us to take a closer look.

Arguments about the role of congressional apportionment in enhancing legislative polarization tend to stress two factors. The first is the creation of majority-minority districts designed to promote the election of racial and ethnic minorities to Congress. The creation of such districts often requires the concentration of black or Hispanic voters into districts where they constitute a large majority. A by-product of such concentration is the "bleaching" of majority white districts by removing minority voters. The result is an increase in African American and Hispanic representatives, who anchor the left end of the scale, and conservative Republicans, who represent almost entirely white districts. Although majority-minority districting undoubtedly has such effects, it is easy to overstate its significance in the big picture. First of all, very few states have majority-minority districts. More than two-thirds of the majority-minority districts are located in just five states: California, Florida, Illinois, New York, and Texas. In many of these cases, minority voters are sufficiently concentrated so that majority-minority districts can be formed easily with minimal effects on the boundaries of other districts. Eliminating these states from the calculations does not qualitatively alter the time series on polarization in the U.S. House.[31] There is a second reason to believe that racial gerrymandering has not had much impact. Earlier in this chapter, we showed that whereas African American legislators have much more liberal voting records than white legislators, if we control for party, white representatives are not particularly sensitive to the size of the black population of their districts. Even if the "bleaching" effect alters the partisan balance, it does not increase partisan polarization among white representatives.[32]

A second common argument about apportionment is that the opportunity and technical ability to engage in partisan gerrymandering have gone up over time. Such gerrymandering is assumed to create much more homogeneous congressional districts, which accommodate more extreme legislators.

Advocates of this hypothesis stress the near absence of incumbent losses in the previous two electoral cycles. In a less anecdotal vein, Cox and Katz (2002) analyzed congressional elections in light of the landmark "one person, one vote" Supreme Court decision in Baker v. Carr. This decision forced every state with more than one representative to redistrict after every decennial census. Cox and Katz show that the decision had a substantial impact on the rise of the incumbency advantage. There are reasons to be skeptical of a large connection between partisan districting and polarization. The first reason is theoretical. A seat-maximizing partisan gerrymander involves creating small majorities for the dominant party in a large number of districts and creating large majorities for the opposition party in a small number of districts. Purely partisan gerrymanders would not necessarily reduce the number of competitive districts.

Consequently, Cox and Katz argue that the incumbency effect arose precisely where pure partisan gerrymanders were politically infeasible. When the dominant party cannot impose its districting preferences, the result is a cross-partisan compromise, incumbency protection. Because such plans often involve enhancing the partisan homogeneity of districts, they have the potential to exacerbate polarization. But the effect is not obvious. Our recent polarization is primarily manifested in new cohorts of legislators that are more extreme than the departing cohorts. The average ideological movement of incumbent politicians has been much smaller.[33] By prolonging the careers of incumbents, incumbent-protecting gerrymanders may have impeded even greater polarization. Of course, the very fixation on incumbency advantage in the political science literature may be overblown. There were very substantial shifts in House seats in the 1994, 2006, 2010, and 2014 elections, all occurring as polarization continued to surge.

The final way in which apportionment may have contributed to polarization has not received nearly so much attention. As a result of the shifts of population from the Northeast and the Middle Atlantic to the South and West, the last four decennial apportionments have resulted in a large net shift of seats to the Sun Belt. Following the 2010 census, for example, the South gained eight congressional seats (four in Texas alone) and the Mountain West gained three of the remaining four (Washington got the other). These gains came almost entirely at the expense of the Middle Atlantic and the industrial Midwest. Because the parties in the Sun Belt (especially in the once solid South) are more polarized than in the Rust Belt, the result has been an increase in polarization due to the regional reallocation of seats.

Consider the mean NOMINATE position of the Democratic and Republican members broken down by whether their state was a winner, a loser, or unaffected by reapportionment. In each of the last three apportionments, the mean difference between the parties in the "winning" states is substantially larger than the partisan differences in "losing" and unaffected states. The last apportionment for which this was not true was in 1970, just before the current wave of polarization began.[34] One way in which reapportionment appears to influence polarization is not through partisan gerrymandering within states. It is the reallocation of seats across states forced by the decennial census.[35]

An important implication of all of the reapportionment-based arguments is that the distribution of voter preferences across districts is more polarized than the national distribution of preferences. But we see little evidence that the difference in those distributions is large. To illustrate this point, let's consider the distribution of presidential vote, a common measure of district partisanship and ideology. If the districting process is contributing to polarization, we would expect the distribution of the presidential vote across districts to have fatter tails than the distribution of the vote across geographic units that are not subject to political manipulation. Figures 2.23a–e show the distribution of the Republican presidential vote across districts and across counties for the last five apportionments.[36] Contrary to the districting hypotheses, these distributions are very similar. The densities in the tails of each distribution are almost identical. For example, following the 2000 and 2012 elections, there are slightly fewer counties voting around 30 percent Republican relative to districts and a few more very anti-Republican districts. This is presumably the effect of majority-minority districting.[37]

A similar effect is apparent following the 1990s apportionment. The 1970s and 1980s apportionment did not produce fat tails either but rather a pro-Republican bias whereby the distribution of presidential vote across districts lies distinctly to the right of the county distribution. That is, although there was a pro-Republican bias in districting, there was no bimodal distribution of districts that would protect incumbents. In all four years captured in figures 2.23a–e—and most emphatically in 1992 and 2000—there were many congressional districts where the Republican presidential vote percentage was close to

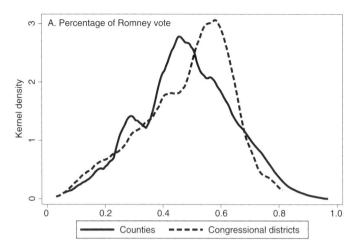

Figure 2.23a
Distribution of the 2012 Romney two-party vote by counties and congressional districts.
Note: Counties are weighted by population. Both densities were estimated using bandwidth = 0.025.

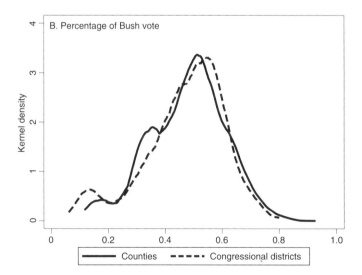

Figure 2.23b
Distribution of the 2000 Bush two-party vote by counties and congressional districts. *Note:* Counties are weighted by population. Both densities were estimated using bandwidth = 0.025.

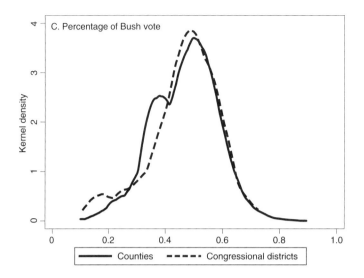

Figure 2.23c
Distribution of the 1992 Bush two-party vote by counties and congressional districts.
Note: Counties are weighted by population. Both densities were estimated using bandwidth = 0.025.

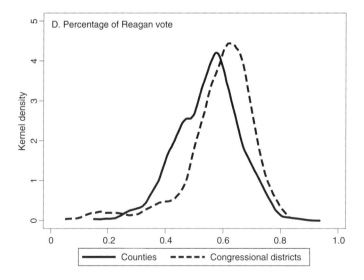

Figure 2.23d
Distribution of the 1980 Reagan two-party vote by counties and congressional districts.
Note: Counties are weighted by population. Both densities were estimated using bandwidth = 0.025.

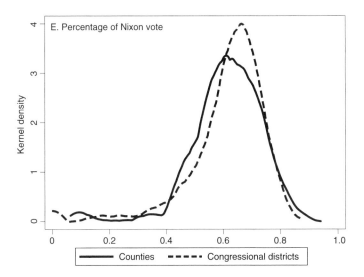

Figure 2.23e
Distribution of the 1972 Nixon two-party vote by counties and congressional districts.
Note: Counties are weighted by population. Both densities were estimated using band-width = 0.025.

50. Incumbents win such districts not because they benefit from gerrymandering but because they enjoy an incumbency advantage. Districting does seem to distort the underlying distribution of prefer-ences, but it would be very hard to argue that there is a significant tendency toward more polarized distributions.

Given the lack of strong evidence of a link to districting in the House, we return to perhaps the biggest objection against such a link: the polarization of the Senate. The Senate is never reapportioned or redis-tricted, so an apportionment story requires that polarization in the House cause polarization in the Senate. It is not clear what sort of mechanism might underlie such an effect. It is possible that changes in House apportionment alter the pool of competitive Senate candidates, or that the effects of apportionment strengthen the hand of each party's extreme factions. But any such mechanism would seem to require that changes in House polarization occur before changes in the Senate. Statistical tests do not support the idea that the House leads the Senate. In the spirit of a Granger causality test, we regressed biennial changes in Senate polarization on the contemporary change in House polariza-tion and the lagged changes in House polarization for the post–World War II period.[38] The results are shown in table 2.4. Only the

Table 2.4
Change in Senate polarization (standard errors in parentheses)

Change	Coefficient
Change in House polarization at t	0.479
	(0.181)
Change in House polarization at $t - 1$	0.065
	(0.172)
Change in House polarization at $t - 2$	−0.041
	(0.193)
Constant	0.0102
	(0.006)
N	34
R^2	0.212

contemporary change in House polarization, not its lagged values, is correlated with changes in the Senate series. Thus, we find no evidence of Granger causation. Similarly, we find little support for an effect of Senate polarization on House polarization.

Although congressional apportionment is obviously an important determinant of the quality of representative government, it plays but a bit part in our choreography.

Party Primaries and Polarization

Another of the common folk explanations of political polarization has to do with the role of primary elections in nominating congressional candidates. It is widely assumed that moderates have an increasingly difficult time winning their party's contests.[39] Such a dynamic would then present increasingly stark choices to the general electorate.

This account has important limitations, however. The first is that the widespread adoption of the primary as a nomination device for Congress took place at the end of the nineteenth century and the first half of the twentieth. As we have seen, this time period corresponds to an era of declining polarization. By the time polarization began escalating, primaries were nearly universal. So any general claim that primary elections are the principal cause of polarization seems weak. Nevertheless, it is still worth entertaining the idea that institutional differences in the selection of legislative candidates do contribute to polarization.

A few studies have found evidence for a polarizing effect of partisan primaries. Kaufman, Gimpel, and Hoffman (2003) found that presidential primary voters in states with open primaries hold political ideologies similar to those of the general electorate, whereas in states with closed primaries, the two electorates are more ideologically distinct. Gerber and Morton (1998) found that the positions of legislators nominated in open primaries hew more closely to district preferences, whereas Brady, Han, and Pope (2007) found that legislators who hew closely to the general election electorate suffer an electoral penalty in primaries.

However, most of the research suggests that the effects of moving to open-primary systems are modest at best. Hirano et al. (2010) studied the history of primary elections for the U.S. Senate. Their findings cast significant doubt on the role of primary election institutions in polarization. First, the introduction of primaries had no effect on polarization in the Senate. Second, despite the common belief that participation in primaries has been decreasing, they found that primary turnout has always been quite low. Thus, it is doubtful that changes in primary election participation can explain the polarizing trends of the past three decades. Third, they found no econometric evidence that either low primary turnout or low primary competition leads to the polarization of senators.

Using a panel of state legislative elections, McGhee et al. (2014) investigated the effects of changing primary systems and found little evidence that such switches affect polarization. Similarly, Bullock and Clinton (2011) investigated the effects of California's short-lived move from a closed primary to a blanket primary, in which any registered voter could participate. They found that the change did lead to more moderate candidates in competitive districts but that these effects were not observed in districts that were dominated by either of the parties. This result suggests that the recent change in California to a top-two primary may affect districts that are not firmly controlled by one or the other party.

Finally, even if one could establish a cross-sectional relationship between primary systems and polarization, the fact that closed-primary systems have not become more common suggests that it cannot explain the long-term trends. Closed primaries should have been producing as much polarization in 1960 as they did in 1990.

Seeking the Sources of Congressional Polarization

In this chapter, we have documented the rise of polarization in the two houses of Congress. We have ruled out a broad spectrum of alternative explanations for our finding. These explanations range from method-ological artifact to the political realignment of the American South to institutional changes within Congress and the structure of congressio-nal elections and primaries. None of the alternatives provides a con-vincing theoretical explanation, nor does any correlate empirically with the time series of polarization. Certainly none of these alternatives is as cheek to cheek with polarization as were the time series of inequality and immigration that we showed in chapter 1.

We did find, however, that constituency characteristics had become more linked to congressional ideology in recent decades and, in par-ticular, that median income had become more linked to conservatism. We therefore turn to economic and demographic factors in the next three chapters.

Appendix 2.1

Table 2.A1
Determinants of NOMINATE scores, 113th House (2013–2014) (standard errors in parentheses)

Variable	Model A	Model B	Model C
Republican		1.050	1.044
		(0.018)	(0.018)
Median family income, in $10,000 (2013 $)	−0.001	0.002	0.000
	(0.002)	(0.007)	(0.007)
% Black constituents	−1.803	−0.153	−0.059
	(0.164)	(0.062)	(0.082)
% Hispanic constituents	−1.112	−0.018	−0.021
	(0.127)	(0.046)	(0.057)
% Some college	2.091	0.814	0.834
	(0.506)	(0.170)	(0.172)
% College degree	−0.896	0.185	0.240
	(0.661)	(0.222)	(0.222)
Southern	0.506	0.062	0.054
	(0.047)	(0.017)	(0.018)
African American member			−0.062
			(0.037)
Hispanic member			0.017
			(0.038)
Female member			−0.024
			(0.019)
N	440	440	440
R^2	0.424	0.936	0.937

Table 2.A2
Determinants of NOMINATE scores, 108th House (2003–2004) (standard errors in parentheses)

Variable	Model A	Model B	Model C
Republican		0.887 (0.015)	0.886 (0.015)
Median family income, in $100,000 (2013 $)	0.078 (0.022)	0.019 (0.008)	0.017 (0.008)
% Black constituents	−1.244 (0.141)	−0.190 (0.051)	−0.063 (0.077)
% Hispanic constituents	−0.588 (0.124)	−0.044 (0.043)	0.043 (0.060)
% Some college	2.240 (0.448)	0.531 (0.155)	0.507 (0.157)
% College degree	−1.381 (0.396)	−0.367 (0.136)	−0.343 (0.136)
Southern	0.336 (0.044)	0.100 (0.015)	0.091 (0.016)
African American member			−0.088 (0.039)
Hispanic member			−0.074 (0.045)
Female member			−0.033 (0.020)
N	441	441	441
R^2	0.337	0.924	0.926

Table 2.A3
Determinants of NOMINATE scores, 103rd House (1993–1994) (standard errors in parentheses)

Variable	Model A	Model B	Model C
Republican		0.686	0.684
		(0.015)	(0.014)
Median family income, in $10,000 (2013 $)	0.058	0.004	0.002
	(0.019)	(0.008)	(0.007)
% Black constituents	−0.897	−0.362	−0.080
	(0.114)	(0.048)	(0.076)
% Hispanic constituents	−0.380	−0.180	−0.110
	(0.116)	(0.047)	(0.069)
% Some college	1.137	0.535	0.533
	(0.359)	(0.146)	(0.148)
% College degree	−0.855	−0.403	−0.352
	(0.374)	(0.152)	(0.150)
Southern	0.207	0.116	0.099
	(0.039)	(0.016)	(0.016)
African American member			−0.189
			(0.040)
Hispanic member			−0.054
			(0.052)
Female member			−0.038
			(0.022)
N	437	437	437
R^2	0.238	0.875	0.883

Table 2.A4
Determinants of NOMINATE scores, 98th House (1983–1984) (standard errors in parentheses)

Variable	Model A	Model B	Model C
Republican		0.545	0.546
		(0.016)	(0.016)
Median family income, in $10,000 (2013,$)	−0.013	0.003	0.002
	(0.020)	(0.010)	(0.010)
% Black constituents	−0.785	−0.366	−0.233
	(0.104)	(0.055)	(0.076)
% Hispanic constituents	−0.800	−0.327	−0.284
	(0.136)	(0.072)	(0.093)
% Some college	1.546	0.866	0.890
	(0.386)	(0.201)	(0.203)
% College degree	−0.600	−0.894	−0.907
	(0.433)	(0.224)	(0.224)
Southern	0.171	0.187	0.166
	(0.034)	(0.018)	(0.019)
African American member			−0.126
			(0.050)
Hispanic member			−0.027
			(0.067)
Female member			-0.038
			(0.033)
N	437	437	437
R^2	0.228	0.793	0.797

Table 2.A5
Determinants of NOMINATE scores, 93rd House (1973–1974) (standard errors in parentheses)

Variable	Model A	Model B	Model C
Republican		0.507	0.509
		(0.016)	(0.016)
Median family income, in $10,000 (2013 $)	−0.016	−0.017	−0.022
	(0.018)	(0.010)	(0.010)
% Black constituents	−0.688	−0.291	−0.050
	(0.105)	(0.059)	(0.081)
% Hispanic constituents	−0.823	−0.304	−0.196
	(0.154)	(0.085)	(0.109)
% Some college	1.685	0.788	0.807
	(0.603)	(0.329)	(0.335)
% College degree	0.121	−0.422	−0.296
	(0.528)	(0.288)	(0.287)
Southern	0.167	0.191	0.152
	(0.037)	(0.020)	(0.022)
African American member			−0.240
			(0.058)
Hispanic member			−0.109
			(0.088)
Female member			−0.013
			(0.039)
N	441	441	441
R^2	0.195	0.762	0.772

Income Polarization and the Electorate

What has happened to voters as politicians have polarized? A hint at the answer is contained in our finding that the liberal-conservative ideologies of members of the House of Representatives are increasingly tied to the median incomes of their constituents. In this chapter, we explore how the political preferences of individual voters have become increasingly related to their incomes. High-income voters increasingly identify with the Republican Party and vote for Republican presidential candidates. Low-income voters are increasingly in the Democratic camp. This finding controverts recent punditry.

The 2004 election in particular was not just a contest featuring Bush, Kerry, and their parties. It was also a battle of pundits over the extent and nature of America's electoral divide. Some saw the country as red and blue, the colors used in the famous electoral maps showing the Democrats winning the coasts, major urban areas, and college towns, with the Republicans getting the rest. Red and blue analysis became fashionable despite some claims that the country is purple, with most areas splitting their votes between the parties at fairly equal rates. A conventional wisdom about the electoral divide quickly emerged. When 22 percent of voters told election pollsters that moral values were their top issue and thirteen states voted to ban same-sex marriage, "guns, God, and gays" became the mantric explanation for Bush's victory in 2004.[1] If social issues can loom large in the minds of pundits, they may only be ephemeral perturbations to the central liberal-conservative conflict over redistribution. By the end of 2014, same-sex marriage was legal in thirty-five states. In 2015, the Supreme Court made same-sex marriage a right throughout the United States.

Below we present evidence that the relationship between income and partisanship is not strengthening to the extent it once was. We argue, however, that this change may have less to do with a change in the salience of religious and cultural issues than with a rightward shift of low-income whites on redistributive issues affected by concerns about immigration and race. The highly redistributive Affordable Care Act is the party-defining issue of the time, yet it has never been embraced by a majority of low-income whites because of concerns that its targeted beneficiaries are largely black and Latino.

Academics have indeed been more circumspect than pundits in their analysis of electoral polarization. Dimaggio, Evans, and Bryson (1996), Evans (2003), and Fiorina (2004) find no evidence that the overall electorate is more polarized on most social and economic issues. Indeed, on many issues the electorate is moving toward consensus. The one not so minor exception in these studies, however, is that those voters who identify strongly with the major parties are increasingly divided, with Democratic identifiers consistently taking more liberal positions and Republicans taking more conservative ones.[2] Similarly, there is evidence that partisan affiliation in the mass public is increasingly polarized by liberal and conservative views. Green, Palmquist, and Schickler (2002) report that the difference between the "percentage of Republicans who call themselves conservatives" and the "percentage of Democrats who call themselves conservatives" has doubled between 1972 and 1996, moving from 25 to 50 percent.[3] Figure 3.1 also shows that the overall percentage of voters calling themselves liberal or conservative has grown steadily since 1990, while the number refusing to take an ideological label has declined, especially over the past two elections.

One thing that public discourse and academic discourse have in common is that neither has paid much attention to how changes in the American economy have contributed to electoral polarization. The journalist Thomas Frank sums up the conventional wisdom this way: "One thing is certain in the search to unravel the mystery of the 'great divide': we know for sure the answer isn't class. We can rule that uncomfortable subject out from the start."[4]

For the most part, political scientists have been no more eager to broach the "uncomfortable subject." Although much recent work in comparative political economy has sought to link inequality to political conflict and back to economic policy, few of these insights have been applied to American politics.[5] Only very recently has interest in the links between inequality and American politics increased. Bartels (2008), Gilens (2012), and Jacobs and Page (2005) find strong evidence that congressional voting and public policy are much more responsive

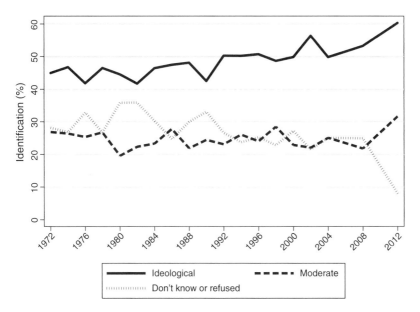

Figure 3.1
Ideological self-placement. *Note:* Respondents to National Election Study. Respondents identifying as liberal or conservative (including "strongly" and "slightly") are grouped into the ideological category.

to the opinions of high-income citizens than to those of poorer ones.[6] Bartels (2008) also finds a significant effect of partisan control of the presidency on the growth of inequality. Despite this progress, however, a recent report of the American Political Science Association declares that "inequality in American government is understudied."[7]

Perhaps one reason for the dearth of interest is that income or wealth has not been seen as a reliable predictor of political beliefs and partisanship in the mass public, especially in comparison to other cleavages, such as race and region, or in comparison to other democracies. For example, the major work on partisan identification by Green, Palmquist, and Schickler (2002) makes little or no use of income as a predictor of partisan attachments.[8] Studies of "class voting," conducted primarily by sociologists, have found that the American electorate has become less divided on occupational and subjective class identities since the New Deal.[9] If political conflict does not have an income basis, it makes little sense that changes in economic inequality would disturb existing patterns of political conflict. Partisanship was, in fact, only weakly related to income in the period following World

War II. In the presidential election years of 1956 and 1960, National Election Study (NES) respondents from the highest income quintile were hardly more likely to identify as a Republican than were respondents from the lowest quintile. In contrast, in the last six presidential election years respondents in the highest quintile were more than twice as likely to identify as Republican as were those in the lowest quintile.[10]

We can measure the income basis of partisanship through an index of party-income stratification. Our index is simply the proportion of Republican identifiers in the top income quintile divided by the proportion of Republican identifiers in the bottom quintile.[11] As seen in figure 3.2, income stratification has shown a clear upward trend over the past forty years, leading to an increasing rich-poor cleavage between the parties.[12]

In figure 3.2, we also plot stratification for the presidential vote. Here we compute the ratio of the fraction of Republican voters among voters

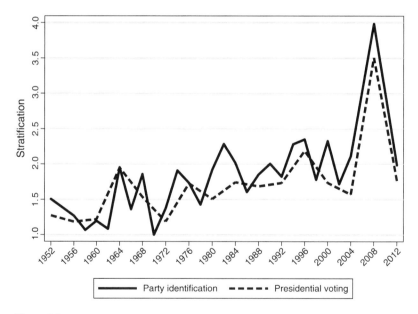

Figure 3.2
Party stratification by income. *Note:* Stratification is computed as the Republican proportion of the top income quintile divided by the Republican proportion of the bottom quintile. The 2012 sample includes only face-to-face interviews and omits the oversample of blacks and Hispanics. *Source:* American National Election Study, Survey Research Center, University of Michigan, Ann Arbor. Various years.

for the two major parties in the top quintile to the same fraction in the bottom quintile. The upward trend in stratification is also evident for the presidential vote.

Of course, the simple bivariate relationship between stratification and income does not show that partisan differences are causally linked to income differences. Increasing stratification could be due to changing income characteristics of party constituencies based on other cleavages. We do not deny this claim (in fact, we present some evidence for it below), but we insist that regardless of the mechanism that created the stratification of partisanship by income, the mere existence of substantial income differences across the constituencies of the two parties has important implications for political conflict. In the 2012 campaign this conflict was expressed in Republican rhetoric about "the 47 percent who will never vote for us" and "job creators" versus "takers." As parties are generally presumed to represent the interests of their base constituencies, income stratification should contribute to the parties pursuing very different economic policies. Fiscal policy, for which the Republican trademark is the Grover Norquist pledge never to vote for tax increases, heads the list. There are also sharp partisan differences over monetary policy, minimum wages, food stamps, the earned income tax credit, low-income housing, Medicaid, and health care subsidies. These policies all have redistributive implications, so there is an obvious interest in studying the income stratification of partisan identification and voting.

We also want to be clear that we are not arguing that the increased propensity for Americans to vote along income lines is an important cause of polarization. Indeed, as we discuss below, much of the income stratification of partisanship can best be explained as a response to parties whose economic policy priorities have sharply diverged. We do suggest, however, that the increased sorting of the electorate along income lines has reinforced partisan polarization by creating a constituency basis for each party's positions.

To explore the relationship between the economic and political transformations we have discussed, the rest of this chapter attempts to provide some explanations for the increased party-income stratification. The main source of data is the National Election Study, conducted by the Survey Research Center of the University of Michigan. The NES has sampled the American electorate every two years starting in 1952 (1954, 2006, and 2010 excepted) and is the only longitudinal data source that has been on the dance floor for the past sixty years. To address directly more recent trends, we also use the much larger recent samples provided by the Pew Research Center for the People and the Press. In our analysis of NES data, we focus on partisan identification because it is the one item present in every study from 1952 to 2012. Moreover, unlike presidential voting, it is less influenced by election-specific factors. We are able, however, to show that our results for partisanship largely replicate for presidential vote choice, although, as is to be expected, the results are somewhat noisier.

There are four non-mutually exclusive reasons why income stratification might have increased. First, there could be a *response* effect. That is, there might be a temporal increase in the coefficient for income in our model of partisanship. Below we argue that this increase is consistent not only with party polarization on economic policy issues but also with the increased salience of economic issues. Second, there may be an *inequality* effect. Increased inequality has made low-income groups relatively poorer and high-income groups richer, so that with even a constant *response* effect, stratification would grow. Third, increased stratification might be a result of a change in the joint distribution of other demographic characteristics and income. Pro-Democratic groups may have gotten poorer while pro-Republican groups got richer. For example, African American partisanship may have remained unchanged, but the relative poverty of African Americans may have increased. Fourth, groups with high incomes may have moved toward the Republicans while poorer groups may have moved toward the Democrats. For example, the relative poverty of African Americans may have remained unchanged but their propensity for Democratic identification might have increased.

To quantify these effects, we estimate a model of party identification and its relationship to income and other characteristics. We then use the estimates of this model as well as data about the changing distribution of income to calculate the level of party-income stratification under many different counterfactual scenarios. The results show that almost all of the increase can be attributed to an increased effect of income on partisanship and changes in party allegiances of certain groups. A significant portion of the stronger income effect reflects a greatly increased income effect in the South. Changes in the incomes of various groups and the widening income distribution do not play as large a role.

A Simple Model of the Relationship between Income and Partisanship

To provide structure for our empirical analysis, we begin with the canonical prediction of political-economic models of voter preferences concerning tax rates and the size of government. These models predict that a voter's preferred tax rate is a function of both her own income and the aggregate income of society.[13] If we assume that tax schedules are either proportional or progressive, people with higher incomes will prefer lower tax rates because they will pay a larger share of taxes but receive only an equal share of public expenditure. Alternatively, when per capita income is larger, higher tax rates produce more money for redistribution and public goods. Thus, ceteris paribus, a citizen with a fixed income will prefer higher tax rates as per capita income increases. But when per capita incomes rise, citizens, especially richer ones, may be able to self-insure against income and other shocks through saving or private insurance. So increased per capita income may reduce the demand for social insurance programs such as unemployment and disability.

Can tax rates go through the roof? In a seminal paper, Duncan Foley (1967) assumed that people paid a proportion of their income as taxes but received, as redistribution, an equal share of the tax revenues. People with incomes below the mean would benefit, as their equal share would be greater than their taxes. Those above the mean would lose. Foley's model implies sharply polarized preferences. All below the mean income would favor a tax rate of 100 percent; all above it would favor 0 percent. What are the political implications of these polarized preferences? In simple models of politics, the median voter is thought to be decisive. Because income distributions are skewed with median income considerably less than mean income, Foley's model suggests that a democracy should have a high degree of redistribution.

Redistribution, however, cannot be carried out without a cost to aggregate income. Specifically, high taxation should reduce labor supply.[14] Alternatively, there could be a deadweight loss that occurs in the collection and redistribution of tax revenues. When taxation is costly, preferences on taxation become a continuous function of income. There is no longer Foley's discontinuity at the mean.

A straightforward, tractable model of the cost of taxation was developed by Bolton and Roland (1997). They assumed that redistribution generates a deadweight loss that is quadratic in the tax rate. Specifically, the deadweight loss from a dollar of taxation is αt^2, where α is a parameter and t is the proportional tax rate. So if $\alpha = 1$ and $t = 1/2$, a quarter is lost for every dollar collected, but if $t = 1$, the entire dollar is lost. In other words, tax increases generate increases in marginal cost. For $\alpha = 1$, tax revenue increases as t is increased from 0 to $1/2$, then fall as t is increased above $1/2$. The Bolton-Roland model is one way to generate the Laffer curve promoted by supply-siders, who claim that government revenue can be increased by cutting taxes.

With the quadratic loss model, the most preferred tax rate of a person decreases as her income rises—the rich want low taxes. In fact, the desired tax decreases linearly with the ratio of a citizen's pretax income to mean pretax income. If $\alpha = 1/2$, the most preferred tax rate of a voter is simply

$$t_{preferred} = 1 - \frac{\text{voter's income}}{\text{mean income}}.$$

Thus, as inequality increases—as the ratio falls for the median voter—there should be higher taxes and more redistribution. Note further that the median voter always wants some redistribution but that the desired tax rate will fall as government efficiency falls (α increases). For any level of efficiency, there will be more support for redistribution as the ratio of median to mean income falls. A shift in the ratio, say from 0.8 to 0.7, has important consequences for policy. These pressures for redistribution are likely to appear even if the median voter is not decisive for policy. In a responsive democracy, more inequality should typically lead to more redistribution. The ratio of median to mean income is a simple way of capturing the pressure to redistribute.

The Bolton-Roland model does carry over an undesirable feature of the Foley model. Those with average or above-average income have a preferred tax rate of zero. To adapt the model to one where voters with above-average income can seek some strictly positive rate of taxation, we allow all voters to derive altruistic benefits from government redistribution. Altruism might alternatively be thought of as a belief that some level of government is necessary for a society. To model this feature, we assume that each voter places a weight of one on the transfers he or she receives from the government and a weight of π on the average transfers to others.

In box 3.1, we explain how voting decisions for a generic voter i will depend on the utility difference between Republican and Democratic

Box 3.1

Voting over Alternative Tax Policies

Let the pretax income of a generic voter i be y_i. Let $\bar{y}$ denote average income. Bolton and Roland (1997) assume that the utility U_i of the voter is simply post-tax income. We supplement that model, however, and assume that voters receive an additional increase in utility from transfers to others based on public-spiritedness, altruism, and the like. So now the utility of a voter is given by $U_i = y_i(1-t) + (1+\pi)\bar{y}(t - \alpha t^2)$, where $\pi > 0$ is the boost to utility received by the voter from transferring to others.

If the political parties are polarized, the median voter is not decisive. Instead, voters must make the best of a bad situation and choose between the tax policies of the Republicans and Democrats, which we denote as t_R and t_D, with $t_D > t_R$. Some straightforward algebra then shows that the utility difference for the voters can be written as

$$U_i^R - U_i^D = (t_D - t_R)y_i + (t_D - t_R)(1+\pi)\bar{y}(\alpha(t_D + t_R) - 1)).$$

The first term is positive, proportional to income, and independent of deadweight loss. The Republicans are favored because they tax less. The second term depends on the tax policies and deadweight loss but is independent of the voter's income. When inefficiency and taxes are sufficiently low $(\alpha(t_D + t_R) < 1)$, the second term will favor the Democrats. Voters trade off taxes and benefits, with higher-income voters tilting to the Republicans. If tax platforms are held constant, the Democrats benefit from increasing government efficiency (i.e., lower α).

To further refine the model, we assume that each party represents a constituency with average incomes $y^R > y^D$. It is straightforward to show that the two tax policies most preferred by the constituencies are given by $t_R = \dfrac{(1+\pi)\bar{y} - y^R}{2\alpha(1+\pi)\bar{y}}$ and $t_D = \dfrac{(1+\pi)\bar{y} - y^D}{2\alpha(1+\pi)\bar{y}}$. If we substitute these back into the utility difference, we obtain

$$U_i^R - U_i^D = \frac{y^R - y^D}{2\alpha(1+\pi)}r_i - \frac{(y^R - y^D)(y^R + y^D)}{4\alpha\bar{y}(1+\pi)},$$

or

$$U_i^R - U_i^D = \frac{y^R - y^D}{2\alpha(1+\pi)}\left[r_i - \frac{y^R + y^D}{2\bar{y}}\right].$$

This simple model has implications for the effects of polarization on party support. First, an increase in polarization (i.e., a larger value of $y^R - y^D$) increases the sensitivity of the voter's choice to changes in relative income. Second, the effect of average income depends not only on the level of polarization but also on the absolute level of the two platforms. The greater $y^R + y^D$, the more an increase in average income benefits the Republicans.[15]

tax policies. This difference works through the voter's income, the average income, the incomes represented by the two parties, y^R and y^D, the extent of deadweight loss, and the degree of altruism. The ratio of the voter's income to average income is termed "relative income" and denoted r_i. Because a voter's party identification may depend on factors other than this income-based utility difference, let x_i be a vector of other factors that determine support for the Republican Party and ε_i be individually idiosyncratic factors. For x_i variables we use standard demographics—race, gender, education, age, and region—and a behavioral variable—church attendance—that represent variables other studies have found to be related to partisanship.[16]

Our model of Republican Party identification is therefore:

$$\text{Republican ID} = \tilde{\gamma} + \beta\left[r_i\frac{y^R - y^d}{2\alpha(1+\pi)}\right] + \boldsymbol{\theta}x_i + \epsilon_i$$

$$= \tilde{\gamma} + \tilde{\beta}r_i + \boldsymbol{\theta}x_i + \epsilon_i, \tag{3.1}$$

where

$$\tilde{\beta} = \beta\frac{y^R - y^D}{2\alpha(1+\pi)},$$

$$\tilde{\gamma} = \gamma - \beta\frac{(y^R - y^D)(y^R + y^D)}{4\alpha\bar{y}(1+\pi)},$$

with γ being a standard regression constant and the remaining term being a constant explained in box 3.1. Given this model, we can identify several factors that in principle could account for the increased stratification of partisanship by income.

1. *Inequality.* Increases in economic inequality may have led to more extreme values of r_i. A standard measure of economic inequality is the ratio of the income of the top quintile to that of the bottom quintile. Thus increased inequality could raise the mean value of r for the upper quintile or reduce the mean value of r for the lowest quintile.

2. *Response polarization.* Party polarization on economic issues as reflected by $y^R - y^D$ has increased. From equation 3.1, this increases $\tilde{\beta}$.

3. *Differential economic success of partisan groups.* Other determinants of party identification such as race, gender, region, education, and age have become more related to income. Therefore income stratification

may be a by-product of the differential economic success of the demographic groups that compose each party.

4. *Partisan demographic shifts.* Poorer demographic and social groups have moved toward the Democrats while wealthier groups have identified more with the Republicans.

Before assessing these different possibilities, we turn to some important data and estimation issues.

Data

We employ NES data from 1952 to 2012 to estimate equation 3.1. Our dependent variable is a seven-point scale of partisanship that ranges from Strong Democrat through Independent to Strong Republican, coded 0 to 6. Unfortunately, NES data pose a number of problems specific to the estimation of our model. Perhaps the biggest problem is that the NES does not report actual incomes but allows respondents to place themselves into various income categories. We use census data on the distribution of household income to estimate the expected income within each category. These estimates provide an income measure that preserves cardinality and comparability over time. The details of our procedure are in appendix 3.1.[17]

In addition to the constructed income variable, we include controls for race, region, gender, age, and education. Race and region are combined to create two categorical variables, African Americans and southern non-African Americans.[18] The residual category is northern non-African Americans. We measure education by distinguishing between those respondents who have "some college" or a "college degree" from those who have a high school diploma or less. We also include the age of the respondent. To capture the effects of "moral" issues, we include a dummy variable for church or synagogue attendance (at least "once or twice a month"). Table 3.1 gives the average value of each of these variables for selected election studies.[19]

In fact, race, gender, age, education, and church attendance are the only demographics that are consistently available on all of the twenty-eight NES presidential and midterm year surveys from 1952 through 2012.

It is important to note that these additional variables are not only statistical controls but also variables that are not distributed randomly across income levels. Therefore, both changes in the joint distribution

Table 3.1
NES sample means of variables (presidential election years)

Year	Party ID	Relative income	Black	Female	Some college	College	Age (yrs)	Southern white	Attends church
1952	2.475	0.902	0.090	0.544	0.083	0.064	44.812	0.221	0.563
1956	2.660	0.951	0.083	0.553	0.108	0.080	44.758	0.237	0.608
1960	2.546	0.945	0.074	0.539	0.114	0.096	48.435	0.263	0.590
1964	2.060	0.889	0.230	0.561	0.121	0.109	45.852	0.191	0.595
1968	2.333	0.846	0.158	0.567	0.136	0.130	46.702	0.227	0.546
1972	2.605	0.896	0.099	0.568	0.161	0.132	44.383	0.240	0.490
1976	2.606	0.885	0.100	0.580	0.181	0.152	45.616	0.235	0.525
1980	2.518	0.912	0.116	0.569	0.206	0.162	44.263	0.271	0.480
1984	2.768	0.831	0.111	0.562	0.247	0.167	44.405	0.227	0.489
1988	2.823	0.776	0.132	0.573	0.225	0.198	45.140	0.243	0.504
1992	2.705	0.741	0.128	0.534	0.236	0.235	45.755	0.241	0.515
1996	2.678	0.807	0.121	0.555	0.271	0.275	47.604	0.242	0.526
2000	2.726	0.838	0.118	0.563	0.303	0.309	47.206	0.268	0.529
2004	2.873	0.891	0.152	0.533	0.317	0.299	47.272	0.229	0.507
2008	2.297	0.794	0.251	0.570	0.307	0.217	47.369	0.222	0.459
2012	2.569	0.673	0.156	0.555	0.336	0.284	46.541	0.220	0.461

of these variables with income and changes in their relationship to partisanship may have effects on the extent to which partisanship is stratified by income.

To control for election-specific effects on partisanship, we include election fixed effects (year dummies) in the estimation.

Estimation
As just noted, we observe only placement on the seven-point partisan identification scale and not the continuous measure of Republican identification that is given in the linear equation 3.1. Our categorical data on partisan identification have, moreover, a bimodal distribution. Consequently, ordinary least squares estimation is inappropriate. A preferable alternative is to treat the partisanship variable as a set of ordered categories and estimate an ordered probit model (McKelvey and Zavoina 1975). In box 3.2, we describe how the ordered probit uses the data from the seven-category partisan identification scale to estimate equation 3.1.

To capture changes in how income and other variables relate to partisanship, we assume that the coefficients of equation 3.1 can change

Box 3.2
Ordered Probit Model of Partisan Identification

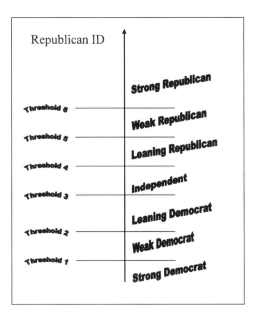

The amount of Republican identification is given by equation 3.1. If the amount is below threshold 1, the respondent is considered a "Strong Democrat." If the amount is between threshold 1 and threshold 2, the respondent is a "Weak Democrat," and so on. Equation 3.1 contains a random error that follows the unit normal distribution (the bell curve). Because the error is not observed, estimates of equation 3.1 give only the probability that a person falls into each of the seven categories of party identification. Ordered probit chooses estimates of both the coefficients in equation 3.1 and the thresholds to maximize the likelihood of the observed responses.

over time. For our relative income variable, we estimate several different specifications that restrict the movement of $\tilde{\beta}$ in various ways. We report four sets of results corresponding to a constant income effect, an effect with a linear trend, an effect with a fourth-order polynomial trend, and a separate income effect for each of the six decades represented in our data set. We also allow the effects of other variables to change over time with linear trends. We assume that the category thresholds estimated by the ordered probit are constant over time.

Therefore, the distribution of responses across categories changes only with respect to changes in the substantive coefficients and the distribution of the independent variables.[20]

Results

Table 3.2 presents the estimates for our four specifications of the income effect. Not surprisingly, across all four specifications, relative income is a statistically significant factor in the level of Republican partisanship. Model 1 has a constant income effect. Although it is statistically significant, the estimate of the constant effect is rather small. A person with twice the average income ($r_i = 2$) has Republican partisanship that is only 0.140 larger than one with an average income. This effect is less than one position on the partisanship scale, as the distance between the category thresholds averages more than 0.4.

The small average effect of income masks a definite trend over the entire period. Model 2 simplifies matters by assuming that the income effect changes only linearly. This model produces a statistically significant growth rate in the income effect of 0.0021 per year. From 1952 to 2012, the estimated income effect more than doubled, rising from 0.078 to 0.206. Roughly similar results appear in model 4, where there is a separate income effect for each decade. In the first two decades, the income effects are below 0.10, while they are above 0.16 in the last three. Even though the growth in the income effect is not monotonic, we find that the estimated income effects have grown substantially over time.

The results on elite polarization in chapter 2 show a decline in polarization after World War II followed by a subsequent rise. In addition, figure 3.2 suggests that there may have been a leveling off or a fall in income stratification at the end of the 1990s. To allow for both these effects, we estimated model 3, where income effects follow a fourth-order polynomial trend. The results are displayed in figure 3.3.

A first observation from figure 3.3 is that the confidence interval is always well above zero—income matters. The results, moreover, through the mid-1990s roughly match our earlier observations about elite polarization and income inequality—low levels followed by a sharp increase. The turning point, however, precedes the turning point in polarization by about a decade. By the twenty-first century, the income effect appears to decline, echoing popular claims that politics has now turned to abortion and other social issues. The decline, however, is imprecisely estimated, as the width of the confidence

Table 3.2
Effects of relative income on Republican partisanship, ordered probit (standard errors in parentheses)

	Constant income effect	Trended income effect	Fourth-order polynomial income effect	Decade income effect
Relative income	0.140 (0.008)	0.078 (0.018)	0.171 (0.046)	
Relative income × (year − 1951)/10		0.021 (0.005)	−0.198 (0.093)	
Relative income × [(year − 1951)/10]^2			0.120 (0.060)	
Relative income × [(year − 1951)/10]^3			−0.022 (0.014)	
Relative income × [(year − 1951)/10]^4			0.001 (0.001)	
Income effect 1952–1960				0.091 (0.023)
Income effect 1962–1968				0.077 (0.019)
Income effect 1972–1980				0.125 (0.016)
Income effect 1982–1990				0.177 (0.017)
Income effect 1992–2000				0.202 (0.020)
Income effect 2002–2012				0.161 (0.022)
N	42,678	42,678	42,678	42,678
Log-likelihood	−78,803.9	−78,796.5	−78,789.0	−78,789.0
Likelihood ratio p-value (H0 = constant effect)		.000	.000	.000
African American	−0.653 (0.037)	−0.673 (0.038)	−0.673 (0.038)	−0.675 (0.038)
African American × (year − 1951)/10	−0.064 (0.011)	-0.057 (0.011)	−0.058 (0.011)	−0.057 (0.011)
Female	0.132 (0.022)	0.127 (0.022)	0.127 (0.022)	0.126 (0.022)
Female × (year − 1951)/10	−0.053 (0.007)	-0.051 (0.007)	−0.051 (0.007)	−0.051 (0.007)
Southern nonblack	−0.571 (0.026)	−0.578 (0.026)	−0.577 (0.026)	−0.578 (0.026)
Southern nonblack × (year − 1951)/10	0.135 (0.008)	0.137 (0.008)	0.137 (0.008)	0.138 (0.008)
Some college	0.302 (0.032)	0.318 (0.032)	0.318 (0.032)	0.320 (0.032)

Table 3.2 (continued)

	Constant income effect	Trended income effect	Fourth-order polynomial income effect	Decade income effect
Some college × (year – 1951)/10	−0.044 (0.009)	−0.049 (0.009)	−0.049 (0.009)	−0.050 (0.009)
College degree	0.421 (0.035)	0.458 (0.036)	0.455 (0.036)	0.457 (0.036)
College degree × (year – 1951)/10	−0.076 (0.009)	−0.089 (0.010)	-0.088 (0.010)	−0.089 (0.010)

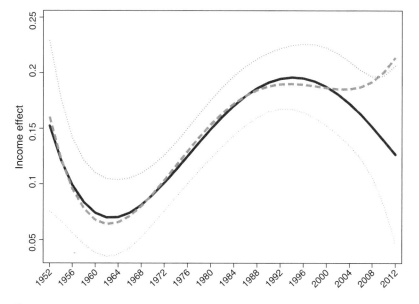

Figure 3.3
Income effect on party identification: fourth-order polynomial estimates. *Note:* The dashed line is an estimate excluding responses to the 2012 NES. The dotted lines represent the confidence interval for the estimates using all years.

interval expands sharply in the 2000s. Caution is in order in gauging the import of recent changes. In particular, much of the decline reflects the impact of the 2012 NES data. Without the 2012 data, the model, as shown by the dashed line in figure 3.3, estimates that the income effect in the twenty-first century is close to its level in the 1990s.

The effect of income in the formal theory represented in equation 3.1 calls for the effect of income to be expressed as the product of an underlying behavioral parameter (β) and the difference in the party tax rates or, more broadly, party platforms. The theory predicts that if we include relative income and the product of the difference in party platforms and income, only the interacted variable should be significant. To do an explicit test, we interacted relative income with the House party polarization measures plotted in figure 1.1. Although the specification did not fit as well as the linear trend specification, the results (not reported) are encouraging. The estimated coefficient of relative income was just 0.063, with a standard error of 0.028. But the estimated coefficient on the interacted variable was 0.125, with a p-value of 0.005.

We now turn to the results for coefficients other than income. The constant in the formal model is contained in the (unreported) year fixed effects. If the term γ was constant in time, the measured fixed effects should, theoretically, be decreasing in time. Observe that the second term in $\tilde{\gamma} = \gamma - \beta \dfrac{(y^R - y^D)(y^R + y^D)}{4\alpha\bar{y}(1+\pi)}$ is negative. In fact, if we assume, consistent with chapter 2, that polarization has taken the form of y^R increasing faster than y^D, the second term should have become more negative over time, leading to a falling value for γ. That is, we should see a decreasing sequence of year fixed effects.

In fact, the reverse occurs. The result is illustrated by the step model, where the year fixed effects are less than 0.20 until 1972 and greater than 0.35 for every election after 1992. The regression of the year fixed effects on time shows an R^2 of 0.86 and a t-statistic of 12.5. These results suggest, given our strong prior beliefs that the second term is negative, that the behavioral parameter γ is growing even more sharply than the fixed effects. That is, certain trends favoring Republican identification are not picked up in the effects of income and demographics, including trends in these effects. This increase in "valence advantage" is one reason why support for the Republican Party did not fall as a consequence of the party's shift to the right.

The effects of the other demographic variables have changed dramatically over the period of our study. These changes should not be surprising to casual observers. African Americans and females have moved away from the Republican Party, just as nonblack southerners have flocked toward it. Older voters supported the Republicans in the mid-twentieth century, but by the twenty-first their allegiance had deteriorated. The effects of education have diminished, in part because college attendance and graduation have skyrocketed.

The effect of income is very important compared to that of the demographic variables. Consider the estimates from column 4 of table 3.2. The upper half of table 3.3 shows how much the income of a respondent at half of the average income would need to increase to match the effect of a change in the other variables as for the 2000 election. Only in the case of race would an extreme income change be needed to match the effect of changes in the other demographics. The lower half of the table captures the effects of the demographic variables in 2012. The changes in income would, for most of the comparisons, have had to have been more substantial, a reflection of both the flattening out of the increase in the effect of income in the twenty-first century and the lengthening, by twelve years, of the effects of the linear trends in the demographics.

What Caused the Increase in Party-Income Stratification?

In this section, we attempt to assess the relative importance of the four hypotheses about the increase in party-income stratification. We use our estimates of equation 3.1 to compute implied levels of stratification under various scenarios. Consistent with testing hypotheses 1, 2, and

Table 3.3
Demographic and income shifts compared

2000	Pro-Republican identification shift	Equivalent relative income shift from one-half average income to:
Nonblack to black	0.953	5.222
Age 25 to 85	0.267	1.822
Female to male	0.124	1.115
No college to college	0.019	0.596
Non-South to South	0.096	0.976
Nonchurch to church	0.197	1.478
2012		
Nonblack to black	1.021	6.848
Age 25 to 85	0.415	3.079
Female to male	0.185	1.653
No college to college	−0.088	−0.046
Non-South to South	0.261	2.124
Nonchurch to church	0.262	2.129

3, we can manipulate the coefficients of the model, the distribution of r_i, and the joint distribution of r_i and the other demographic variables. To assess the relative importance of each of these changes, we compute the levels of party-income stratification in 1960, 2000, and 2008 under different scenarios, using the results of the fourth-order polynomial specification in column 3 of table 3.2.

Before asking what accounts for the change in party-income stratification, we first consider the types of demographic changes that have occurred over this period. Table 3.4 gives the profiles of the lowest and highest income quintiles for the 1960, 2000, and 2008 surveys. A respondent in the lowest quintile has a family income (or single income) below the 20th percentile point of the March Current Population Survey family income distribution and in the highest quintile if above the 80th percentile point. A comparison of the quintile ratio columns shows the magnitude by which the income distribution and the joint distribution of income and other attributes have changed over the past forty years.

Table 3.4
Characteristics of income quintiles, 1960, 2000, and 2008

	2008			2000			1960		
	Top quintile	Bottom quintile	Ratio	Top quintile	Bottom quintile	Ratio	Top quintile	Bottom quintile	Ratio
Average relative income	2.37	0.21	11.55	2.14	0.22	9.81	2.27	0.26	8.59
% African American	0.09	0.35	0.26	0.06	0.20	0.27	0.01	0.18	0.03
% Female	0.42	0.59	0.72	0.45	0.66	0.69	0.55	0.60	0.91
% Southern nonblack	0.22	0.22	0.98	0.30	0.30	1.00	0.29	0.30	0.95
% With some college	0.30	0.19	1.57	0.23	0.24	0.96	0.22	0.05	4.52
% With college degree	0.50	0.05	9.52	0.63	0.10	6.25	0.33	0.04	8.88
% Church attendance	0.54	0.50	1.08	0.53	0.50	1.06	0.69	0.50	1.38
Average age	45.93	46.83	0.98	44.93	50.48	0.89	46.35	59.47	0.78

The top-bottom quintile ratio for average relative income has increased from 8.59 to 11.55.[21] Beyond this striking change in the distribution of income, we find large changes in the placement of groups within the distribution.

Some changes have worked against the increased stratification of partisanship on income, for example in education. Both measures of education are distributed more equitably in 2000 than in 1960, whereas their correlation with Republican partisanship diminished substantially. But by 2008, inequality in education had grown. College degrees were more unequal in 2008 than in 1960. The changing distribution of age and its relation to partisanship also has worked against the increased overrepresentation of Republican identifiers in the top quintile. This change reflects the relatively lower age for the bottom quintile in 2000 and 2008; age is negatively correlated with Republican identification in the 2000s, whereas it was positively correlated in 1960.

Changes in the income distribution of the other demographic categories, however, clearly has worked to increase stratification. With the increase in single females from 1960 to 2008, females have become a notably larger share of the lowest quintile respondents and a smaller share of the top quintile.[22] Because females have moved steadily toward the Democratic Party, the effects on party-income stratification are quite apparent.[23] Conversely, the move of high-income southerners into the Republican Party contributes to stratification.

The changes with respect to race are more ambiguous. Income inequality *among* African Americans has increased dramatically, so that blacks now compose a greater portion of *both* of the extreme income quintiles. African Americans as a group are largely Democratic identifiers. If the propensity to choose a Democratic identification were independent of income, the black increase at the top quintile would decrease stratification, and the increase at the bottom would increase it. If we control for income, however, we find that the propensity of African Americans to identify with the Democrats has increased. Because blacks remain substantially overrepresented at the bottom and underrepresented at the top, that they have become more Democratic increases stratification. This effect of increased African American identification with the Democratic Party outweighs the effects arising from the changes in the income distribution of blacks.

To quantify the magnitude of some of these effects, we simulate stratification scores for 1960, 2000, and 2008 using the results of the fourth-order polynomial income effect model. We manipulate the model and the profiles in order to assess which factors most contributed to the increased stratification. These results are shown in table 3.5.[24]

The first three rows of table 3.5 reflect the estimated stratification for each year using the actual model. That is, for each respondent in the top quintile, we use the estimated coefficients to compute the probability that the respondent is a Republican (strong and weak) identifier. We then average these probabilities to estimate the fraction of the top quintile that are Republican identifiers. We do the same for the bottom

Table 3.5
Determinants of party-income stratification

Number	Scenario	Average Republican probability of lowest quintile	Average Republican probability of highest quintile	Party-income stratification
1	1960	0.206	0.326	1.581
2	2000	0.207	0.380	1.832
3	2008	0.180	0.349	1.937
4	2000 with 1960 sample	0.198	0.410	2.065
5	2008 with 1960 sample	0.198	0.381	1.924
6	1960 with 2000 Sample	0.220	0.346	1.573
7	1960 with 2008 Sample	0.187	0.345	1.843
8	1960 with 2000 Income	0.205	0.322	1.572
9	1960 with 2008 Income	0.211	0.388	1.839
10	2000 with 1960 income	0.210	0.389	1.854
11	2008 with 1960 income	0.182	0.344	1.891
12	2000 with 1960 income effect	0.201	0.294	1.464
13	2008 with 1960 income effect	0.177	0.285	1.607
14	1960 with 2000 income effect	0.214	0.419	1.957
15	1960 with 2008 income effect	0.211	0.388	1.839

quintile. The ratio of the two fractions is our stratification measure. These results are our benchmarks for comparison with other counterfactuals. They are somewhat greater for 1960 and somewhat less for 2000 than the actual stratifications reported in figure 3.2.

Our first exercise untangles whether the change in stratification is driven by changes in estimated model effects or by changes in demographics. In rows 4 and 5, we estimate stratification using the estimated coefficients for 2000 and 2008, respectively, applied to the 1960 sample respondents. The exercises show how much the change in stratification is due to changes in the structure of partisanship. Both the 2000 and 2008 experiments are much larger than the 1960s baseline, demonstrating the important effect of the changing parameters of the partisanship model. That the 2008 estimate is smaller than the 2000 estimate suggests that recent changes in the model have slightly lowered the expected level of stratification, holding demographics constant.

Alternatively, rows 6 and 7 flip the experiments and show the estimated stratification when the 1960 coefficients are applied to the 2000 and 2008 respondents to capture the effects of the demographic shifts. The resulting stratification of 1.573 for 2000 is almost identical to the estimated stratification for 1960 (row 1), suggesting that demographic changes had little net effect through 2000. But the 2008 estimate is much larger at 1.843, suggesting that demographic effects have had a substantial impact over the last decade. Together these results suggest two phases in the relationship between income and partisanship, an earlier phase through the 1990s that was driven primarily by changes in the relationship between demographics and partisanship and a later phase dominated by demographic changes.

The remaining rows of table 3.5 deal specifically with the direct effects of relative income. Rows 8 to 11 correspond to counterfactual estimates of stratification in each year using the degree of income inequality in another year. For row 8, we use the estimates in table 3.2 but multiply top 1960 quintile incomes by 2.14/2.27 (see table 3.4) and bottom quintile incomes by 0.22/0.25. Otherwise, we use the 1960 sample and coefficients. The experiment for row 9 is analogous but uses the numbers for 2008.

For rows 10 and 11, we reverse the process to simulate 2000 and 2008 stratification with the 1960 income distribution. These results show that changes in the distribution of income barely affected stratification through 2000. In both rows 8 and 10, the counterfactual stratification indices are almost identical to the actual ones. The contribution of income inequality is much more substantial through 2008. The comparisons of rows 1 and 9 suggest that the change in income distribution accounted for a 0.3 increase in stratification. The reverse experiment based on the comparison of rows 3 and 11 shows a much smaller impact, however.

To see this link, we turn to the effects of the increased impact of relative income on partisanship. In row 12, we estimate 2000 stratification using the 2000 sample and all coefficients except for the one for relative income, where we substitute the 1960 coefficient. We do the same for 2008 in row 13. In row 14 (15), we reverse the roles of 1960 and 2000 (2008).

In all of the experiments, the resulting stratification is very close to the actual value for the year whose income effect is being used. The stratification for 2008 using a 1960 income effect is 1.607, slightly larger than the baseline of 1960 (1.581). Similarly, the stratification of 1960 using a 2008 income effect is 1.839, a smidgen less than the 2008 baseline of 1.937.

These results suggest that the driving force behind the increased stratification was the increased correlation between income and partisanship. If we interpret this increase as party polarization, these findings suggest that the changes in the bivariate relationship can best be accounted for by the actions of the party elites and not the voters. In other words, as the parties have become differentiated in fiscal and other economic policies, they have cued the voters to vote more on the basis of income.

Political Competition in a Richer Society

The 2000 presidential election ended in a dead heat, and the final outcome rested with a decision by the Supreme Court. From Bill Clinton's election in 1992 through Barack Obama's reelection in 2012, the presidential winner has never obtained as much as 53 percent of the popular vote. The close races remind us that the American political system has remained remarkably competitive. Indeed, the NES sample percentages of Republican partisans from 1952 to 2002 have fluctuated, with no apparent trend (Green, Palmquist, and Schickler 2002, 15). (There has been a decline for the Democrats, to the benefit of independents.)

Should such a balance have been maintained? Real median income doubled between 1952 and 1996. Average income increased even more sharply. Should not this change have benefited the Republicans?

If respondents computed their relative income not on the basis of average income in the year of the survey but on the basis of average income in 1960, Republicans clearly would have been advantaged. Table 3.6 shows the actual fraction of Republican identifiers in the

Table 3.6
Republican identification and the change in real income

Year	Actual	Estimated from model	Estimated using 1960 mean income to compute relative income
1952	0.281	0.235	0.226
1956	0.303	0.257	0.254
1958	0.294	0.210	0.208
1960	0.297	0.248	0.248
1962	0.297	0.233	0.234
1964	0.220	0.171	0.173
1966	0.251	0.236	0.240
1968	0.231	0.214	0.220
1970	0.232	0.224	0.232
1972	0.238	0.263	0.272
1974	0.237	0.242	0.251
1976	0.242	0.259	0.270
1978	0.211	0.242	0.255
1980	0.230	0.255	0.266
1982	0.244	0.228	0.241
1984	0.276	0.281	0.298
1986	0.256	0.263	0.287
1988	0.280	0.298	0.322
1990	0.249	0.254	0.277
1992	0.255	0.267	0.289
1994	0.307	0.321	0.347
1996	0.278	0.271	0.299
1998	0.268	0.269	0.301
2000	0.254	0.275	0.312
2002	0.320	0.316	0.361
2004	0.290	0.309	0.347
2008	0.188	0.240	0.270
2012	0.210	0.259	0.277

sample, the estimated fraction using the model coefficients, and the estimated fraction replacing average real income in the relevant year with average real income in 1960 in computing relative income, r_i.

The comparison to the estimated model predictions shows that from 1986 onward, the increase in real incomes would have generated a gain in the 2 to 4 percent range in Republican identification had respondents compared their current incomes to 1960 average incomes. With respect to the actual sample fractions, the gain would have been in the 2 to 8 percent range. Insofar as the actual system is very competitive, a gain of 2 percent or more would likely have swung many offices to Republicans. Arguably, the real incomes represented by the parties have increased in a way that preserves a competitive two-party system.

Did the South Do It?

After the Second World War, the American South evolved from a one-party system centered on the Democrats to a two-party system dominated by Republicans. Our results show that southern nonblacks switched from being substantially more Democratic than northern nonblacks to being substantially more Republican. This change in partisan identification has already been examined by Green, Palmquist, and Schickler (2002). Our contribution is to indicate that pocketbook voting is an important part of the story of the dramatic switch of partisan allegiances in the South.

What happened in the South with respect to income is vividly illustrated by figures 3.4 and 3.5. Figure 3.4 shows results for the quartic polynomial estimation when the model is estimated with only nonblack respondents in the South. Figure 3.5 is the comparable figure for northern nonblacks.

The South shows a sharply increasing income effect. Income had essentially no effect on southern partisanship in the 1950s. The confidence interval shown in figure 3.4 includes zero as late as 1966. A likelihood ratio test of the linear effect rejects the null hypothesis of a constant income effect. As the figure suggests, testing a quartic model against the linear model does not lead to rejection of the null hypothesis that the increase is linear. The increase shows signs of abatement only when we include the 2012 NES data.

The results for the North form a stark contrast to the South. Although the confidence interval always lies above zero, the constant income

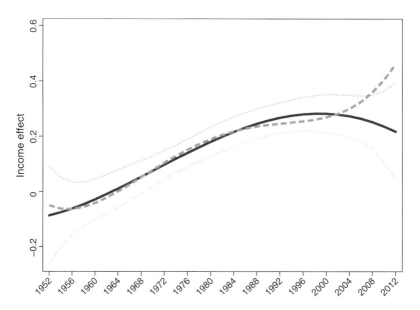

Figure 3.4
Income effect on party identification: fourth-order polynomial estimates for southern non-African Americans. *Note:* Dashed line is an estimate excluding responses to the 2012 NES. The dotted lines represent the confidence interval for the estimates using all years.

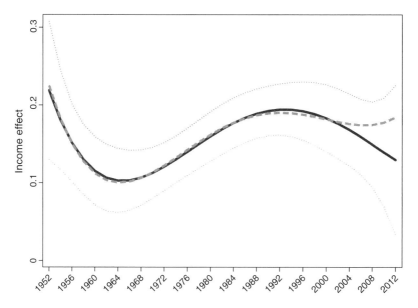

Figure 3.5
Income effect on party identification: fourth-order estimates for northern non-African Americans for the estimates using all years. *Note:* Dashed line is an estimate excluding responses to the 2012 NES. The dotted lines represent the confidence interval.

effect model is not rejected for the linear model but is rejected for the quartic model. The North went through a declining income effect in the 1950s, when elite polarization was low, and an increasing effect in the 1970s and 1980s, when elite polarization was increasing. But, intriguingly, the income effect in the North plateaued from the 1990s onward and even declined to a level no higher than it was in the mid-1970s once we include the 2012 NES data.

The 2000s

We can also take a closer look at recent years by using surveys conducted by the Pew Research Center for the People and the Press. Pew surveys, in the field almost every month in both election and nonelection years, generally include partisanship, income, and demographic variables compatible with our NES analysis. The advantages of the Pew surveys are that they take place at reasonably regular intervals and that large sample sizes can be obtained by pooling surveys. One important difference is that there are only five responses to the party identification question (Democrat, Leans Democrat, Independent, Leans Republican, and Republican). If we assume that Pew's Democrat and Republican responses are equivalent to collapsing the NES's weak and strong partisan categories, however, estimates of equation 3.1 are comparable across the NES and Pew samples. The other difference is that questions about the frequency of church attendance are asked only sporadically by Pew. Instead, we can use the perhaps more politically appropriate question: "Would you describe yourself as a 'born-again' or evangelical Christian?"

The Pew data allows us to examine whether there has been a general attenuation of the income effect during the past eight years. In figure 3.6 we show the income coefficient (and confidence interval) for each year since 1997 from the Pew studies.[25] Through 2008, any attenuation of the income effect is relatively mild. The 2008 estimate is within the 1999 confidence interval. After 2008, the income effect drops sharply, consistent with the findings from the 2012 NES. (Exceptionally, the NES did not conduct a midterm survey in 2010.) This finding also holds when we examine only nonblacks outside the South.

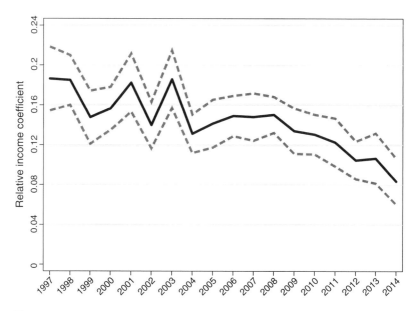

Figure 3.6
Annual income effect. *Note:* From PEW surveys conducted between 1997 and 2014 (N = 325,704). The dotted lines represent the confidence interval.

Moral Issues

As we mentioned at the beginning of the chapter, most popular analyses of recent elections have focused on moral and cultural issues.[26] These are certainly factors. Both the NES and the Pew surveys indicate that regular churchgoers and evangelical Christians identify more strongly with the Republican Party than in the past. Nevertheless, it is hard to make the case that the emergence of these cleavages helps to explain the polarization of the past thirty years. First, moral and social issues are not a large part of the congressional roll call agenda and thus cannot explain the divergence in NOMINATE scores between the two parties. Second, the rising effect of church attendance on Republican identification did not begin until the 1990s. If we estimate equation 3.1 just on the basis of the NES studies before 1992, the coefficient on church attendance is not significantly different from zero. The NES did not even ask about evangelical Christianity until 1984. This item, like church attendance, is insignificant in equation 3.1 until the 1990s. Even in the 2000 NES, church attendance is worth only about 1.5 units of relative income. If we replace church attendance with the NES's born-again variable, the effect of being a born-again Christian in 2000 is also about the same as 1.5 units of relative income (about $50,000 in family income).[27]

Perhaps the biggest fallacy about conservative Christian voters is that they systematically vote against their economic interests. There seem to be two reasons for this misunderstanding. The first has to do with the observation that blue states have higher average incomes than red states. This observation is true but misleading. It certainly does not imply that richer people are more Democratic. The NES and Pew studies show that this pattern is not true for party identification, and we will show that it is not true for voting. The second misconception is that conservative Christians are systematically poorer than other groups. They are, but the difference is much smaller than conventional wisdom would have it. Using the Pew studies from 2012, we find that there is only about a $16,000 average difference between the family incomes of born-again respondents and those of all other respondents.[28] About half of this difference can be accounted for by demographic differences such as region, age, gender, and education.

Another reason that the "voting against economic interest" story is not compelling is that income is an extraordinarily good predictor of partisanship even among conservative Christians. Figure 3.7 shows the percentage of born-again white Pew study respondents who call themselves Republicans by relative income (r_i). For born-again Christians and evangelicals, the percentage Republican increases steeply with income. This income gradient is even larger than for non-born-again whites. The difference across groups is about ten percentage points with those for the lowest relative incomes but grows to a difference of more than twenty percentage points at the highest incomes. This bivariate finding holds up well in our econometric model. If we run equation 3.1 just on white born-again Christians, the estimated income effect is 0.235, 70 percent higher than the overall effect.

These results suggest that low-income conservative Christians do not completely ignore their economic interests (see also Bartels 2008). Certainly, they feel cross-pressures between their Bible and their pocketbook, and they do support the Republicans more than other low-income voters do. Nevertheless, support for Republicans is much lower than among other conservative Christians with higher incomes whose Bible and pocketbook point in the same direction.

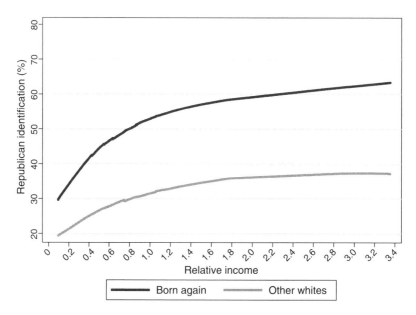

Figure 3.7
Republican identification, religion, and relative income. *Note:* Computed from Pew surveys conducted between 1997 and 2014. The figures are based solely on the responses of white, non-Hispanic respondents.

Presidential Voting

To this point, we have concentrated primarily on partisanship. There are good reasons to focus on partisanship, but elections are won and lost by voting, so we turn to vote choice.

Fortunately, our results for partisan identification replicate nicely in a probit analysis of presidential vote choice. The dependent variable is coded 1 for Republican and 0 for Democrat. Our sample here is defined only by those respondents who expressed a choice for one of the major party candidates in the presidential year. Declared abstentions, votes for minor party candidates, and nonresponses resulted in our having only about two-thirds as many observations per year as for the partisan identification analysis. We use the same independent variable specifications as in our analysis of partisan identification. In table 3.7 we show the results.

For presidential voting, relative income continues to have a significant effect, as shown in column 1 of table 3.7. The result for the linear trend model in column 2 is very similar to that for partisan

Table 3.7
Effects of relative income on presidential vote choice, probit (standard errors in parentheses)

	Constant income effect	Trended income effect	Fourth-order polynomial income effect	Decade income effect
Relative income	0.229 (0.017)	0.152 (0.033)	0.223 (0.071)	
Relative income × (year − 1951)/10		0.025 (0.009)	−0.320 (0.162)	
Relative income × [(year − 1951)/10]^2			0.260 (0.108)	
Relative income × [(year − 1951)/10]^3			−0.063 (0.026)	
Relative Income × [(year − 1951)/10]^4			0.005 (0.002)	
Income effect 1952–1960				0.135 (0.038)
Income effect 1962–1968				0.154 (0.046)
Income effect 1972–1980				0.237 (0.033)
Income Effect 1982–1990				0.315 (0.042)
Income Effect 1992–2000				0.267 (0.038)
Income Effect 2002–2012				0.254 (0.040)
N	16,727	16,727	16,727	16,727
Log-likelihood	−10,131.5	−10,127.9	−10,122.9	−10,124.4
Likelihood ratio p-value (H0 = constant effect)		0.007	0.002	0.014

Table 3.7 (continued)

	Constant income effect	Trended income effect	Fourth-order polynomial income effect	Decade income effect
African American	−1.127	−1.148	−1.152	−1.152
	(0.096)	(0.097)	(0.096)	(0.096)
African American × (year − 1951)/10	−0.137	−0.132	−0.130	−0.130
	(0.029)	(0.029)	(0.029)	(0.029)
Female	0.092	0.085	0.085	0.084
	(0.040)	(0.040)	(0.040)	(0.040)
Female × [(year − 1951)/10]	−0.061	−0.059	−0.059	−0.059
	(0.012)	(0.012)	(0.012)	(0.012)
Southern nonblack	−0.126	-0.135	−0.134	−0.135
	(0.049)	(0.049)	(0.049)	(0.049)
Southern nonblack × (year − 1951)/10	0.062	0.064	0.064	0.065
	(0.014)	(0.014)	(0.014)	(0.014)
Some college	0.318	0.334	0.338	0.338
	(0.058)	(0.058)	(0.058)	(0.058)
Some college × (year − 1951)/10	−0.044	−0.049	−0.051	−0.051
	(0.016)	(0.016)	(0.016)	(0.016)
College degree	0.294	0.338	0.337	0.336
	(0.061)	(0.063)	(0.063)	(0.063)
College degree × (year − 1951)/10	−0.068	−0.082	−0.082	−0.082
	(0.017)	(0.017)	(0.017)	(0.017)
Age	0.080	0.076	0.075	0.075
	(0.013)	(0.013)	(0.013)	(0.013)
Age × (year − 1951)/10	−0.012	−0.011	−0.010	−0.010
	(0.004)	(0.004)	(0.004)	(0.004)
Attends church	0.040	0.040	0.043	0.042
	(0.041)	(0.040)	(0.040)	(0.040)
Attends church × (year − 1951)/10	0.083	0.083	0.083	0.083
	(0.012)	(0.012)	(0.012)	(0.012)
Constant	−0.438	−0.347	−0.381	−0.322
	(0.079)	(0.086)	(0.098)	(0.088)

identification, particularly after we consider the effects of sample size on precision. Similarly, the pattern of the time polynomial coefficients for the quartic model is quite similar in comparing models 3 from table 3.2 and table 3.7.

Red and Blue

At this point, readers may wonder how our analysis jibes with the red and blue maps they saw on election nights starting in 2000. It is unmistakable from these maps that the Democratic candidates drew heavy support from the high-income coasts while Republicans won the lower-income middle of the country. Nevertheless, suggesting that this pattern holds because Republicans draw support from low-income voters is a classic example of the ecological fallacy of inferring individual behavior from aggregate statistics. If there is regional variation in Republican support spuriously correlated to average income, the red-blue maps are entirely consistent with our results.

To demonstrate that there is indeed a strong income effect in partisanship within regions, we use the Pew studies from 1997 to 2014 to compute the partisan attachments of high- and low-income voters by state. Figure 3.8 shows the percentage of Republican identifiers in the

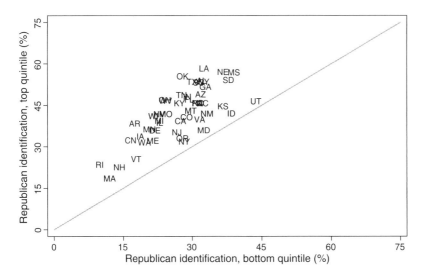

Figure 3.8
Party-income stratification by state. *Note*: Computed from Pew surveys conducted between 1997 and 2014. The figures are based on the responses of white respondents.

top income quintile (based on the national income distribution) and the percentage of Republicans in the bottom quintile. To focus on cleavages among white voters, we exclude nonwhites and Hispanics.

This figure reveals that there is at least some income stratification in each of the forty-eight states included in Pew's sample, as all the tokens lie above the 45-degree line. Although a couple of states, such as Massachusetts and Utah, have very small income gaps in party identification, most states have cleavages on the order of that for the United States as a whole. Perhaps surprisingly, within-state income stratification does not seem to be a "red state" phenomenon. Many of the states that voted for Gore, Kerry, and Obama have large gaps in the party identification of rich and poor.

To show that the election maps provide incorrect inferences about the role of income in presidential voting, we examine county-level voting returns for president for each election from 1968 to 2012. Our dependent variable is the Republican share of the two-party vote. We then use census data to construct an aggregate version of equation 3.1. For each election, we match each county to its demographic profile from the most proximate census. As an income variable, we use the natural log of median family income for each county. As the Census Bureau does not ask about religion, we use data on the number of churches per capita (Glenmary Research Center 2010).[29] We do not include gender because there is not much variation across counties.

We pool all of these election returns into one large panel. We allow linear trends in the demographic characteristics but estimate a separate income coefficient for each year.[30] In model 1, we regress the Republican vote on just the annual income coefficients and year fixed effects. This model captures the annual bivariate relationship between county income and Republican voting. The income coefficients are given in column 1 of table 3.8.[31] According to the estimates, the income effect peaked in 1980 and has declined since. From 1996 forward, the effects are negative, and are statistically significant starting in 2004. This finding explains why the maps look the way they do. In column 2, the demographic characteristics (with time trends) are added to the model. The income effect now peaks in the most recent elections, 2012, and is statistically significant for all years starting in 1988. In comparison to column 1, this finding suggests that the perceived negative correlation between income and Republican voting in the maps is accounted for by geographic variation in other

Table 3.8
Republican support by county, 1968–2012 (standard errors in parentheses)

Income measure	Model 1	Model 2	Model 3	Model 4
Ln family income 1968	0.010	−0.019	0.072	0.012
	(0.019)	(0.025)	(0.022)	(0.023)
Ln family income 1972	−0.120	−0.145	0.027	−0.029
	(0.018)	(0.022)	(0.020)	(0.020)
Ln family income 1976	0.114	0.094	0.132	0.076
	(0.017)	(0.022)	(0.021)	(0.021)
Ln family income 1980	0.129	0.108	0.148	0.084
	(0.028)	(0.032)	(0.024)	(0.026)
Ln family income 1984	0.042	0.030	0.126	0.069
	(0.031)	(0.032)	(0.029)	(0.025)
Ln family oncome 1988	0.040	0.110	0.155	0.174
	(0.020)	(0.027)	(0.021)	(0.022)
Ln family income 1992	0.008	0.098	0.127	0.159
	(0.021)	(0.028)	(0.022)	(0.023)
Ln family income 1996	−0.030	0.078	0.114	0.159
	(0.024)	(0.029)	(0.024)	(0.024)
Ln family income 2000	−0.044	0.090	0.082	0.160
	(0.034)	(0.033)	(0.031)	(0.025)
Ln family income 2004	−0.080	0.076	0.036	0.129
	(0.033)	(0.033)	(0.032)	(0.027)
Ln family income 2008	−0.108	0.136	0.039	0.205
	(0.031)	(0.033)	(0.033)	(0.026)
Ln family income 2012	−0.104	0.169	0.057	0.244
	(0.034)	(0.036)	(0.036)	(0.030)
N	37,368	37,069	37,368	37,069
R^2	0.157	0.481	0.421	0.749
Year fixed effects	Yes	Yes	No	No
Demographics	No	Yes	No	Yes
State × Year fixed effects	No	No	Yes	Yes

variables, notably the percentage of African Americans (and, to a much lesser extent, the number of churches). In column 3, we drop the demographic variables but use state-by-year fixed effects to capture regional variation in Republican support. Now the income coefficient is positive in all elections but, parallel to our results from the NES and Pew studies, atrophies in the twenty-first century. Column 4 contains the results from the model with demographics and state-by-year fixed effects. The results reinforce our results from column 2. Again, 2012 has the largest, highly statistically significant coefficient, more than three times the value for 1984 and earlier years. Clearly, it is important to control for demographics in assessing how income affects voting.

These results show that while Republicans have gained support in lower-income *regions*, they have not lost support among higher-income *voters*. Within each state and demographic group, the higher the income, the more Republican the outcome.

Conclusion

High-income Americans have consistently, over the second half of the twentieth century and into the twenty-first, been more prone to identify with and vote for the Republican Party than have low-income Americans, who have sided with the Democrats. The impact of income persists when one controls for other demographics, and the magnitude is important. Moreover, there has been a rather substantial transformation in the economic basis of the American party system. Today, income is far more important than it was in the 1950s. American politics is certainly far from purely class-based, but the divergence in partisan identification and voting between high- and low-income Americans has been striking. This trend helps to explain the conflicts over taxation of estates and dividends in an era generally presumed to be dominated by "hot-button" social issues like abortion and guns.

In our simple theoretical model, we posited that relative, not absolute, income was important to voting behavior. As average incomes rose in the last half of the twentieth century, voters and political parties, we believe, made adjustments that maintained an extremely competitive two-party system, most strikingly in the 2000 presidential race. Indeed, a simulation suggested that the Republicans would have had an additional advantage in partisan identification of around three percentage points if voters had compared their current incomes to the 1960 average income.

The fact that the political system has remained largely competitive because parties and voters have adapted to the large increases in real income should not mask some important observations about American politics and an important finding in this chapter. First, although the system is competitive, the system appears to have shifted from a slight advantage for Democrats to a slight advantage for Republicans. This shift is most notable in the Republican control of Congress, which began after the 1994 elections and continued, in spurts, to a post–Great Depression high after the 2014 elections. Moreover, the Republicans have won five of the last nine presidential elections. Second, as we showed in chapter 2, the Republicans appear to have become more competitive while shifting to the right. As for taxes, the vigorous cuts of the Reagan and George W. Bush administrations were offset by relatively mild increases under Clinton. Obama just partially restored some of the Clinton-era tax rates. Third, we have seen an increase in year fixed effects in our estimates of partisan identification. Something has, at the least, compensated the Republicans for the shifts in the effects of relative income and demographics.

One possibility is that the Republicans have benefited from "moral values" shifts that are not captured in our church attendance variable. But other analysis in this chapter suggests that this possibility cannot be a complete explanation because born-again and evangelical Christians are particularly sensitive to income effects on political preferences. Another possibility is that the increase in real income has led a majority of the electorate to be less favorable to redistribution and social insurance than were the counterparts of these voters a half century earlier. The diminished need for social insurance is perhaps marked by increases in net worth and wealth (Guiso, Haliassos, and Jappelli 2002), home ownership, and securities ownership. Home ownership rose from 63 percent in 1965 to 69 percent in 2004 before declining following the Great Recession.[32] In particular, Duca and Saving (2008) have argued, using econometric analysis, that the increase in the Republican share of the popular vote for Congress can be attributed to the rise in securities ownership from 25 percent in 1964 to nearly 50 percent in 1998. In any event, the Republicans have prospered by moving strongly away from redistribution to the poor as income stratification of voters has intensified.

There are, of course, multiple sources for the increased political divergence between high- and low-income voters. But our evidence shows that changes in both overall income inequality and the incomes of various demographic groups have only marginally contributed to increased partisan stratification on income; the most important contributions seem to come from partisan polarization and the southern realignment. Consistent with our model, the coefficient of relative income roughly tracks patterns of elite polarization derived from congressional voting studies. That is, the basic pattern is a decline or leveling in the 1950s and 1960s, followed by an increase in the 1970s and 1980s. In fact, we used both relative income and relative income interacted with our elite polarization measure in one variant of our statistical analysis. As called for by our theoretical model, only the interaction term was significant. Moreover, as our simulation results showed, the increased importance of the relative income variable seems to be primarily responsible for the increased connection between income and partisanship.

It is not terribly surprising that the southern realignment also plays an important role in our findings because it is the most important change in the American party system during the twentieth century. Our results about the changes in southern politics, however, differ substantially from arguments stressing the role of race and social issues. We do not deny the importance of these factors, but we find that the political attachments of the contemporary South are driven by income and economic status to an extent even greater than in the rest of the country. Even if a decline in income-based voting in the North, most notably in 2012, proves to be fundamental and enduring, the role of income in southern politics and the South's increasing share of the national electorate will likely prevent any significant depolarization of American politics in the near future.

We note, in closing this chapter, that we have found a discrepancy in the change in the income effect between our analysis of survey data and our analysis of county-level election results. The county analysis shows an increasing effect of income through 2012. We address this discrepancy in the concluding chapter. For now, we note that the increasing role of income in the county analysis matches the raw increase in stratification presented at the beginning of this chapter. Income stratification, regardless of how it works its way through covariates, is likely to substantially impact public policy.

Appendix 3.1   Approximating Incomes for NES Categories

Given categorical income data, there are two typical approaches to comparing income responses at different points in time. Let $x_t = \{x_{1t}, \ldots x_{kt} \ldots, x_{Kt} = \infty\}$ be the vector of upper bounds for the NES income categories at time t.[33] The first approach is to use the categories ordinally by converting them to income percentiles for each time period.

This approach, however, throws away potentially useful cardinal information about income. Further, as it is unlikely that income categories will always coincide with a particular set of income percentiles, some respondents will have to be assigned ad hoc to percentile categories. A second approach is to assume that the true income is a weighted average of the income bounds. Formally, one might assume that the true income for response k at time t is $\alpha x_{k-1,t} + (1-\alpha)x_{kt}$ for some $\alpha \in [0,1]$. The true weight will depend on the exact shape of the income distribution. When the income density is increasing in $[x_{k-1,t}, x_{kt}]$, the weight on x_{kt} should be higher than when the density is decreasing over the interval. The same weights cannot be used for each category at a particular point in time or even for the same category over time.

As neither of these two approaches can be used to generate the appropriate data, we use census data on the distribution of income to estimate the expected income within each category. These estimates provide an income measure that preserves cardinality and comparability over time.

To outline our procedure, let $y_t = \{ y_{1t}, \ldots, y_{Mt}\}$ be the income levels reported by the census corresponding to a vector of percentiles $z_t = \{z_{1t}, \ldots, z_{Mt}\}$. We use family income quintiles and the top 5 percent. Therefore, for 1996, $y_{1996} = \{\$18,485; \$33,830; \$52,565; \$81,199; \$146,500\}$ and $z_{1996} = \{0.2, 0.4, 0.6, 0.8, 0.95\}$. We assume that the true distribution of income has a distribution function $F(\cdot | \mathbf{\Omega}_t)$ where $\mathbf{\Omega}_t$ is a vector of time-specific parameters. Therefore, $F(\mathbf{y}_t | \mathbf{\Omega}_t) = \mathbf{z}_t$. In order to generate estimates of $\hat{\mathbf{\Omega}}_t$, let $w(\hat{\mathbf{\Omega}}_t) = F(\mathbf{y}_t | \mathbf{\Omega}_t) - \mathbf{z}_t$. We then choose $\hat{\mathbf{\Omega}}_t$ to minimize $w(\hat{\mathbf{\Omega}}_t)'w(\hat{\mathbf{\Omega}}_t)$. Given an estimate of $\hat{\mathbf{\Omega}}_t$, we can compute the expected income within each NES category as

$$EI_{kt} = \begin{cases} \left[F\left(x_{1t}|\hat{\mathbf{\Omega}}_t\right)\right]^{-1} \displaystyle\int_0^{x_{1t}} x \, dF\left(x|\hat{\mathbf{\Omega}}_t\right) \text{ if } k = 1 \\ \left[F\left(x_{kt}|\hat{\mathbf{\Omega}}_t\right) - F\left(x_{k-1,t}|\hat{\mathbf{\Omega}}_t\right)\right]^{-1} \displaystyle\int_{x_{k-1,t}}^{x_{kt}} x \, dF\left(x|\hat{\mathbf{\Omega}}_t\right) \text{ otherwise} \end{cases}.$$

We assume $F(\cdot)$ is log-normal with $\hat{\mathbf{\Omega}}_t = \{\mu_t, \sigma_t\}$. These parameters have very straightforward interpretations. The median income at time t is simply e^{μ_t}, and σ_t^2 is the variance of log income, which is a commonly used measure of inequality. Table 3A.1 gives the estimates of $\hat{\mathbf{\Omega}}_t$ for each presidential election year. These results underscore the extent to which the income distribution has become more unequal.

Table 3

A.1. Estimates of the log-normal income distribution, by election year

Election year	μ_t (mean)	σ_t (standard deviation)
1952	7.894	0.817
1956	8.172	0.804
1958	8.269	0.798
1960	8.356	0.793
1962	8.419	0.822
1964	8.508	0.812
1966	8.607	0.796
1968	8.793	0.763
1970	8.959	0.756
1972	9.026	0.776
1974	9.179	0.786
1976	9.306	0.792
1978	9.455	0.803
1980	9.641	0.809
1982	9.794	0.822
1984	9.900	0.831
1986	10.016	0.839
1988	10.105	0.852
1990	10.215	0.848
1992	10.260	0.855
1994	10.300	0.877
1996	10.386	0.864
1998	10.470	0.881
2000	10.568	0.882
2002	10.613	0.888

Note: There was no NES study in 1954.

Figure 3.A1 plots $F(\mathbf{y}_t \mid \mathbf{\Omega}_t)$ against $\mathbf{z}_t$ and shows how well the log-normal approximates the distribution of income—if it were a perfect fit, the lines would track 20, 40, 60, 80, and 95 exactly. Although the approximation is generally very good, the log-normal is a poor approximation of incomes at lower levels, as the lowest line is generally below 20, because the true distribution of income has a larger mass near zero and a larger tail than the log-normal. The effect is that EI_{kt} has a slight positive bias for low incomes and a slight negative bias for large incomes.

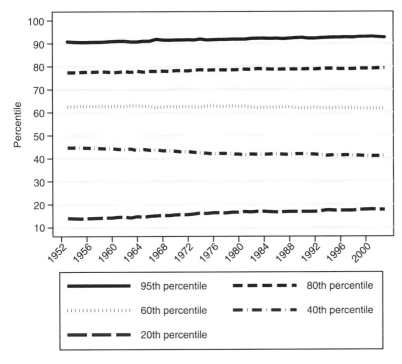

Figure 3.A1
Fit of log-normal income approximation. *Note:* If the fit were perfect, each plotted line would be horizontal at the corresponding percentile.

Appendix 3.2   Measuring Party-Income Stratification

Three complications arise in using the NES to measure the partisanship of the top and bottom income quintiles:

1. *Some NES samples are unrepresentative.* In several years the distribution of respondents' income is very unrepresentative of the income distribution reported by the Census Bureau.

2. The *NES sample matches neither the "Family" nor "Household" samples for which the Census Bureau reports income quintiles.* The NES asks respondents for the income of their family for the previous year. For single voters, the NES asks their individual income. Thus the NES sample includes families and single-person households. The census Family sample, on the other hand, does not include single persons living alone, and the Household sample aggregates multiple families living at

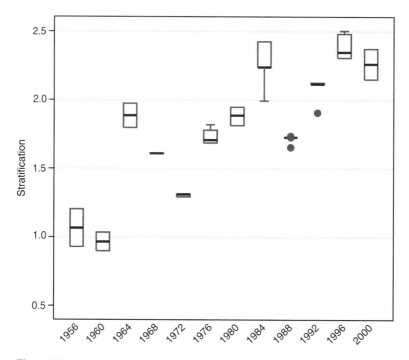

Figure 3.A2
Box plot of stratification measures in presidential election years. *Note:* The bottom of each box is the 75th percentile, the top is the 25th percentile, and the middle bar is the median.

the same household but does include single householders. Therefore, neither census sample matches the NES.

3. *Income quintile measures will often fall within NES income categories.* When a quintile measure falls within an income category, one must decide how to allocate the respondents in that category into the adjoining quintiles.

It is very difficult to solve all three of these problems for the entire period from 1952 to 2012. Problem 1 necessitates matching the NES sample with the income distribution from the Current Population Survey (CPS), but problem 2 necessitates recomputing that distribution for units more closely resembling those of the NES. Nevertheless, even with appropriate measures of the income quintiles, problem 3 has no obvious solution. To compute figure 3.2, we used our log-normal approximation of the distribution of household income to compute expected income for each NES category. We then used these estimates to classify respondents into income quintiles on the basis of the Census Bureau's reported income limits for household income quintiles.

Given the limitations of these choices, we did a number of other calculations to see if the results in figure 3.2 are robust. To deal with problem 1, we recomputed the stratification measures using both household and family income distributions to classify respondents. We also use samples from the November CPS for 1972 and 1996 that include single individuals and families so as to approximate the NES population and minimize problem 2.[34] Because the November CPS data are categorical, we use both linear and exponential extrapolation to compute the 20th and 80th percentiles. Thus, combining all of these data sources, we have four quintile estimates for 1972 to 2000 and two for each of the other years.

To deal with problem 3, we experiment with various ways of allocating respondents into quintiles. We do four computations for each quintile measure by including or excluding the relevant NES category in the top and bottom quintiles. Thus we have sixteen stratification measures for 1972–1996 and eight for other years. Figure 3.A2 is a box-and-whiskers plot showing the variation across the different measures in each year. Fortunately, the variation is small, and the central pattern is close to that of figure 3.2.

4 Immigration, Income, and the Voters' Incentive to Redistribute

Economic inequality in the United States has increased sharply (chapter 1). Until very recently, income differences had become more important in determining where a congressional district's representative would likely fall on the liberal-conservative dimension (chapter 2) and how voters identified with parties and made voting decisions in presidential elections (chapter 3). However, for 2006–2014 there is evidence that the movement of lower-income whites and an increase in importance of lifestyle and identity issues have dampened the income effect, even though income and wealth inequality has greatly increased in the wake of the Great Recession. Why has the increased importance of income not translated into policies that would curtail the sharp growth in inequality? At least in part, noncitizens who are ineligible to vote are concentrated at the bottom of the income distribution, so politicians feel little pressure to respond to their interests. Although economic inequality has increased, the relative income of the vast majority of *voters* did not markedly deteriorate until the Great Recession of 2008–2009.

This chapter focuses on the median voter, whereas chapters 2 and 3 emphasized polarized parties that represented voters of different income characteristics. There is no contradiction. We simply use median incomes to shape the discussion. If, in contrast, redistributive policy reflected, for example, the 98th percentile voter under unified Republican government and the 40th when the Democrats are leading the dance, this chapter's conclusions would most likely remain unchanged. An effect of immigration is that voter preferences as filtered through political parties and institutions are likely to have been tilted against redistribution.

In 1972, noncitizens were a small fraction of the U.S. population. They were also relatively well-to-do. In fact, the median income of a noncitizen was actually higher than that of citizens reporting themselves as having not voted in the presidential race between Nixon and McGovern. Noncitizens today are growing in number, and they tend to be at the bottom of the income distribution. In contrast, the relative economic position of voters and nonvoters has had relatively less change since 1972.

The changing economic position of noncitizens is politically relevant. It is likely to contribute to the failure of the political process in the United States to generate redistribution that would eliminate growing disparities in wage and income inequality. The income of the median voter did *not* witness a relative decline from the mid-1980s until the Great Recession of 2008–2009. How was the median voter's economic position sustained, while that of the median family declined? Part of the answer, as we show, is that lower-income people are increasingly likely to be noncitizens. The median income of noncitizens has shifted sharply downward, and the fraction of the population that is noncitizen has increased dramatically. From 1972 to 2012, the median family income of noncitizens fell from 78 percent of the median income of voters to 56 percent, while the fraction of the population that is noncitizen rose from 2.7 percent to 8.8 percent.[1]

One of the main reasons for the dramatic change in the number and poverty of noncitizens is federal legislation that has opened the doors to increased legal immigration while doing little to control illegal immigration. During the late nineteenth and early twentieth centuries, immigration was made more difficult for Europeans. The Chinese and Japanese were excluded entirely. The Immigration Acts of 1921, 1924, and 1929 set up permanent quotas by national origin that both restricted total immigration and favored the relatively wealthy people of northwestern Europe. The barriers of the 1920s were broken down only by the 1965 amendments to the Immigration and Nationality Act of 1952. The amendments largely ended discrimination on the basis of national origin. Annual immigration quotas were greatly increased by the Immigration Act of 1990.

Economists have recognized that immigration, through low-wage competition, has had an effect on inequality. But how big is the effect? Borjas, Freeman, and Katz (1997) argue that immigration accounts for only a small share of the increase in inequality. Studies by Borjas (1987), Altonji and Card (1989), and Lalonde and Topel (1989) also find only a small effect. Lerman (1999), on the other hand, finds that immigration explains 25–70 percent of the growth in the Gini index presented in figure 1.1. More recent work by Borjas (2003) points to a substantial negative impact of immigration on wages for low-wage workers after controlling not only for education but also for work experience.

We stress that the direct economic effects must be combined with the indirect political effects. Changes in such public policies as minimum wages, income taxation, and estate taxation, on balance, held the median voter's relative position in place. More redistributive policies would have occurred, we conjecture, had there been a sharp deterioration in the position of *voters* in the middle of the income distribution.

There is a large literature, including the references above, that focuses on immigration. In contrast, this chapter emphasizes citizenship because many immigrants eventually become naturalized citizens who are eligible to vote. Our results suggest that naturalized immigrants are likely to look, in terms of income, much like native citizens. At least, it is clear that the relative income of the median voter did not greatly decline during the wave of naturalizations that started in the 1990s.[2] In contrast, as some immigrants have become naturalized, they have more than been replaced by the continuing surge of poor immigrant noncitizens.

The analysis of this chapter is all in terms of relative incomes. In the economic model of redistribution discussed in chapter 3, only relative incomes, and not the real levels, differentiated voters in how they respond to party platforms in a given election year. The real levels shift the response from one election to another with, ceteris paribus, increases in real average income being favorable to Republicans. Over the period of our study, real median income has in fact increased. The effect of real income increases in the model can be interpreted in terms of redistribution as social insurance (such things as unemployment benefits, old-age benefits, and medical benefits). The increase in real income should diminish support for redistribution, complementing the results of this chapter.[3] The effects of income inequality, however, are all on relative incomes.

We explore the relationship between income and voting in a way that differs from the standard approach taken by political scientists. (See Brady 2004 for an example.) The usual approach is to see if the rich in fact vote more than the poor. We take a different approach, comparing characteristics of the income distribution of voters to the same characteristics for nonvoters and noncitizens. We ask how the income characteristics have changed over time. In the standard approach, one is also concerned with verifying that income has an effect when one controls for demographic factors. We are less concerned with this issue because public policy depends less on covariates than on income. A person's taxes are not lower because he or she is a college graduate, an African American, or an evangelical. (One's labor market experience may differ, however.) Taxes may be slightly less if a person is over sixty-five, but the monthly Social Security check still depends on lifetime earnings and not on race, education, or gender. So if we want to study redistribution, we should start with income, at least as a first cut.

In most political economy models, the income inequality that has arisen since the 1970s would have self-equilibrated. As inequality increased, there would have been more pressure to redistribute.[4] This prediction is apparent in the model of Bolton and Roland (1997) introduced in chapter 3. As inequality, defined as a decrease in the ratio of median voter income to mean income, went up, more redistribution should have occurred. In the United States, however, public policy veered in the opposite direction. As we detail in chapter 6, the real value of the minimum wage has been allowed to fall; taxes on income from capital have fallen, as have top marginal income tax rates and the estate tax.[5]

Other industrial nations have been exposed to the same technological change or opportunities as the United States. Although economic inequality might be driven by technological change, the responses elsewhere have not been the same. For example, Piketty and Saez (2003) and Saez (2015) show that in the last three decades, the share of national income going to the top 1 percent of the population remained unchanged in France, Japan, and Sweden but sharply increased in the United States. We also note, in keeping with the theme of this chapter, that France has had a dramatically different experience with noncitizenship. The percentage of noncitizens in France decreased from 1975 to 1999, falling from 6.5 percent of the population to 5.6 percent.[6] There was only a slight increase, to 6.2 percent, by 2013. Perhaps the more relevant comparison is that only 3.2 percent came from non-EU nations. Sweden similarly had 6.9 percent noncitizens, with only 3.9 percent from non-EU nations.[7] In Japan, the percentage of the population that was foreign or foreign-born in 2010 was just 1.7.[8] Other developed nations and the United States thus have had contrasting trends in income inequality and in citizenship. How might these trends have been reflected in political processes?

To answer this question, we return to the Bolton and Roland (1997) model and focus on median/mean ratios. From the perspective of that model, noncitizenship has both a *disenfranchisement effect* and a *sharing effect*.[9]

The *disenfranchisement effect* can be viewed as a change in the numerator of the median/mean ratio. The median income of voters is higher than that of all families. This fact reflects not just voters having higher incomes than eligible nonvoters but also voters having higher incomes than noncitizens. The effect of disenfranchising noncitizens will increase either if noncitizens become more numerous or if they become poorer.

If all citizens voted, the appropriate ratio would be median citizen income/mean family income. If all those over eighteen voted, the appropriate ratio would be median family income/mean family income. By comparing these ratios to median voter income/mean family income, we can study how much "disenfranchisement" is the result of nonvoting by citizens and how much the result of the ineligibility of noncitizens.

The presence of noncitizens in the population not only affects the numerator of the median/mean ratio, it also changes the denominator. Because noncitizens are poorer than citizens, mean family income is less than mean citizen income. Noncitizens thus increase the ratio, making redistribution less attractive to the median voter. Noncitizens shrink the per capita pie that has to be shared equally with all residents. The sharing of benefits with noncitizens has, of course, become a political hot potato. To assess the *sharing effect*, we will compare redistribution when mean family income for citizens is substituted for mean family income in the ratio. This counterfactual presumes that mean citizen income is unaffected by the presence of noncitizens. Although citizen income may well be affected by immigration, it is hard to argue that it would fall below realized mean family income. Some sharing effect must be present.

The sharing effect will drive all citizens to be less favorable to redistribution. The disenfranchisement effect decreases the political influence of relatively low-income families and increases the influence of higher-income families. We focus, for convenience, on median incomes, but our findings can be viewed as indicative of the incentives to redistribute that face a large segment of the electorate with incomes not very distant from the median. The main point of this chapter is that the relative income of the median income *voter* in the United States did not

deteriorate over a long period of rising inequality. The disenfranchisement effect and the sharing effect are consistent with lessening voter
support for redistribution.

Although the ratio of family income of the median *individual* to mean
family income fell in the United States, the ratio of the family income
of the median *voter* to mean family income stayed remarkably constant.
The political process did appear to have equilibrated in the sense that
the median voter was not worse off compared to the mean.

How has this distinction between the median voter and the median
individual arisen? First, not every eligible individual votes. U.S. citizens who do not vote have lower incomes than those who do. This
income difference has always been the case. The income of nonvoters
does fluctuate with turnout. Nonvoters have had lower incomes as
turnout increased in 2006 and later years. Otherwise, the income difference does not appear to have shifted much over time. An argument
that it may have shifted originates in the observation that many states
bar voting by convicted felons and that convictions and incarcerations
have trended sharply upward (Uggen and Manza 2002). Convicted
felons—Bernie Madoff, Rajat Gupta, and Martha Stewart aside—tend
to be poor. Making felons ineligible might make nonvoters disproportionately poor. But we don't see such effects in our data. It is possible
that the Census Bureau undersamples convicted felons and therefore
consistently overestimates the incomes of nonvoters. But it is also possible that people susceptible to felony convictions always had very low
turnout, so that changing conviction rates and eligibility would have
minimal impact on the income distribution of nonvoters. In any event,
the impact of ineligible felons has to be small relative to that of noncitizens. McDonald, extending McDonald and Popkin (2001), for example,
estimates that in 2014, noncitizens outnumbered ineligible felons by
more than six to one.[10] Uggen and Manza (2002) estimate that ineligible
felons were 2.3 percent of the adult population in 2000, in contrast
to the 7.8 percent of the Current Population Survey sample that is
noncitizen.

Second, and more important, the percentage of residents who are
noncitizens has risen sharply, tripling between 1972 and 2000 and continuing to increase, slowly, in the twenty-first century. Moreover, as
emphasized by Bean and Bell-Rose (1999) and Borjas (1999), noncitizens are increasingly low wage and poor. Our most striking observation is the rapid decline in the median income of noncitizens relative
to the median income of voters. In a nutshell, continuing immigration

has created a large population of noncitizens. These noncitizens are an important component in the fall of median family income relative to mean income. Voters are doing much better.

We have a second interesting finding. There is a midterm cycle in the income of nonvoters. The median income of nonvoters increases in off years and declines in presidential years. In other words, marginal voters who vote in presidential elections but not in off years have higher incomes than persistent nonvoters. The smaller set of citizens who vote in neither presidential nor off-year elections have particularly low incomes. In presidential elections, then, the median family income of a voter is sharply higher than that of the median income of a nonvoter and much, much higher than that of a noncitizen. A corollary finding is that the median family income of nonvoters, relative to that of voters, declined as turnout increased in recent years.

Data and Methods

Our data are drawn from the November Current Population Survey (CPS) conducted by the Census Bureau. In even-numbered years, those with congressional or presidential elections, the CPS asks each respondent whether he or she is a citizen and whether he or she voted in the election held on an early Tuesday in November. The citizenship question has appeared every two years starting in 1972.[11] The CPS has long been used to study voter turnout, most notably by Raymond Wolfinger and Steven Rosenstone (1980) in their classic book, *Who Votes?*

The CPS contains no information about voter behavior other than turnout. Its advantage is that the sample sizes are far larger than in surveys like the National Election Study. We analyze all respondents age eighteen and over who provided information about income and citizenship and who, if they are citizens, provided information about voting. Respondents with complete information on citizenship, voting, and income range from a low of 69,584 in 2000 to a high of 110,588 in 1980. Figure 4.1, taken from Bonica et al. (2013), shows the 2008 and 2010 distributions of respondents by citizenship and voting for each income category. The figure illustrates the strong relationship between income and voting. Bonica et al. (2013) report:

There are two effects. First, higher fractions of the poor are non-citizens. Second, among the poor who are citizens, turnout is very low. Fewer than half the households with incomes under $15,000 reported voting in the presidential election of 2008 even though the Obama campaign increased turnout of the

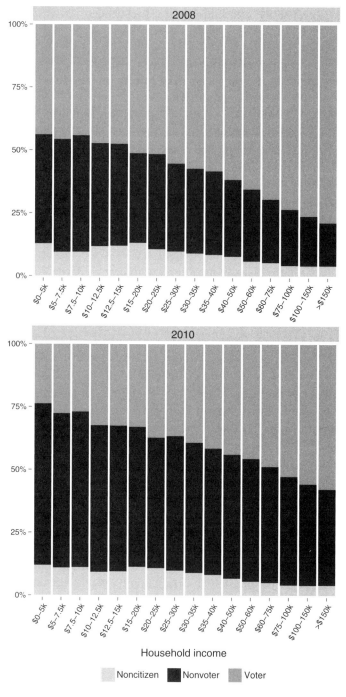

Figure 4.1
Citizenship and voting in 2008 and 2010. *Source:* Figure redrawn from from Bonica et al. (2013) with permission.

poor over what it had been in 2000. In contrast, over four-fifths of those with incomes over $150,000 reported voting. The contrast is greater for midterm elections. Turnout decreased only slightly for top income earners but decreased substantially for those with incomes below $15,000, so that only about one-third reported voting. In 2008, those reporting incomes above $150,000 represented 9.9 percent of the voters as against 8.0 percent of the voting age population. In 2010 the numbers were 9.6 percent and 7.4 percent.

There are, however, many negatives that detract from using the CPS data, despite the large sample size. First, people lie. We know that voting is overreported. When we compare actual voter turnout data from the Federal Election Commission with self-reported turnout data in the CPS, we find that respondents overstate voter participation by seven to twelve percentage points (see Rosenthal and Eibner 2005 for details). We suspect that citizenship is overreported as well. If the set of nonvoters who lie and claim to be voters had an income distribution identical to that of voters, we would still get correct estimates of the median and mean income of voters, but we would underestimate the median income of nonvoters. This effect would make the income contrast between voters and nonvoters less stark than the data indicate. If, on the other hand, the income distribution of nonvoters who lie is identical to that of honest nonvoters, we will underestimate the median and mean income of voters, implying that the true differences are even stronger than those we report. One hopes that lying nonvoters have an income distribution somewhat in between honest nonvoters and true voters, in which case the bias will not be severe.[12] An encouraging observation is that more voting is reported for presidential election years than for off years, paralleling actual turnout. We also hope that there are no severe problems of bias generated by those who lie about their citizenship and, a fortiori, by noncitizens who claim to be voting citizens. People, of course, also lie about their incomes, a nasty problem swept under the rug by those who analyze census data.

Second, there are sampling problems with the census. The two tails, particularly the lower tail, of the income distribution are likely to be undercounted. We acknowledge the potential for bias here and move on.

Third, there is a top-coding problem. The Census Bureau top-coded income at $75,000 from 1982 through 2002.[13] Economic growth and inflation combined to increase sharply the fraction of the sample that was top-coded. In 1982, only 2.41 percent of voters were in the top category; in 2000 and 2002, 28.2 and 31.3 percent were, respectively. The top coding reduces the accuracy of our estimation of the income distribution, particularly for voters. More detailed data on individual income can be found in the March CPS, but these data cannot be linked to the November survey.[14] It is regrettable that the federal government waited until 2004 to adjust the income brackets in the November CPS, but we have to play the cards we are dealt.

In analyzing the CPS data, we first cross-tabulated income with citizenship and voting to obtain the income distributions of voters, nonvoting citizens, and noncitizens. These three categories are important to our purposes. For each of the three groups and for the entire sample, we estimate mean income and median income using the estimated mean and variance of a two-parameter log-normal distribution. The method is described in detail in appendix 3.1 of chapter 3. As there were as few as eleven categories in a given year, we chose parsimony and did not estimate a richer distribution with a larger number of parameters. The accuracy of the estimates is very likely to deteriorate with the severity of the top-coding problem. For centiles of the income distribution, we can, in contrast, obtain highly accurate estimates (except for centiles above the top code) by interpolation from category bounds.[15] The large N of the CPS makes interpolation accurate.

Results

We begin, following the discussion in chapter 3 and earlier in this chapter, by examining ratios of median income to mean income. To recap: as this ratio falls, there should be more pressure to redistribute. Put simply, as the median voter's income falls relative to the mean, the voter's share of the initial pie falls and the voter will seek to get a larger piece. The pressure to redistribute persists even if the total pie shrinks somewhat as a result of changes in labor supply, deadweight loss from tax collection, and so on. We focus first on the disenfranchisement effect by making all families the baseline for comparison.

Using the ratio of the median to the mean as our measure of inequality, we find that income inequality significantly increased in the United States in the last three decades. The bottom line of figure 4.2 shows a decrease from 0.75 in 1972 to less than 0.65 in 2012.[16] Now let's contrast the lower line and the upper one in figure 4.2, which shows the same ratio when we substitute the median income of *voters* for the median

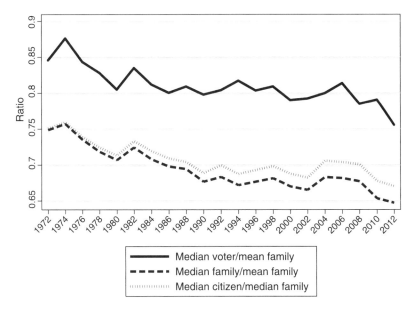

Figure 4.2
Median/mean income ratios. *Source:* November Current Population Survey, various years.

income of *all* families but still keep mean income as the denominator. Notice that this ratio is always substantially higher than that for the median individual in the entire sample. That is, the median voter has much less incentive to redistribute than the median individual. Moreover, there is less of a trend. There is a less significant increase in inequality.[17]

Median citizen income has deteriorated at about the same rate as median voter income and consequently remains well below it. The big drop is in median family income. The difference between citizens and all families is, of course, the sharp drop in the median income of noncitizens. We further note that the contrast between voters and all families would be stronger were it not for the Great Recession of 2008–2009. Between 1978 and 2006, there was very little fluctuation in the median/mean ratio for voters. The ratio then declined in 2008 and 2010, and had a particularly large drop in 2012.

In any case, what is clear is that the median voter's situation has deteriorated much less than the median family's. How much less? One way to assess the import of the differences shown in figure 4.2 is to assess their importance for taxation. We argued earlier in this chapter that a disenfranchisement effect would result in lower taxes, with the effect being greater the lower the income of the disenfranchised residents. We therefore turn to calculations of tax rates based on the data.

The information displayed in figure 4.2 permits us to calculate the disenfranchisement effect implied by the Bolton and Roland model (see chapter 3). We will work with $\alpha = 1/2$ and $\pi = 0$. The preferred tax rates of the median voter calculated from this assumption average to 19.0 percent over the twenty-one CPS biennial samples from 1972 to 2012. The federal income tax has averaged about 14 percent of total adjusted gross income (AGI). But since most voters also pay state and local income taxes, the $\alpha = 1/2$ assumption looks fairly reasonable. It is straightforward to explore the sensitivity of the results to variation in α.

Most of the disenfranchisement effect comes from the failure of all citizens to vote. Were the median citizen decisive, the tax rates would average 10.3 percentage points higher than in the median voter model, increasing from 19.0 to 29.3 percent. But as we have seen, this difference is fairly constant across time. Only in 1994 would the median citizen, relative to the median voter, have raised taxes more than in 1974. The additional increases brought about by the disenfranchisement of non-citizens, while smaller, show an important trend in time. From 1972 through 1988, the median family would have desired a tax less than 1.1 percentage points more than the tax desired by the median citizen. From 1990 through 2002, the increase would have been between 1.1 and 1.8 percentages points before increasing further to more than two percentage points.

Actual tax policy since 1972 has clearly headed in a direction opposite to that implied by these calculations but certainly is more akin to median voter preferences than to median citizen or median family preferences.

We are concerned, however, with the accuracy of our log-normal estimates of mean and median income.[18] Standard alternative measures used by economists compare ratios of centiles of the income distribution. We can compute centiles with reasonable accuracy by using log-linear interpolation from the categorical data.[19] A common ratio is 50–90, the ratio of the median to the 90th centile. We cannot use this ratio because of top coding. We can look at the 50–80 ratio but need to drop the years 1998–2002 because of top coding. This ratio is shown in figure 4.3.

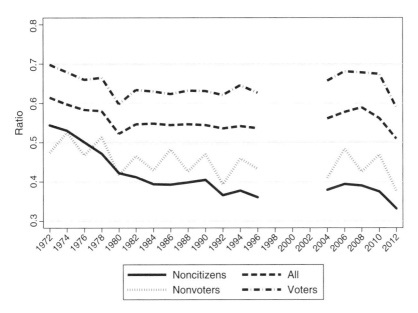

Figure 4.3
Ratio of median income to 80th centile income, all families, various categories. *Source:* November Current Population Survey, various years. Years 1998–2002 not shown because data was top-coded.

Figure 4.3 shows a more complex picture than figure 4.2. Overall, in terms of 50–80 ratios, income inequality does increase through 1996. But the damage here was done by 1980, before Reaganomics took hold in the United States. Between 1980 and 1996, all families and nonvoters basically treaded water. Even with the slight decrease that took place in 1996, the relative situation of the median voter markedly improved after 1980. As the median voter improved, the position of the median noncitizen continued to deteriorate. The presence of increasing numbers of relatively poor noncitizens bumped up voters in the overall income distribution. For the years 2004–2010, the ratios for all families, voters, and nonvoters improve, reaching levels not seen since the 1970s. The one exception—an important one—is noncitizens, for whom the ratio remains at the low level of the 1990s. But in 2012, consistent with the results shown in figure 4.2, there is a sharp increase in inequality for all groups.

The story told by the picture is echoed by the simple regression analysis shown in table 4.1. In each column, we regress the 50–80 ratio on a time trend and a dummy for presidential election years. The first thing to note from the results is that, parallel to our results for mean/median comparisons, the median voter has much less incentive to redistribute than does the median family. This is shown by the regression constants reported in table 4.1. The median voter's income is 66 percent of that of the 80th percentile family, whereas the median family is at only 57 percent, even in 1972, before trend effects kick in. The median voter is also far better off than the median nonvoter and the median noncitizen.

A second observation is that the estimated position of the median voter did not deteriorate over time. The trend effect, though negative, is small and statistically insignificant. In contrast, there are significant negative trends for nonvoters, and especially noncitizens, whose trend coefficient is more than double the magnitude of that of nonvoters. A third observation, one we return to later, is that there is a significant midterm cycle in the ratio for nonvoters. The cycle is captured in the sawtooth pattern for nonvoters shown by figure 4.3. Nonvoters are very significantly poorer in presidential election years. This income difference results from the fact that relatively well-off nonvoters, who have income profiles much like those of midterm voters, turn out in presidential years. In contrast, there is no opposite midterm cycle for voters, partly because the additional voters in presidential years are small relative to the pool of midterm voters and partly because the additional voters, though well off relative to other midterm nonvoters, are not richer than midterm voters.

Table 4.1
Median (50th) to 80th centile income comparisons (t-statistics in parentheses)

Variable	Median noncitizen/80th centile family	Median nonvoter/80th centile family	Median voter/80th centile family	Median family/80th centile family
Presidential election year	−0.0068 (−0.37)	−0.0569 (−5.84)	−0.0149 (−1.02)	−0.0062 (−0.48)
Year − 1972	−0.0036 (−5.05)	−0.0014 (−3.66)	-0.0002 (−0.36)	−0.0007 (−1.35)
Constant	0.4849 (25.98)	0.5093 (50.78)	0.6578 (43.76)	0.5741 (42.86)
R^2	0.631	0.768	0.075	0.124

Note: Years are 1972–1996 and 2004–2012.

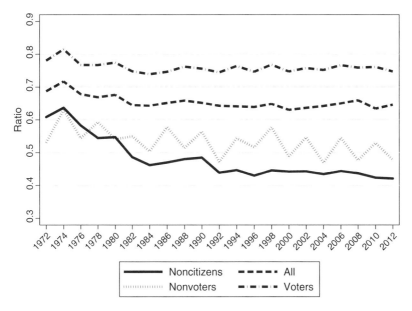

Figure 4.4
Ratio of median income to 72nd centile income, all families, various categories. *Source:* November Current Population Survey, various years.

Very much the same story is told by figure 4.4. When we drop down from the 80th centile to the 72nd centile, we can cover all years through 2012. A main theme carries over directly from figure 4.3—the relative position of noncitizens has deteriorated sharply over time. Similarly, the sawtooth pattern of the midterm cycle for nonvoters repeats in figure 4.4. The relative situation of nonvoters also declines, but not as severely as that of noncitizens. In contrast, the relative position of voters is remarkably stable after a decline in the 1970s. Relative to the family in the 72nd centile of the overall income distribution, the median voter is no worse off today than he or she was thirty years ago.

The relative decline in median family income, shown most strongly by figures 4.2 and 4.3, has in large part been the result of the substantial immigration that has flowed into the United States every year since the passage of the Immigration Act amendments of 1965. As table 4.2 shows, noncitizens as a percentage of our sample have steadily increased, tripling between 1972 and 2012.[20] Changes like these are significant in an electorate that is divided nearly 50–50. It is comforting to see that, whatever the bias in the reporting of citizenship, the bias

Table 4.2
Sample percentages by voting and citizenship

Year	Noncitizens	Nonvoters	Voters
1972	2.68	32.19	65.13
1974	2.86	49.82	47.32
1976	3.04	34.24	62.72
1978	3.40	47.43	49.18
1980	3.79	33.09	63.12
1982	3.96	43.38	52.66
1984	4.19	31.84	63.97
1986	4.39	45.83	49.77
1988	4.03	34.14	61.84
1990	5.47	44.92	49.61
1992	6.20	28.05	65.75
1994	6.36	44.22	49.42
1996	6.31	34.02	59.67
1998	6.82	45.86	47.33
2000	7.76	30.28	61.96
2002	7.95	42.82	49.23
2004	8.23	24.97	66.80
2006	8.66	39.89	51.45
2008	8.63	23.35	68.02
2010	9.17	39.85	50.98
2012	8.78	25.58	65.64

appears to be fairly constant and unaffected by whether the year is a presidential election year or not.

In contrast to the rapidly increasing noncitizen population, the percentage of the over-eighteen population that votes has been remarkably constant. Of course, turnout continues to be strongly affected by whether the election is midterm or presidential. A regression of the percentage of voters *among citizens* in table 4.2 on a time trend (1972 = 0) and a presidential year dummy gives (*t*-statistic in parentheses):

$$\text{Voters} = \underset{(31.06)}{50.87} + \underset{(2.43)}{0.154}(\text{Year} - 1972) + \underset{(9.35)}{14.39}(\text{Pres. Year}), R^2 = 0.84.$$

Thus, as first observed by McDonald and Popkin (2001), there has been no decline in turnout.[21] It is hard to blame increasing inequality on citizen apathy at the polls. In fact, increased turnout in the twenty-first century resulted in a small, statistically significant, upward trend in the fraction of those respondents who claim citizenship and who also claim to have voted. Reported citizen turnout in presidential election years peaked at over 74 percent of citizens in 2008, when Barack Obama energized voters, and hit a low of 63 percent in 1996, when Bob Dole produced about as much excitement as a candidate as his postelection Viagra TV ads did. Similarly, midterm turnout hit a low of 48.7 percent in 1974, when Watergate drove away Republicans, and a high of 56.3 percent in 1986. In a nutshell, the rise in inequality and polarization in the last three decades of the twentieth century was not accompanied by a reduction in the reported turnout of reported U.S. citizens.

So what sustained the ratio of the median income of voters to the mean income of the population? Certainly not that the voters had become a narrower slice of the eligible population. Figure 4.1, however, demonstrates that turnout is strongly correlated with income. Has voting just become more correlated with income, with apathetic poor citizens sitting out elections?

We can begin to answer this question by comparing the median incomes of voters to the median incomes of nonvoters and noncitizens. If low-income citizens became apathetic and failed to vote, while overall citizen turnout remained roughly constant, we would expect to find the median income of nonvoters to have declined relative to voters. This decline didn't happen in a noticeable way in the last quarter of the twentieth century. What did happen is that the median income of noncitizens relative to the median income of voters declined sharply. The evidence is in figure 4.5 and table 4.3, which use medians calculated by linear interpolation.[22]

As table 4.3 indicates, the income of the median noncitizen is falling sharply relative to that of the median voter. The ratio is unaffected by whether the year has a presidential election. The median income of nonvoters has also fallen, but less than the median income of noncitizens. The coefficient estimate for nonvoters of −0.0019 is less than one-half the magnitude of the −0.0052 coefficient estimate for noncitizens. Much of the negative trend for nonvoters results from the high-turnout presidential election years that began in 1992 and repeated in 2000 and later years, years that were likely to have left nonvoters poorer than usual. Clearly, it is noncitizens, not nonvoters, who have experienced a sharp decline in relative income.

What happens systematically, in contrast, is that high-turnout elections draw the better-off nonvoters into voting, tending to leave

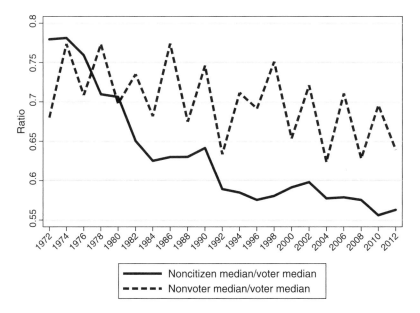

Figure 4.5
Income ratios, 1972–2012. *Source:* November Current Population Survey, various years.

Table 4.3
Comparisons of median noncitizen and median nonvoter incomes to median voter income (*t*-statistics in parentheses)

Variable	Median noncitizen/ Median voter	Median nonvoter/ Median voter
Constant	0.777	0.736
	(89.88)	(46.07)
Presidential election year	−0.0019	−0.0052
	(−5.77)	(−8.72)
Year − 1972	−0.0746	0.0028
	(−9.47)	(0.19)
R^2	0.88	0.81

only the poorest as nonvoters. As we discussed earlier, we have a significant midterm cycle—the median nonvoter is relatively poorer in a presidential election year than in the preceding or succeeding midterm elections.

To show how the midterm effect operates, we compare the midterm election of 1998 to the high-turnout presidential election year of 2000.

If turnout in presidential election years among off-year nonvoters were not correlated with income, we would expect to see a larger fraction of nonvoters with high nominal incomes in 2000 than in 1998. Inflation was low but positive, and, moreover, there had been real economic growth between November 1998 and November 2000. Yet the percentage of non-voters earning more than $40,000 actually declined from 41.6 percent in 1998 to 39.0 percent in 2000. Therefore, the higher-income nonvoters in off years tend to vote in presidential election years. A perhaps simpler way to see what underlies the midterm cycle is to note that while the nominal median income of voters increased in every two-year period through 2002, the nominal median income of nonvoters actually fell in 1988, 1992, and 2000.

There is an implication for the study of national elections in these results. The trend of Republican success in the three decades that inequality has increased (Duca and Saving 2002) can, as we argued in chapter 3, hardly be solely a matter of very poor social conservatives voting against their economic interests. A large segment of the truly poor does not have the right to vote. Whereas in 2010, noncitizens were 9.2 percent of the general population, they were 12.9 percent of families with an income below $7,500 per year (see figure 4.1). Similarly, in 1996, noncitizens were 10.0 percent of families earning less than $10,000 but only 6.3 percent of the general population.

Our results comparing medians for nonvoters to the medians for voters do contrast with the earlier results where we compared medians for nonvoters to the 72nd or 80th percentiles of all families or families of citizens. There the result was a much more statistically significant decline for nonvoters. The results can be reconciled by observing that income growth has been increasing most in the higher centiles of the income distribution. When compared to the median income of voters, the median income of nonvoters has not deteriorated much. But because median income among nonvoters is much less than that for voters, the position of nonvoters has fallen more sharply in comparison with that of relatively high-income families.

The main thrust of our analysis, moreover, rests on the increase in economic differences between citizens and noncitizens. Our results bear out research by economists and demographers. As, for example, Borjas (1999) explains, in 1972 these immigrants came predominantly from first world nations. Their median income was not far behind that of voters and was higher than that of nonvoters. Over time, the immigrants came predominantly from the third world, in large part Mexico.

By 1982, median noncitizen income had fallen permanently behind that of the median nonvoter.

The changing pattern of income of noncitizens, as indicated by the November CPS, is echoed by the changing racial-ethnic composition of this group. We graph the ethnic-racial composition of noncitizens in figure 4.6.[23] We break out Hispanics from non-Hispanics. Within non-Hispanics, we distinguish between white, black, and other. In 1974, noncitizens were 42 percent white.[24] The white percentage plummeted to 16 percent by 2012. The decrease among whites was made up by an increase in the "Other" category in the 1970s and by Hispanics in the 1980s and, increasingly, in the 1990s and beyond. Our results are likely to overestimate the income of noncitizens if illegal immigrants are less likely to be sampled and more likely to be Hispanic. We will also overestimate the income of noncitizens if illegal immigrants with low incomes overreport citizenship more frequently than legal immigrants.[25]

To this point, our analysis has focused on the disenfranchisement effect. We have shown a steep and increasing difference in the tax rates that the Bolton-Roland model associates with the median voter, as

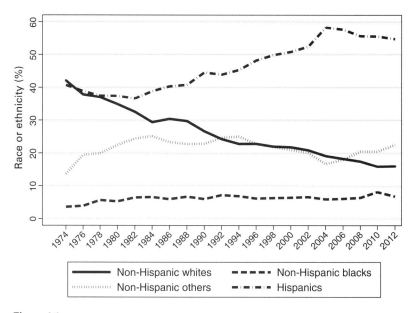

Figure 4.6
Noncitizens by race and ethnicity. *Source:* November Current Population Survey, various years.

opposed to the median family, being pivotal. Taxes would be higher, however, were it not for the sharing effect. Our analysis of the sharing effect presumes that there would not have been major changes in relative income had there been a closing of the immigration floodgates. This assumption is perhaps not outrageous. Cutting off immigration might have raised the wages of citizens at the very low end. It might also have, for example, eliminated the supply of nannies that permits two spouses to work and obtain very high incomes. Here the impact is likely to be greatest at very high incomes. The impact at the median would have been lower. So the comparisons we make have some credibility, especially 50–72 and 50–80.

We begin the comparisons, however, with the median/mean ratios first seen in figure 4.2. In figure 4.7, we compare the previously plotted ratio of median voter income to mean *family* income and the ratio of median voter income to mean income for all *citizen* families. The figure shows that the median voter's position relative to the mean family deteriorates, as inequality increases, until 1984. From 1984 until 2006 the position holds steady, reflecting the rapid increase in noncitizens. With the Great Recession, there is a rapid deterioration, not anticipated

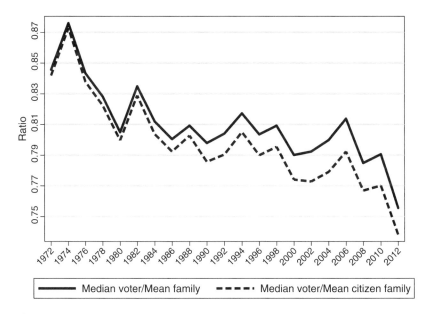

Figure 4.7
Ratio of median voter income to mean family income and mean citizen income. *Source:* November Current Population Survey, various years.

in our first edition. We return, in the conclusion to this chapter, to this new spurt of inequality.

There is little difference in the series using mean citizen income rather than mean family income in the denominator of the ratio until 1984, when the gap widens. The lack of a gap before 1984 is not surprising, given the relatively small noncitizen population. With immigration, the breach eventually widens. The decline for the mean citizens ratio is very statistically significant ($t = -7.89$, $R^2 = 0.766$).

At the level of the gap in the twenty-first century, the median voter would want substantially higher taxes if the income distribution were that of citizens rather than all families. In the benchmark Bolton-Roland scenario with $\alpha = 1/2$, the tax rate in the twenty-first century would be about 2 percent higher were the income distribution that of citizens rather than all families. The overall tax rate would be in the low to mid-twenties. Note that in this range of tax rates, we have not chosen an unreasonable value for government inefficiency. The cost, modeled as $(1/2)t^2$ in the Bolton-Roland model, would only be about two cents on the dollar.

The results for the median/mean ratios are confirmed by analysis of the 50–80 and 50–72 ratios. In figure 4.8, we produce the 50–80 comparisons of medians of voters and nonvoters to the 80th percentiles of all citizen families. In the same figure, we include the previous comparisons to the 80th percentiles of all families. The curve for citizens lies below that for all families. In the 1970s, however, the curves are indistinguishable, reflecting that noncitizens were few and of relatively similar income to citizens. As noncitizens become both more numerous and relatively poorer, a gap opens up, small but increasing. The gap becomes much larger in 2008 and somewhat larger in 2012, two years when our calculations from the CPS data showed large increases in 80th centile citizen income before the depth of the Great Recession and after the recovery. The 2008–2012 results are largely consistent with the analysis of median/mean ratios in figure 4.7.

In table 4.4, we report regressions similar to those in table 4.1, replacing families with citizens. The pattern for nonvoters changes little from table 4.1. Voters do show a statistically significant negative trend (at the $p = 0.10$ level for a one-tailed test) when compared to citizens, unlike the comparison to families. That is, noncitizens are bumping voters up a bit in the income distribution, compensating in part for the

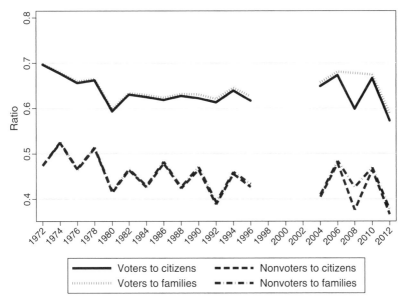

Figure 4.8
Ratio of median income to 80th centile income of citizens and families compared. *Source:* November Current Population Survey, various years. Years 1998–2002 not shown because data was top-coded.

Table 4.4
Comparisons of median voter income (50th centile) to 80th centile income of all families (t-statistics in parentheses)

Variable	Median nonvoter/80th centile family, citizens	Median voter/80th centile family, citizens
Constant	0.5127	0.6641
	(52.42)	(45.73)
Presidential election year	−0.0018	−0.0009
	(−4.84)	(−1.53)
Year − 1972	−0.0614	−0.0228
	(−6.47)	(−1.62)
R^2	0.82	0.26

Note: Years are 1972–1996 and 2004–2012.

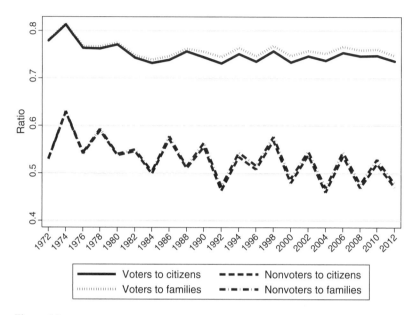

Figure 4.9
Ratio of median income to 72nd centile income of citizens and families compared. *Source:*
November Current Population Survey, various years.

rise in income inequality. The bump up captures the sharing effect on
willingness to redistribute.

In figure 4.9, we show a similar comparison for 50–72 ratios. This
figure shows a larger gap between the citizen and the family comparison than does figure 4.8. Although the gap between the family series
and the citizen series has widened over time, implying an increasing
reluctance to "share," this figure shows that the median voter's position has not deteriorated since the early 1980s in comparison to those
twenty-two centiles higher in the income distribution. The deterioration, as shown in figures 4.7 and 4.8, has been relative to the largest
incomes.

Conclusion

Until the Great Recession of 2008–2009, the median income *voter's*
incentive to redistribute did not increase as overall economic inequality
rose in the United States. The reason is partly that the rise in inequality
was offset by immigration, which has changed the location of citizens
in the income distribution. Those ineligible to vote are substantially

poorer than those eligible to vote. Moreover, poorer citizens have not become increasingly apathetic, at least as measured by the tendency to vote. Most citizens, and voters in particular, have been "bumped up" by the disenfranchisement of poorer noncitizens. At the same time, a voter of a given income is less eager to redistribute if that redistribution has to be shared with the noncitizen poor.

In any event, immigration cannot have been a driving force in the onset of the increase in income inequality and political polarization. In the early 1970s, noncitizens were quite a small share of the population of the United States, and their income profiles were close to those of citizens. Increasingly, however, noncitizens became a larger, poorer share of the population. From 1990 on, this change placed a number of ineligibles at the bottom of the income distribution, sufficient to make a substantial impact on the redistributive preferences of the median income voter. Even if immigration occurred too late to have produced the increases in inequality and polarization, it may well be contributing to the blocking of efforts to redress these trends.

Our results argue against the claim of Lijphart (1997) in his American Political Science Association presidential address that low voter participation is responsible for the much greater inequality in the United States than in Europe. Lijphart's claim may make sense in terms of contemporary cross-national comparisons, but it does not hold up in the time series. Piketty and Saez (2003) present evidence that inequality fell in the United States just as much as in France and Britain from World War I until 1970. During this period, there was considerably lower voter turnout in the United States than in France. Since 1970 the three nations have diverged in inequality, but the turnout of eligible citizens in the United States has not fallen. Turnout in France fell, but inequality has remained in check. It is true that the turnout of *residents* of the United States over eighteen has fallen, but few would be prepared to extend the right to vote to noncitizens. Compulsory voting for citizens, proposed by Lijphart, might indeed lead to more redistribution, but the absence of compulsory voting cannot by itself explain the failure to address inequality in the United States since 1970. The explanation is likely to be more closely related to the rise in noncitizenship. The increase reflects two political outcomes. First, immigration reforms in the 1960s and 1990s permitted a large increase in legal immigration. Second, the United States did little to contain illegal immigration. The two outcomes have changed the relationship of income to voting.

A look back at the results in this chapter should emphasize that the incentives of the median voter to redistribute were stabilized by immigration, despite rising inequality, in a period that ran roughly from 1984 until 2006. Rising inequality had made the median voter relatively worse off in the 1970s, when the noncitizen population was relatively small. The Great Recession of 2008–2009 and the subsequent weak recovery have increased the incentives of the median voter to redistribute. These incentives are particularly evident in the 2012 data. So why has a Democratic president gone back on his 2008 campaign promise to fight housing foreclosures, failed to put through a government finance program for infrastructure, and failed to fully raise taxes back to the Clinton level? The Affordable Care Act has increased redistribution somewhat, but the effects will not be known with certainty until 2016–2017. Why the redistribution has not been much greater owes in part to institutional constraints, which we address in chapter 6. But another part of the answer may lie in the increased influence of money in politics, an influence that may have shifted the United States from a democracy to a plutocracy. We therefore next turn our attention to campaign contributions.

5   Campaign Finance and Polarization

coauthored with Adam Bonica

Cryogenically preserved in the 1960s, Austin Powers's nemesis Dr. Evil emerged in the 1990s to continue his quest for world domination. As a first step toward his goal, Dr. Evil and his minions plot to extort vast sums of money from the United Nations by hijacking a nuclear weapon from Kerpla- chistan. His initial proposal to his followers is to demand a hefty ransom of one million dollars. After an uncomfortable pause, Evil's second-in- command, Number Two, responds, "Don't you think we should maybe ask for more than a million dollars? A million dollars isn't exactly a lot of money these days."

Indeed, even a *billion* dollars isn't that much money these days. The *Forbes* 400 list of the wealthiest Americans for 1982 identified seventeen fortunes exceeding a billion dollars. Everyone on the list in 2014 was a billionaire and then some, since $1.6 billion was the minimum wealth required for inclusion. In inflation-adjusted 2014 dollars, the 400 were worth a collective $2.2 trillion in 2014, compared to just $0.2 trillion in 1982.

America's megarich have a problem that many of us wish we had— figuring out what to do with all that money. For many on the *Forbes* 400 list and the exploding numbers of the merely rich, politics has been the answer. They have entered politics through two routes. Some have used their fortunes to jump-start their own careers in electoral politics, while others have become generous patrons of other candidates and causes.

The most spectacular examples of the first path are former presi- dential candidate Ross Perot (at age eighty-four, in 2014 he was still in the *Forbes* 400, at number 146, with assets of $3.8 billion) and former New York City mayor Michael Bloomberg (number 10, with $35.1 billion). During two runs for the presidency, Perot spent in excess of $70 million, and Bloomberg spent $69 million to win the mayoralty.

After Bloomberg left office, his activities as a high-profile donor kept him in the headlines, for he spent $16.2 million in 2012 and $27.4 million in 2014 to fund Independence USA, his personal super-PAC, and various other organizations.[1] These are enormous sums, but trivial in terms of each man's net worth.[2] In addition to a half dozen other *Forbes* listees who have made the jump to electoral politics,[3] such not-quite-so-superrich Americans as Jon Corzine (D-NJ) and Maria Cantwell (D-WA) have entered politics by self-financing expensive Senate campaigns.[4] Since 2000, at least thirty-five individuals have spent $10 million or more to further their personal political ambitions. According to opensecrets.org, ten House candidates spent more than $1.4 million of their own money on their own campaigns in 2014, though all but three lost. The Senate had ten candidates who spent more than $1.6 million in personal funding, but only two won their elections.[5] Despite the seemingly low returns on self-financing, twenty-five U.S. senators each had a net worth exceeding $6 million and twenty-five House members had wealth exceeding $28 million.[6] If Austin Powers had not foiled his plot, Senator Evil might now be serving on Capitol Hill.

Entering politics through the purely financial route has become even more common these days. In the 2004 election, new campaign finance regulations sent the big money into so-called 527 groups (named after Section 527 of the Internal Revenue Code under which they are organized), such as MoveOn.org and the Club for Growth.[7] Twenty-five individual donors contributed more than $2 million apiece to these, led by George Soros at $23.5 million.[8] It is not surprising that fifteen of the twenty-five belong to the *Forbes* 400. In the 2012 election cycle, Sheldon and Miriam Adelson contributed $104 million, largely in a futile effort to secure the Republican nomination for Newt Gingrich. The Koch brothers have become the bêtes noires of progressives as they spend millions of dollars on candidates and a network of conservative organizations. Environmentalist Tom Steyer spent $57 million helping Democratic candidates in the 2014 midterm elections.[9] The contributions as a percentage of the respective contributor's wealth remain small, but the pocket change of billionaires is a lot more valuable than the sofa cushion change of millionaires.[10]

One striking aspect of the big money in politics is how partisan it is. One might expect the wealthy to support pragmatically powerful incumbents regardless of party. If this behavioral pattern was ever dominant, it is certainly no longer the case. Of the one hundred largest individual contributors in 2012, only one, Michael Bloomberg, split his contributions more evenly than 85 percent to 15 percent between the major parties.[11]

Reformers have not failed to notice the rise of big money or its partisan nature. In 2002, Congress passed and the president signed the Bipartisan Campaign Reform Act (BCRA), popularly known as McCain-Feingold. For many of its supporters, BCRA was essential to mitigate the disproportionate political influence of large donors. Though less often articulated, a second motivation was the belief that effective reform could lower the temperature of national politics. As we shall see, however, campaign finance reform has done little to achieve either of these goals. By 2014, moreover, McCain-Feingold was undone by the courts in a series of rulings that included *Citizens United* and McCutcheon v. FEC.

The Escalation in Campaign Spending

In the contemporary period of polarized politics, campaign expenditure has escalated rapidly. Figure 5.1 shows the total spending by House and Senate candidates in year 2012 dollars.[12] Real spending roughly doubled over twenty years, peaking at just over $2 billion for the 2010 election.[13]

There are two obvious hypotheses about the link between campaign spending and polarization. The first is that increased financial demands make congressional candidates more responsive to the positions of extreme interest groups. If this scenario were true, we would expect to observe financial rewards for more extreme members of Congress. A second hypothesis reverses causality. Perhaps campaign spending increased because polarization increased the stakes of winning elections to such a degree that ideological contributors became willing to contribute ever greater sums. Both hypotheses could, of course, be rejected. The correlation of polarization and campaign spending could be entirely spurious. Television in particular may have increased both polarization and campaign costs.

Legal developments also appear to have spurred the acceleration of campaign contributions. The "soft-money" loophole and independent expenditure committees have dramatically enhanced the role of very wealthy contributors by allowing unlimited contributions. As we will see, the Democrats have become just as dependent as the Republicans, if not more so, on the largesse of multimillionaire contributors. Such

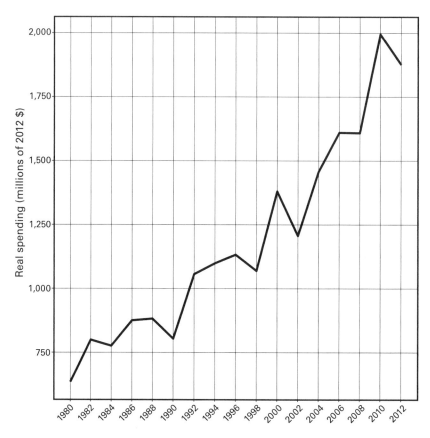

Figure 5.1
Real spending on House and Senate campaigns, 1980–2012. *Note:* Adjusted for inflation, spending has nearly tripled in thirty years. The inflation adjustment is to 2012 using the CPI-U series. *Source:* Data from the Federal Election Commission (http://www.fec.gov).

dependence is obviously consistent with the Democrats not moving further to the left on economic issues in response to increasing inequality. In this chapter, we examine these hypotheses more closely.

The Legal Environment of Campaign Finance

From early in the twentieth century, direct electoral contributions from corporations and labor unions have been illegal. The Tillman Act (1907) banned direct campaign contributions from corporations, and the Labor Management Relations Act of 1947 (Taft-Hartley) banned them from labor unions. Consequently, campaigns were financed primarily by unregulated individual contributions. These restrictions, however, were a far bigger hindrance for organized labor than for businesses, which could count on wealthy individuals to contribute on their behalf. To level the playing field, labor unions devised the political action committee (PAC), an independent organization that would raise money from union members for disbursement to political campaigns. The first one was the AFL-CIO's Committee on Political Education (COPE). PACs, however, had an uncertain legal status. Numerous legal challenges argued that these PACs violated the provisions of Taft-Hartley. A favorable decision in the 1972 case of Pipefitters Local Union No. 562 et al. v. United States and the passage of the Federal Election Campaign Act (FECA) of 1971 secured the legal status of PACs. Amendments to FECA in 1974 put limits on the contributions individuals could make to PACs and the contributions that PACs could make to candidates.[14] Subsequently the Federal Election Commission ruled that organizations could pay the administrative costs of their PACs (Sorauf 1992, 15).

With new legal and statutory protections, the number of PACs proliferated, increasing almost fourfold by the early 1990s. Corporation and single-issue interest groups were especially active in creating new PACs. Correspondingly, candidates became increasingly reliant on PACs for campaign funds, although individual contributions always predominated (Bonica et al. 2013).

The campaign finance system that emerged was predicated on a set of trade-offs. Interest groups could play a greater role in campaign finance, but there were limits on contributions and provisions for disclosure and transparency. Nevertheless, there were plenty of loopholes, the biggest of which led directly to "soft money." FECA did not regulate contributions to state and local affiliates of the national political parties. Individuals, corporations, and unions could make unlimited contributions to these organizations. Subsequent court decisions held that even the national parties could set up "nonfederal" accounts to pay for "party-building" expenditures. By the time the Supreme Court ruled that parties could spend these funds to make "independent expenditures" on behalf of its candidates, the soft-money loophole had become the central feature of campaign finance.

As figure 5.2 shows, soft-money contributions to the national parties went from $100 million to almost $500 million in real terms in just ten

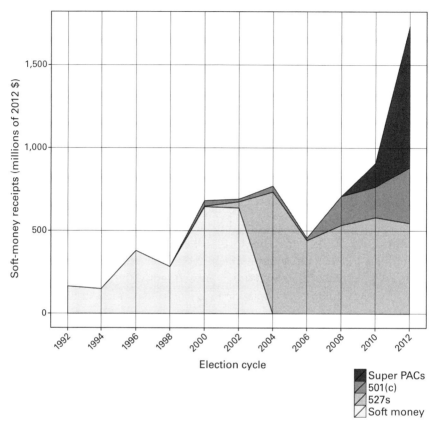

Figure 5.2
Real soft-money receipts of national parties, by donor type, 1992–2012. *Note:* Spending deflated to year 2012 using the CPI-U series. "Soft money" represents contributions to party organizations. *Source:* Data from the Federal Election Commission (http://www.fec.gov).

years. The ban on soft-money contributions to the national parties did little to stem the rise of unlimited contributions. Contributions to 527 organizations jumped from $37 million in the 2001–2002 election cycle to $734 million in the following cycle. By 2012, the combined independent expenditure totals going to 527s, super-PACs, and 501(c) nonprofit organizations had reached $1.7 billion.[15]

Soft money and independent expenditures have exacerbated unequal access to the political process. As spending on independent expenditures has proliferated, inequality of financial participation in elections has increased dramatically. To measure the extent to which the sources of campaign funds have become more concentrated, figure 5.3 presents the trend lines for two different measures of inequality. On the right axis is the Gini index for the size of total contributions, hard and soft money, by individuals from the Federal Election Commission itemized contribution file.[16] If all individuals made equal total contributions, the index would be zero. If there were a single contributor, the index would be one. A very important initial observation is that the distribution of campaign contributions is much less equal than the distribution of income, as can be seen by comparing figure 5.3 to figure 1.1. Because our Gini index for contributions is biased downward (see note 16), the difference between contribution inequality and income inequality is even greater than the difference indicated by a comparison of the two figures. On the left axis, we track the share of all contributions to federal elections made by individuals contributing an aggregate amount of more than half of median income over the course of the election cycle. No voter earning median income could conceivably contribute even half of her income to political campaigns. The index thus shows how strongly campaign spending virtually

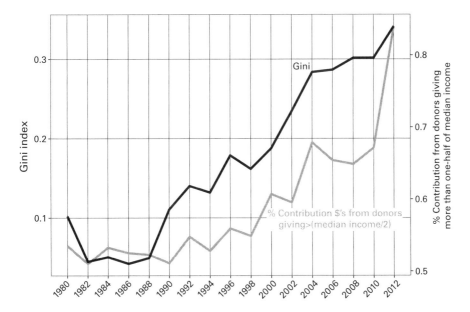

Figure 5.3
Measures of inequality in individual campaign contributions, 1980–2012. *Note:* Measures based on the inequality of contributions sizes for all individual contributions over $200.
Source: Database on Ideology, Money in Politics and Elections.

excludes the bottom half of the income distribution. This index reveals an even starker increase in the concentration of campaign contributions. The proportion of contributions made by large donors contributing more than half of the median income, which remained below 10 percent during the 1980s and much of the 1990s, accounted for 46 percent of all federal contribution dollars by 2012. The correlation between the two indices is 0.90.

A very small number of people account for most of the money in politics. As shown in figure 5.3, the soft-money loophole greatly exacerbated inequality in contributions in the 1990s because a few wealthy people began making six- and seven-figure donations to political parties.[17]

Unease with the escalating prominence of soft money contributed to the passage of McCain-Feingold. This act banned all soft-money contributions to the national political parties and made it harder for state parties to funnel soft money to the national committees. In an attempt to reduce the influence of PACs, it also increased the amount that individuals could give in "hard money" to campaigns but maintained the current limits on PACs, which have not been adjusted for inflation since 1974. In addition, the act restricted the ability of corporations, nonprofit organizations, and labor unions to run "electioneering" ads featuring the names or likenesses of candidates close to an election, the provision infamously struck down by *Citizens United*.

If McCain-Feingold aimed to depolarize American politics, the evidence suggests that it failed, even prior to *Citizens United*. The legal framework for wealthy individuals to donate unlimited amounts had been set in place decades earlier by Buckley v. Valeo (424 U.S. 1 [1976]). What has changed is the relative ease of facilitating large contributions and restrictions on how those funds, once raised, can be used to influence elections. Money that had flowed into the soft-money accounts of the national parties shifted to 527 groups, which spend it freely on campaign advertisements. In the 2004 presidential campaign, groups ranging from the Swift Boat Veterans for Truth to MoveOn.org ran numerous attack ads against John Kerry and George Bush. So just two years after a reform designed to minimize the effect of large donors, billionaires like George Soros could spend tens of millions of dollars directed at influencing the presidential election. *Citizens United* marked a continuation of this trend in helping to pave the way for SpeechNOW.org v. FEC and the creation of super-PACs. Although super-PACs are in many respects functionally equivalent to 527s, their introduction helped clarify much of the regulatory uncertainty surrounding 527s and allowed for express advocacy on behalf of or against candidates.

Contributor Motives: Ideology or Access?

Although the institutional changes and the increased demands of campaign funding are clearly important, these developments exacerbate polarization only if contributors are primarily motivated by ideological concerns and have extreme preferences. If contributors behaved in such a way, we would expect to see them concentrating their money on the candidates who agreed with them most.

Contributors, however, might have any number of motivations. Political scientists and economists have often assumed that most contributors seek to use their money to buy access to critical decision makers. Accordingly, campaign money should flow to key legislators such as committee chairs, party leaders, or the pivotal voter on an important roll call.[18] Because much legislation needs some votes from both sides of the aisle, access contributors may wish to contribute to members of both parties. If contributors are access-oriented, we would expect some concentration of contributions in the middle of the spectrum but also a broad dispersal to obtain crucial support from both the majority party and the minority party. If most individual contributions are in fact widely dispersed, it would be hard to argue that the increased campaign spending and fundraising has contributed to the polarization of Congress.

Identifying Ideological Motivations in PAC Contributions

Clearly, any assessment of the role of campaign finance in party polarization hinges on our ability to identify the motives of contributors. We have developed a simple yet powerful tool for identifying ideological contribution behavior.[19] Our method is based on two summary statistics for each individual contributor. The first is the *ideological position of the contributor*, or CF. CF is the campaign finance score that Bonica (2013b, 2014) developed by scaling campaign finance data, analogous to the NOMINATE scoring of roll call data. The second measure is the *ideological standard deviation of contributions*, or S. This measure is simply the standard deviation of the normalized rank ordering of CF scores of the recipients, weighted by contribution amounts. The CF scores reflect the contributions to all candidates in primary and general federal elections and to soft-money groups.

To minimize distortions in standard deviation S caused by the bimodal distribution of candidate ideal points, we use the rank orderings of the CF scores and normalize them from −1 to +1. To distinguish the normalized rank orderings, we refer to them as F scores. Thus, the ideal points are approximated by the uniform distribution on the interval [−1,1]. Also note that the computation of S is restricted to direct contributions to the set of congressional candidates who appeared on the general election ballot for one of the two major parties and ignores contributions to presidential candidates, party committees, and 527s.

To see how these measures relate to ideological contribution behavior, we consider the contributions of a purely ideological group that spends a total of $\$B$. An ideological group should concentrate its money on the candidates closest to its ideal point. To be precise, if C is the maximum legal contribution to any candidate, the group should contribute to the $N = \text{int}(B/C)$ nearest candidates and $B - CN$ to the next closest. Let K be the number of candidates. Then it is straightforward to show, for the normalized rank orders, that (approximately)

$$S = \frac{N}{\sqrt{3K}}.$$

Now consider a group that uses criteria other than the candidate's policy positions in making contribution decisions. The extreme case is a group that contributes randomly with respect to ideology. Then the expected value of F is 0, and $S = 1/\sqrt{3} \approx 0.577$. Because $N < K$, the ideological contributor has a lower S than the nonideological contributor. Furthermore, we can identify ideological contributors as those who have the lowest value of S given a particular number of contributions.

We begin our analysis by examining F and S for PACs. To work with reasonably large samples, we study only PACs making contributions to at least thirty distinct candidates within an electoral cycle. Table 5.1 provides some important summary statistics on PAC contributions from the 2012 election. We break the data down by the FEC's classification of interest group affiliations.[20]

Table 5.1
Summary PAC statistics, 2012 elections, House and Senate

Federal Election Commission PAC classification	No. of PACs	Contributions		Mean F	Mean S
		Mean no. of contributions	Mean size ($)		
Corporate	343	81	3,933	0.133	0.379
Labor unions	51	135	4,766	−0.358	0.300
Trade, membership, and professional associations	7	106	3,626	0.101	0.474
Nonconnected PACs	230	94	3,677	0.120	0.381
Cooperatives	16	78	3,912	0.007	0.402
Corporations without stock	22	46	2,201	0.459	0.251
Unclassified	276	62	3,710	0.074	0.327

Source: Database on Ideology, Money in Politics and Elections.

The FEC groupings show some noticeable differences in contribution behavior. In particular, labor unions appear to engage in more ideological behavior than the other groups. While most groups have values of F close to zero (the median candidate), labor unions concentrate their contributions at −0.36. Labor also has concentrated contributions with an average $S = 0.30$. Although corporate and trade groups tilt slightly to the right, their contributions are spread more evenly across the spectrum. As the nonconnected and unclassified categories tend to contain the ideological and issue-oriented PACs, it is not surprising that their average values of S are lower than those of the trade and corporate groups. In addition, it is worth noting that all the group classifications have lower values of S than 0.577, the theoretical benchmark for random contributions.

Although informative, table 5.1 masks considerable heterogeneity in behavior within the FEC classifications. Thus, in figure 5.4, we plot F versus S for the 1988, 1996, 2004, and 2012 elections for all PACs making more than thirty contributions.[21] The type of PAC is denoted by its token—corporate (C), labor (L), trade (T), nonconnected (N), unaffiliated (U), cooperative (V), and corporation without stock (W). The fitted values from a locally weighted (lowess) regression of S on F are included in the figure.[22] The horizontal dashed lines indicate the mean S. Plots for other elections since 1980 are similar.

Each of these plots reveals an inverted-U relationship in which some PACs concentrate on liberal or conservative members while others

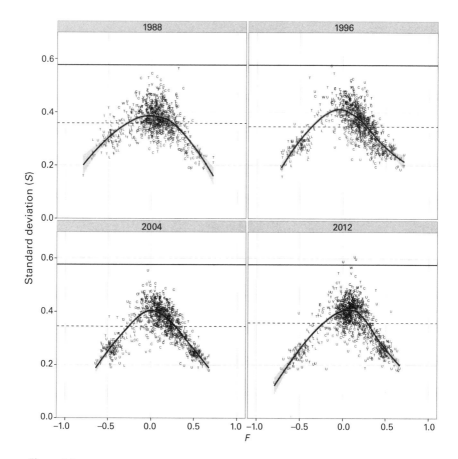

Figure 5.4
PAC contribution patterns.
Note: Each token in the plot represents a PAC. The letter denotes the PAC type—corporate (C), labor (L), trade (T), nonconnected (N), unaffiliated (U), cooperative (V), and corporation without stock (W). Moderate PACs, with *F* near zero, spread their contributions more widely than do more extreme ones. Almost all PACs, however, disperse their contributions less than the random giving benchmark of 0.577, shown as a dark black line. The horizontal dashed lines indicate the mean *S*. The figure includes committees making contributions to thirty or more distinct candidates.

spread their largesse across the spectrum. Few groups, if any, concentrate their money on the middle of the ideological spectrum. Very few moderate groups have values of *S* as low as those for extreme groups. Indeed, some moderate groups have values of *S* very near or above the theoretical value (*S* = 0.577) for purely random contributions.[23]

These figures reveal substantial ideological contribution behavior, but they suggest that any increase in such behavior over time is quite modest. In particular, there seems to be no trend toward more groups concentrating at the edges of the spectrum.

One of the problems with evaluating these figures is that they do not control for the relationship between F and N (K is the same across all groups). Perhaps moderate ideological PACs make more contributions and therefore have higher values for S. To control for this possibility, we estimated the following model:

$$S = \beta_0 + \beta_1 F + \beta_2 F^2 + \beta_3 N.$$

In this specification, the relationship between F and S is assumed to be quadratic. The quadratic closely approximates the pattern shown in figure 5.4. The estimates of the model for each year are given in the appendix 5.1 to this chapter. More important than raw coefficient estimates are the implications of the model for the change in ideological contributions over time. As we mentioned above, if we hold F constant, a decline in S represents greater ideological consistency in contributions. Such an effect would be polarizing if the decline in S were greater for extreme values of F than for moderate values. In figure 5.5, we plot

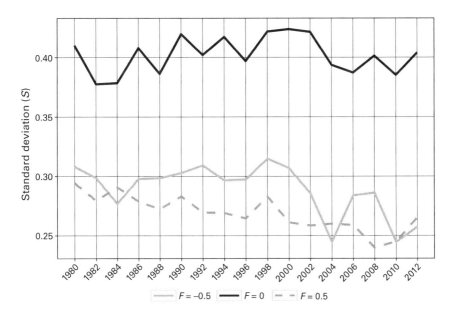

Figure 5.5
Estimated standard deviations (S) as a function of F, 1980–2012. *Note: F* and *S* are defined in the text.

the biennial estimate of the expected value of S for $F = 0$, $F = -0.5$, and $F = +0.5$.

Clearly, S has declined overall, reflecting an increase in ideological consistency. The declines at $F = -0.5$ and $F = 0.5$ are larger in magnitude, suggesting more polarization. Although the differences seem modest, it is important to note that they surely underestimate the polarization of PAC contributions. Recall that the estimates of F are based on the normalized rank-ordered CF scores. Because the distribution of actual scores has become increasingly bimodal, $F = -0.5$ and $F = +0.5$ have moved much farther apart. Despite this divergence, contributions became more, not less, concentrated.

It is important to note that the increasing ideological consistency of campaign contributions does not necessarily imply that extreme legislators receive a contribution windfall. First, as is obvious from figure 5.4, there continue to be far more "access-seeking" PACs than ideological PACs. Nor is it the case that ideological PACs are larger and contribute more to legislators. Figure 5.6 shows the total hard-money contributions to incumbents as a function of F for PACs making at least thirty contributions. There is only a slight liberal bias as labor unions tend to be more ideological and larger on average than corporate or trade-access PACs.

One might suspect that figure 5.4 suggests an extremist advantage, insofar as members of Congress receive the largesse of ideological PACs and are not harshly penalized by access PACs. Nevertheless, the data show that they are penalized enough by the access groups (at least those with $S < 0.577$) to eliminate a financial advantage. Figures 5.7a–c plot candidate receipts from PACs as a function of rank-ordered NOMINATE scores for House members[24] (figure 5.7a) and then as a function of F for House (figure 5.7b) and Senate (figure 5.7c) candidates for the 1988, 1996, 2004, and 2012 elections. These figures reveal that there seems to be no ideological advantage with respect to PAC receipts and that in the 2012 election, extremists suffered a small financial penalty.[25]

Of course, as shown by figure 5.4, without the ideological groups the penalty would have been more severe. Nevertheless, there is not a large amount of support for the hypothesis that PACs have contributed greatly to polarization.

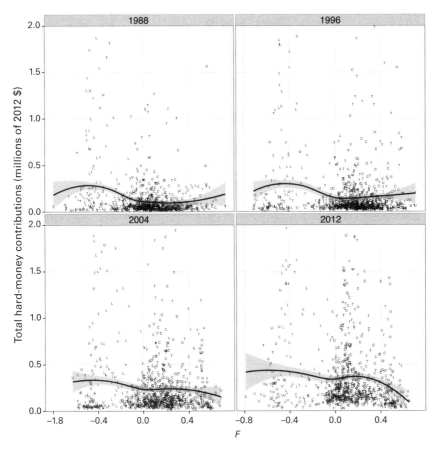

Figure 5.6
Total hard-money contributions to incumbents by PACs in 1988, 1996, 2004, and 2012.
Note: Each token in the plot represents a PAC. The letter denotes the PAC type—corporate (C), labor (L), trade (T), nonconnected (N), unaffiliated (U), cooperative (V), and corporation without stock (W). Groups contributing more than $2 million are excluded from the figure.

Ideology and Contributions by Individuals

PACs often receive the lion's share of the scrutiny, but individual contributors matter even more. Their contributions constitute more than
one-half of all monies raised by congressional candidates. Individuals
have also donated hundreds of millions of dollars in soft money and
to independent expenditure committees. The increasing restrictions on

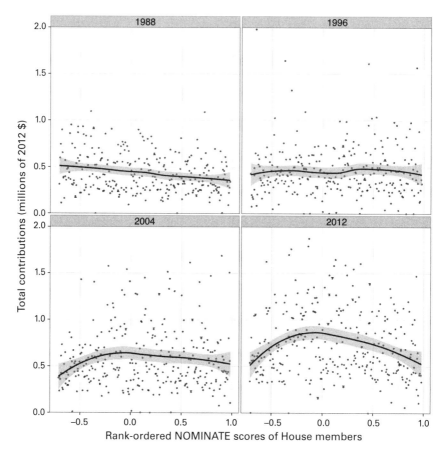

Figures 5.7a–c
Candidate receipts by candidate ideological position in 1988, 1996, 2004, and 2012. *Note:*
Figure 5.7a orders House members by their NOMINATE scores. Figure 5.7b uses *F* scores
for House candidates and figure 5.7c for Senate candidates. There is little correlation
between ideological position and fund raising. The NOMINATE scores are from
DW-NOMINATE scores, found at voteview.com.

PAC giving, with contribution limits not indexed to inflation, has
increased the importance of individual expenditures.

We can analyze individual contributions in a manner very similar
to the way we analyzed PACs. For each contributor, we can plot *F*
and the standard deviation *S*. Figure 5.8 shows the scatterplots and
lowess curves for individual contributors making more than eight
contributions in four congressional elections. Notice that once again,
the relationship describes an inverted U. The relationship is not as

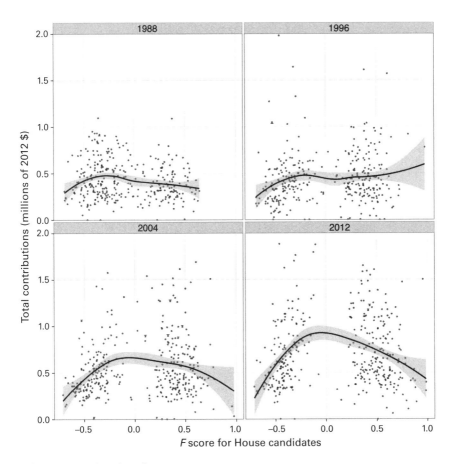

Figures 5.7a–c (continued)

tight, and there are a few ideologically moderate contributors, but there appears to be a far smaller concentration of access-oriented contributors.

Another development revealed in figure 5.8 is the proliferation of individuals who make numerous contributions to legislators. In 1980 there were just 209 such contributors, whereas by 2012 there were 6,536. It is clear from figure 5.8 that much of the proliferation is accounted for by donors who concentrate on the extreme ends of the spectrum.

Despite this growth, just as we found for PAC contributions, there does not seem to be an important financial advantage in being extreme. Figure 5.9 plots the total individual contributions as a function of the

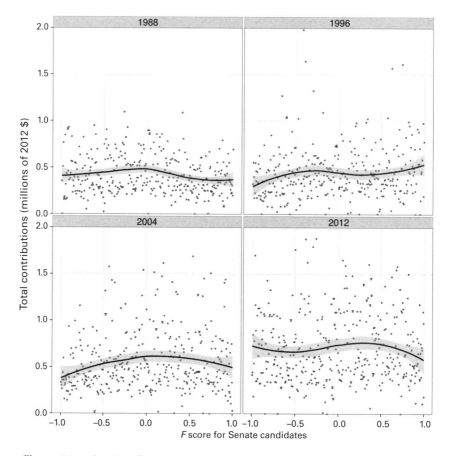

Figures 5.7a–c (continued)

recipient's rank-ordered DW-NOMINATE score for House members. In the most recent presidential election year, 2012, extremists at both ends were receiving somewhat less individual hard money than were moderates.

Independent Expenditures

Although the polarizing effects of hard-money contributions are modest, unlimited contributions made to independent expenditure committees have had a much bigger effect. Figure 5.10 plots the contributions to independent expenditure committees in the 2011–2012

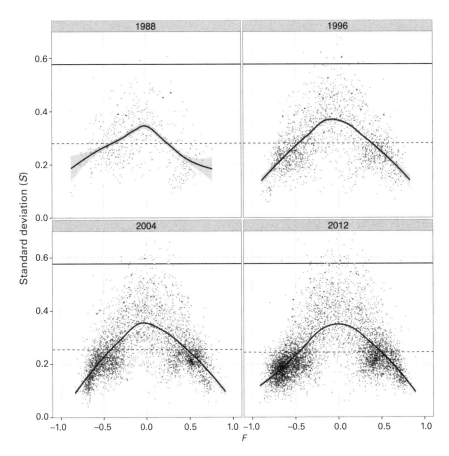

Figure 5.8
Individual contributions by F and S in 1988, 1996, 2004, and 2012. *Note:* Each point represents an individual donor who made more than eight contributions in four election cycles. The solid horizontal lines represent the random contribution benchmark while the horizontal dashed lines indicate the mean S.

election cycle for all individual contributors who gave $50,000 or more to super-PACs and 527 organizations for whom we were able to estimate F. Clearly, most very large soft-money contributors have extreme values of F.

Almost all the large contributors are extremists. The 286 individual donors in our data set who contributed more than $250,000 in 2012 are plotted in figure 5.10. They have values of F that are on average 0.48 away from zero (the median). This distinguishes large contributors from PACs, which have an average $|F|$ of 0.29, but put them in line

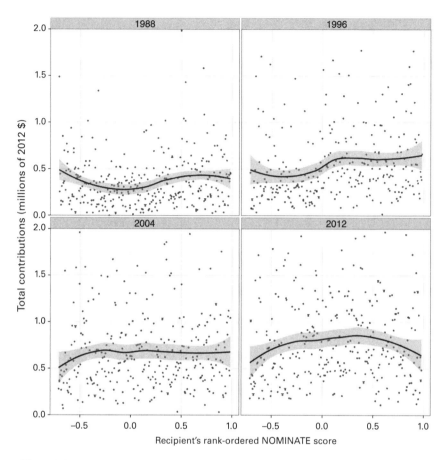

Figure 5.9
Individual contributions to House members in 1988, 1996, 2004, and 2012. *Note:* The figure plots individuals making more than eight contributions.

with other individual donors in the sample (average $|F|$ of 0.47). Large contributors, on average, are slightly less extreme than congressional candidates (including nonincumbents) but are more extreme than the members of Congress (average $|F|$ of 0.40). The results from previous elections tell exactly the same story as figure 5.10.

To take a closer look at the role of extreme views in individual soft-money contributions, we estimate two econometric models. In the first, we estimate a probit model of the decision to make an independent (not "hard"-money contributions directly to candidates) campaign contribution as a function of F, F^2, and S. The results of

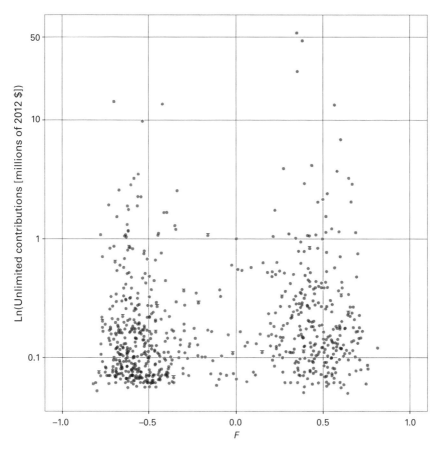

Figure 5.10
Large individual contributions by ideology (*F*) of contributor. *Note:* The figure plots individuals contributing more than $250,000 in the 2012 election cycle.

this model are presented in table 5.2. The large and statistically significant coefficient on F^2 confirms that extreme contributors are the most likely to make unlimited contributions. Minimizing the estimated probabilities with respect to *F*, we find that the least likely to make these contributions are those located at $F = -0.08$. The independent effect of contribution dispersion *S* is negative and consistent with ideological independent expenditures but just short of statistical significance.[26] Assuming a value of $S = 0.25$, contributors located at $F = 0.75$ make unlimited contributions at a probability greater than 0.28. Those at $F = 0.0$ are about 5 percent less likely to make an unlimited contribution. In the second model, we use ordinary least squares regression to estimate how the size of contribution relates to F and S for those who do contribute.[27] Here our dependent variable is the natural log of contributions because of the skew in the distribution of contribution sizes. These results are reported in column 2 of table 5.2. Here we find significant effects for both F^2 and S. Estimated contributions are minimized at $F = -0.06$, reflecting a slight rightward bias in the really large contributions. Contributions for $F = -0.75$ are about 30 percent larger than those for $F = 0$. The estimated effect of S is substantial as well.

Of course, it is hard to estimate the effect of the extreme independent expenditure contributions directly. Presumably the parties have an

Table 5.2
Contributions to independent expenditure groups, 2002–2012 (standard errors in parentheses)

	Probit	OLS on contributions
Constant	−1.538	11.659
	(0.059)	(0.120)
F	0.046	0.071
	(0.020)	(0.038)
F^2	0.291	0.558
	(0.072)	(0.156)
S	−0.506	0.502
	(0.134)	(0.262)
2004	0.342	−0.459
	(0.044)	(0.087)
2006	0.132	−0.594
	(0.044)	(0.089)
2008	0.523	−0.686
	(0.042)	(0.083)
2010	0.149	−0.359
	(0.043)	(0.087)
2012	0.354	−0.144
	(0.041)	(0.083)
AIC	19,209.008	
Log likelihood	−9595.504	
No. of obs.	31,341	2,944
R^2		0.054

Source: Database on Ideology, Money in Politics and Elections.

incentive to use these contributions for the electoral benefit of all their candidates, not just those who share the donor's views. But if the parties prove to be poor agents of the donors, contributions might dry up. Therefore, even if the parties do not use these contributions exclusively for the benefit of their extreme members, such large sums from ideological contributors must make the parties more responsive to the extreme ideological views.[28]

Campaign Finance and the 527 Organizations and Super-PACs

McCain-Feingold sought to diminish the influence of large contributors by eliminating soft-money contributions to the federal parties. The legislation, however, did not prevent the emergence of the 527 groups or super-PACs. Matters have only gotten worse. The major contributors to the 527 groups and super-PACs are exactly the same people who made large soft-money contributions. To make matters worse, as the parties cannot control these expenditures, the groups can better target the money in ways that support extreme candidates, in both general and primary elections. Here we consider the Club for Growth, a libertarian-conservative outside spending group. An important goal for the group is the defeat of RINOs (Republicans in name only) in the primaries. In 2004, the Club for Growth spent $2.3 million in a failed attempt to defeat Republican moderate Arlen Specter in Pennsylvania's Senate primary.[29] By 2010, former Club for Growth's president Pat Toomey's potential primary challenge spurred Specter to switch parties. Specter nonetheless lost the Democratic primary to a liberal Democrat, who was defeated by Toomey in the general election. On the left, groups like MoveOn.org have moved on from trying to defeat Bush to trying to push the Democratic Party to the left. Of course, there are groups dedicated to a more centrist politics, such as the New Democrat Network, but they are dwarfed financially by their more ideological rivals. In addition to the New Democrat Network, of the remaining fifteen largest 527 organizations during the mid-2000s, ten were groups pursuing an explicitly liberal or conservative agenda, two were labor unions, and one was the Swift Boat Veterans for Truth, whose only agenda was beating John Kerry. Nearly all super-PACs were formed to promote an expressly liberal or conservative agenda. In fact, the estimated CF scores for 74 percent of super-PACs would place them to the extremes of the average members of the parties in Congress.

In 2016 the Koch brothers intend to spend vast sums of money duplicating the high-tech 2012 Obama campaign. They aim to build an organization completely independent of the Republican Party that will be able to match the get-out-the-vote efforts of Obama.[30]

Conclusion: The Big Soft Money Comes from Ideological Extremists

The past forty years have been a period not only of political polarization but also of rapidly increasing campaign spending, which has led many to speculate that the two are linked. Our analysis shows no simple causal link leading from the demand for more campaign cash to polarization. Extreme candidates are not better funded than moderates, so there is little evidence that candidates have an incentive to move to the extremes to please their donors. This finding is especially true of our analysis of organized groups. The evidence seems more consistent with a causal arrow pointed in the other direction. Over the past twenty years, the numbers of individual donors contributing large sums have gone up enormously. Many of them are concentrating their largesse on the most extreme candidates. As we have shown, it is the most ideological of these contributors who most exploited the soft-money loopholes and continue to be active in the 527 groups. It is not unreasonable to speculate that the impetus for the greater financial involvement was the increase in polarization and the increased ideological stakes of who wins elections.

Despite the large increases in campaign spending, Ansolabehere, de Figueredo, and Snyder (2003) puzzle over "why there is so little money in politics." We ask, however, why there is so much more money in politics today than at the beginning of the century. The answer lies in unequal riches. More than three million Americans now contribute money to federal election campaigns. But over 99 percent of them are contributing small amounts. Most Americans can afford only relatively small contributions. They can be expected to free ride, either by not contributing at all or by making small contributions, while richer Americans contribute amounts that exceed the annual income of most of their fellow citizens. From the perspective of free riding, it is not surprising that inequality in campaign contributions is far greater than inequality in income. The tithes made by all adults not in the top 1 percent of the income distribution pale in significance compared to the open spigots of the large contributors. These large contributors are drawn from the thousands of not-so-typical American multimillionaires and billionaires who have the resources to make contributions substantial enough to have a major effect on electoral outcomes. That many of these wealthy Americans have ideological agendas, while perhaps not the cause of polarization, certainly provides its sustenance.

Appendix 5.1

Table 5.A1
Estimates of the Dependence of S on F for 1980–2012

Election	1980	1982	1984	1986	1988	1990	1992	1994	1996	1998	2000	2002	2004	2006	2008	2010	2012
Constant	0.408	0.373	0.373	0.400	0.379	0.416	0.393	0.415	0.390	0.415	0.422	0.417	0.389	0.381	0.398	0.379	0.393
	(0.003)	(0.003)	(0.003)	(0.003)	(0.003)	(0.003)	(0.003)	(0.002)	(0.003)	(0.003)	(0.003)	(0.003)	(0.003)	(0.003)	(0.003)	(0.003)	(0.003)
F	−0.048	−0.042	0.002	−0.027	−0.037	−0.039	−0.049	−0.040	−0.045	−0.049	−0.060	−0.038	0.004	−0.032	−0.056	−0.006	−0.002
	(0.010)	(0.008)	(0.007)	(0.006)	(0.007)	(0.007)	(0.007)	(0.006)	(0.006)	(0.006)	(0.005)	(0.006)	(0.005)	(0.004)	(0.005)	(0.005)	(0.006)
F^2	−0.351	−0.309	−0.355	−0.458	−0.375	−0.454	−0.404	−0.471	−0.459	−0.487	−0.552	−0.569	−0.554	−0.470	−0.524	−0.531	−0.554
	(0.025)	(0.018)	(0.016)	(0.016)	(0.018)	(0.018)	(0.017)	(0.018)	(0.016)	(0.016)	(0.015)	(0.017)	(0.016)	(0.013)	(0.014)	(0.015)	(0.016)
N	0.419	0.288	0.260	0.213	0.249	0.089	0.138	0.193	0.214	0.204	0.173	0.156	0.161	0.203	0.215	0.159	0.207
	(0.139)	(0.091)	(0.082)	(0.072)	(0.063)	(0.040)	(0.038)	(0.054)	(0.051)	(0.057)	(0.045)	(0.045)	(0.040)	(0.035)	(0.035)	(0.032)	(0.042)
Labor	−0.059	−0.046	−0.025	−0.024	−0.028	−0.052	−0.039	−0.053	−0.036	−0.049	−0.045	−0.037	−0.035	−0.037	−0.046	−0.034	−0.027
	(0.012)	(0.009)	(0.009)	(0.008)	(0.008)	(0.008)	(0.008)	(0.008)	(0.008)	(0.008)	(0.007)	(0.008)	(0.007)	(0.007)	(0.007)	(0.007)	(0.008)
Trade	−0.004	0.009	0.012	0.016	0.008	0.005	0.010	−0.005	0.012	0.016	0.002	0.005	0.008	0.008	0.001	0.005	0.015
	(0.005)	(0.004)	(0.004)	(0.004)	(0.004)	(0.004)	(0.004)	(0.004)	(0.004)	(0.004)	(0.004)	(0.004)	(0.003)	(0.003)	(0.003)	(0.004)	(0.004)
Unassigned	−0.062	−0.037	−0.023	−0.013	−0.009	−0.013	−0.026	−0.025	0.010	0.010	0.004	−0.005	0.002	0.005	−0.010	−0.006	0.002
	(0.019)	(0.014)	(0.012)	(0.010)	(0.009)	(0.009)	(0.008)	(0.007)	(0.006)	(0.006)	(0.005)	(0.005)	(0.004)	(0.004)	(0.004)	(0.004)	(0.004)
Cooperative	0.095	0.054	0.060	0.074	0.069	0.054	0.069	0.044	0.048	0.051	0.045	0.045	0.013	0.003	0.044	0.025	0.084
	(0.022)	(0.015)	(0.016)	(0.012)	(0.013)	(0.012)	(0.012)	(0.013)	(0.013)	(0.014)	(0.013)	(0.014)	(0.013)	(0.014)	(0.015)	(0.014)	(0.018)
Corporations without stock	0.035	0.006	−0.008	0.009	0.009	−0.005	0.022	0.004	0.024	0.021	0.009	0.015	0.003	0.011	−0.000	0.017	0.014
	(0.028)	(0.015)	(0.012)	(0.011)	(0.011)	(0.010)	(0.010)	(0.011)	(0.010)	(0.011)	(0.010)	(0.010)	(0.010)	(0.010)	(0.009)	(0.010)	(0.012)
Nonconnected															−0.007	−0.010	0.004
															(0.019)	(0.011)	(0.011)
R^2	0.540	0.472	0.506	0.611	0.445	0.584	0.540	0.640	0.572	0.637	0.689	0.658	0.665	0.643	0.683	0.673	0.645
Adj. R^2	0.532	0.465	0.501	0.607	0.440	0.580	0.535	0.637	0.568	0.633	0.686	0.655	0.662	0.640	0.680	0.670	0.641
No. of obs.	491	652	767	796	835	806	841	839	881	856	923	914	912	1,045	1,017	1,040	945

6 Polarization and Public Policy

Politicians have become more polarized, and the rightward move and electoral success of the Republicans have moved the political system away from public policy that might alleviate income inequality. The current surge in polarization started in the 1970s. Since then, voters have increasingly aligned their incomes and their voting behavior, more ineligible adults have become concentrated at the bottom of the income distribution, and soft-money campaign contributions have emerged as a polarizing force.

These political changes can directly exacerbate income inequality. Redistributive policies such as income tax rates, estate tax rates, and minimum wages evolve in a similar fashion to polarization, income inequality, and immigration. As we argued earlier, the rise in real income and the absence of a severe economic downturn between World War II and the Great Recession of the late 2000s should have made voters less favorable to policies like unemployment insurance and welfare, which smooth the current consumption of people of working age. At the same time, support for social insurance for the elderly has been strong. In contrast to taxes on income and wealth and to minimum wages, taxes for Social Security and Medicare programs have increased as polarization has grown.

In politics, change is difficult and punctuated. There is no market to fine-tune allocations to demand and supply. An example highly pertinent to our story is the estate tax. Rates and exemptions were fixed in nominal dollars in 1942 and received no adjustment until 1977. With inflation, smaller and smaller estates in real value were subject to tax. Kopczuk and Saez (2004) estimate that fewer than 1 percent of the adult population were required to file an estate tax return in 1941. By 1976, filing was required for 6.5 percent.[1] Taxable estates of a given inflation-adjusted size were subject to increasing rates.

The estate tax example illustrates what social scientists term the status quo bias of American politics. Polarization accentuates status quo bias to produce *gridlock*. Major legislation is produced less frequently as polarization increases. Gridlock in turn can affect the government's capacity to reduce inequality.

What is surprising is the national move to the right in the wake of the Great Recession. Democrats gained control of Congress in the midterm elections of 2006, which in all likelihood were a reaction to the Iraq War more than a call to reduce inequality or provide social insurance. Democrats solidified these gains in 2008 and added the Obama presidency. The financial crisis, as we detailed in *Political Bubbles*, may well have had electoral consequences. But the congressional elections of 2010, 2012, and 2014 moved the nation sharply to the right. By 2014, the Republicans, with many new highly conservative members, had garnered their largest House majority in decades and had captured control of the Senate. In our concluding chapter, we address why public policy in recent years has done so little to break either polarization or inequality, even in the presence of economic crisis.

Polarized politics is not the only source of income inequality. There are abundant alternative hypotheses about the rise of inequality. The list includes greater trade liberalization, increased levels of immigration, declining rates of trade unionization, the fall in the real minimum wage, the decline in progressive taxation, technological change increasing the returns to education, the increased rates of family dissolution and female-headed households, the aging of the population, pure racism, America's federal political system, gridlocked national politics, and the absence of proportional representation in elections. (See Atkinson 1997 for an overview of some of these topics; see also Alesina and Glaeser 2004.)

Most of the factors listed above are either directly political or potentially affected by public policy. Technological change, however, would appear to respond to many forces that are independent of government policy. Similarly, the decline of marriage is universal throughout the Western world. The roots of the decline may lie just as much in technological changes that affect work in the household and in changes in lifestyle as in changes in incentives produced through welfare and other public policies. Similarly, immigration is driven not just by the American economy and public policy but also by the economies and policies of the source nations. We acknowledge these exogenous factors but keep our focus on the public policies produced in the American political system.

The Turnaround in Public Policies Affecting Inequality

Let us look at time trends in public policy. We focus on minimum wages, estate taxes, and income taxes, largely because we can report long time series of these policies. The policies reverse in a manner that parallels the reversals in inequality and politics.

Federal minimum wages were introduced in 1938.[2] The real value of the minimum wage follows a sawtooth pattern, as shown in figure 6.1. The teeth reflect the fact that the wage is not indexed to inflation. Without new legislation, the real wage will decline. The Democrats attempted to index minimum wages in the 1960s and the 1970s. On September 15, 1977, an amendment sponsored by Congressman Phil Burton of California to index the wage for five years failed by the relatively narrow margin of 232 to 191.[3] The vote was strongly along liberal-conservative lines, with moderate Democrats joining Republicans to defeat the amendment. Had Burton succeeded, the

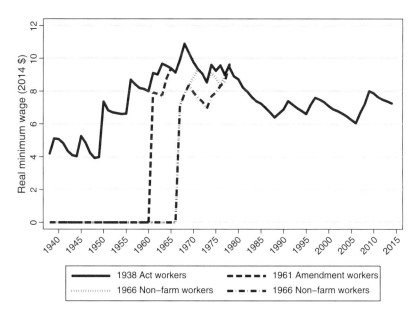

Figure 6.1
Real minimum wages, 1938–2015. *Source:* U.S. Department of Labor. Chart available at http://www.dol.gov/whd/minwage/chart.htm. Deflator: CPI-U.

minimum wage might be far higher today. It might have been as difficult to remove indexation as it now is to pass meaningful increases.

The sawteeth, however, were only temporary interruptions in an upward trend that persisted until 1968, at the very end of Lyndon Johnson's Great Society. Minimum wages have always engendered liberal support and conservative opposition. Both because of their desire to redistribute income to low-wage workers and to avoid competition with non-unionized labor, liberals have favored a high minimum wage covering large segments of the workforce. Conversely, conservatives have sought to keep the minimum wage low and to limit its scope, as they believe that it creates unemployment by artificially inflating the cost of labor and that it imposes too great a burden on small businesses. Minimum wages initially failed to cover large categories of workers, largely as a matter of concessions to southern Democrats.

Despite these general differences, increases in the minimum wage and expansions of coverage historically generated a fair amount of bipartisan support. For example, in 1949, Republicans overwhelmingly supported a near doubling of the wage. Moreover, Republican support was pivotal in the 1961 and 1966 amendments that increased the wage and extended it to new groups of voters. That is, as long as polarization was low, liberals were able to overcome the status quo bias in the non-indexed policy. This relationship is shown in figure 6.1. The figure also shows that coverage was expanded at the same time that the basic minimum wage was increasing. The postwar period was indeed one of generous increases. Although the largest increase occurred in the Truman years, there was a real increase even under Eisenhower, a Republican president.

This bipartisanship disappeared, as it did on so many other issues, as polarization rose in the 1970s. When Congress passed increases in 1977, it did so with a majority of Republicans in each chamber voting in opposition. Subsequently, Reagan's election and the Republican takeover of the Senate blocked further increases until 1989. Although Republicans did support the 1989 bill on final passage, the three-step increase was so modest that it failed to reverse the long decline of the 1980s. In 1996, the minority Democrats managed to force a minimum-wage bill onto the agenda with a deft combination of obstruction of the Republican agenda and symbolic election-year politics. Nevertheless, the result was again a very modest increase, at the

cost of $20 billion in new business tax breaks. The only new success-
ful minimum wage bill since 1996 was a three-stage increase passed
in 2007 after the Democrats had recaptured control of Congress. This
legislation ultimately increased the nominal hourly wage from $5.15
to $7.25.

The consequence of increasing Republican opposition in the period
of polarization is a dramatic decline in the real value of the minimum
wage. The decline began when Richard Nixon took office. Even though
there was some increase after Watergate, minimum wages did not
recover even half of the losses of the first six Nixon years. Increases in
minimum wages were passed under President Carter, but they were
quickly eroded by the high inflation at the end of his four years. In
Carter's last year in office, 1980, real minimum wages were actually
less than in the last year, 1976, of his predecessor, Gerald Ford. The
Reagan years saw much further erosion of the minimum wage. The
"kinder, gentler" increase accepted by George H. W. Bush restored very
little of the losses. Bill Clinton was then barely able to better the Bush
restoration. By 2014, real minimum wages were only fractionally higher
than the level when Clinton took office in 1993.

Politically, the reversal in the minimum wage chart is consistent with
the end of Democratic dominance in American politics, which can
probably be dated from the Nixon election in 1968. But it is also possible that preferences on minimum wages have changed for individual
legislators. Two of us (Poole and Rosenthal 1991) did an admittedly
crude calculation of preference shifts by comparing the votes of senators who had voted on minimum wages in both 1977 and 1989. We
found that the real wage these senators would support had fallen by
about 15 to 20 percent from 1977 to 1989. The decline in this support
might reflect the academic debate over the employment effects of
minimum wages, but it might also reflect a shift in preferences of
increasingly better-off citizens in the upper half of the income distribution. Both a shift in these preferences and an overall shift to Republicans would be consistent with a shift in an electorate that immigration
has increasingly tilted toward the well-to-do.

The real minimum wage today is no higher than it was in the 1950s.
But because real wages have generally risen, this wage is less and less
a binding constraint on employers.[4] The public does appear to support
increases in the minimum wage. Indeed, many states, including red
ones, have overridden the polarization in Washington and set minimum
wages higher than the federal minimum. In 2015 twenty-nine states

have minimum wages higher than the federal minimum of $7.25. The highest state minimum wage in 2014 was Oregon's $9.10. This is still below the real value of the federal minimum in 1968.[5]

Lee (1999) exploits the cross-sectional variation induced by state minimum-wage laws to conclude that the fall in real minimum wages in the 1980s was a leading source of wage inequality. He estimated that declining minimum wages accounted for about half of the increase in the ratio of median wages to wages at the tenth percentile. The reduction in inequality in the 1950s and 1960s could, conversely, reflect the increase in real minimum wages during this period. But changes in the minimum wage obviously cannot account for all of the long-term trends in inequality; there was no minimum wage in the United States before 1938, yet, as we showed in chapter 1, inequality fell in the 1930s. We should also consider taxation. The story is clearest for the estate tax, cleverly relabeled the "death tax" by its Republican detractors. Because it is difficult to reduce complex tax codes to single numbers, we focus on two series for the estate tax. The first is the maximum estate tax rate, or how much the taxpayer would have to pay without giving away or sheltering wealth. The second is the maximum estate without tax liability, that is, the minimum taxable estate. Both series are shown in figure 6.2. To make the series comparable with each other and with the various inequality graphs, we have graphed 1.0 minus the maximum tax rate.

The influence of partisan politics is even clearer for estate taxes than for minimum wages. The first estate taxes were introduced under unified Democratic government during World War I. More estates were subject to tax until a unified Republican government in 1926 both lowered the tax and increased the minimum estate subject to tax from $669,000 to $1,361,000 (in year 2014 dollars). Taxes were increased and the minimum decreased when the Democrats took control of the House in the 1930 elections. Taxation of the wealthy increased in the Roosevelt years until the maximum estate tax rate reached 77 percent in 1941. Rates then remained unchanged for thirty-six years, until 1977. During this time, inflation eroded the minimum until, by 1976, estates under $250,000 were subject to tax. The failure to increase the minimum for so many years resembles the failure of California to adjust real estate taxes during the real estate price boom that preceded the passage of Proposition 13 in 1978. The lack of adjustment meant a broader base for an antitax movement.

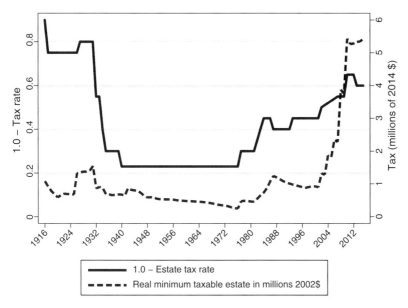

Figure 6.2
Estate tax, 1916–2014. *Note:* Those dying in 2010 were given the option (1) pay no estate tax but receive a smaller step up in the capital gains basis or (2) pay 35% on the value of the estate over $5m. The figure assumes option 2. *Source:* For 1916–2010, Darien B. Jacobson, Brian G. Raub, and Barry W. Johnson, "The Estate Tax: Ninety Years and Counting," http://www.irs.gov/pub/irs-soi/ninetyestate.pdf. For 2011–2015, http://www.bankrate.com/finance/taxes/estate-tax-and-gift-tax-amounts.aspx, http://www.irs.gov/Businesses/Small-Businesses-&-Self-Employed/Estate-Tax, http://en.wikipedia.org/wiki/Estate_tax_in_the_United_States, http://wills.about.com/od/understandingestatetaxes/a/estatetaxchart.htm. Deflator: CPI-U

Estate taxes then reversed with legislation in 1976 (effective in 1977) passed under the Ford presidency. The reduction in rates and the increase in the minimum were minor. The phased-in minimum adjustments failed to outstrip inflation in the Carter years. Reagan did lower taxes on large estates substantially. His bill, which would have eventually lowered the top rate to 50 percent, was replaced by the Tax Reform Act of 1986. The 1986 act, enacted in a time of large deficits, temporarily increased the rate from 55 percent to 60 percent. Clinton's legislation in 1993 made 55 percent, not 50 percent, permanent. Moreover, the minimum again decreased as a result of inflation. The minimum was stabilized, but not substantially increased, after the Republicans took control of Congress in the 1994 elections. Finally, a unified Republican government made drastic changes in 2001. The Bush tax cuts were only partially reversed by the "2012" tax bill passed, when gridlock finally broke, on New Year's Day in 2013. Moreover, the minimum estate subject to taxation is now indexed, so the gains of the wealthy will no longer be eroded by inflation. The inflation-adjusted minimum is now four times its level during the Republican administration of Herbert Hoover.

The picture just given, of gradual change from Ford through Reagan, followed by a "big bang" with Bush 43, is to some degree misleading. A generous exclusion, of about $1,000,000 (in year 1998 dollars), for a closely held business was introduced in 1977.[6] In 1986, the marital deduction was increased from 50 percent to 100 percent (see Carroll 2002, 393). "Family limited partnerships" for limiting estate taxes began to be mass-marketed, apparently in the late 1980s. In other words, when one considers features of the tax other than maximum rates and minimum taxable estates, the changes in the 1970s and 1980s were more substantial.

A somewhat different story holds for top minimum federal income tax rates, shown in figure 6.3. Marginal tax rates increased in the period of decreasing inequality. The Kennedy-era tax cuts, however, led to a decrease in marginal tax rates before the turnaround in inequality. While inequality has grown, however, top marginal tax rates have continued to fall.

Wolff (2002, 28) provides marginal rates on the real incomes of $135,000, $67,000, and $33,000 from 1947 to 2000 (in year 2000 dollars). His data provide a pattern more in accord with what we found for estate taxes. These marginal rates were fairly steady throughout the period of declining inequality after World War II. In 1980, the marginal rate was 59 percent on $135,000, 49 percent on $67,000, and 28 percent on $33,000, consistent with strong progressivity in taxation. By 1991, the three marginal rates were nearly equal, 31 percent, 28 percent, and 28 percent, respectively.

The picture of income taxes drawn from marginal rates is echoed by the effective rate on the top 1 percent by income. The effective rate adjusts for shelters and other gimmicks used to reduce taxes. Carroll (2002, 393) presents data for various years from 1963 to 1995. The effective rates on the rich rose from 24.6 percent in 1963 to 27.8 percent in 1977 and then declined to 19.2 percent in 1985. Pressures to reduce the deficit thereafter led to an upward trend, but after the Clinton bill of 1993, the effective rate reached only 23.8 percent in 1995, still slightly below the 23.9 percent during 1980, Carter's last year in office. Phillips

Figure 6.3
Top federal income tax rate, 1913–2014. *Note:* This table contains a number of simplifica-
tions and ignores a number of factors, such as a maximum tax on earned income of
50 percent when the top rate was 70 percent and the current increase in rates due to
income-related reductions in the value of itemized deductions. Perhaps most important,
it ignores the large increase in the percentage of returns that were subject to this top
rate. *Source:* Historical Parameters Tax Policy Center pdf, downloaded from http://
www.taxpolicycenter.org/taxfacts/displayafact.cfm?DocID=543&Topic2id=30&Topic
3id=39.

(2002, 96) presents effective rates for those earning more than $1 million
from 1948 to 1970, which peaked in the 1955–1960 period at 85.5 percent
and then declined to 66.9 percent in 1965. Phillips also shows rates with
FICA tax included for 1977 onward. These declined during the Carter
years from 35.5 percent in 1977 to 31.7 percent in 1980. Under Reagan,
the rate dropped further, to 24.9 percent in 1985, before rebounding to
26.9 percent in 1988.

We can summarize the three public policies of minimum wages,
estate taxes, and income taxes:

• Consistent with the trend in inequality in the twentieth century,
redistributive policies were first strengthened and then relaxed.

• The dates of a move away from redistribution are somewhat
different—early 1960s for marginal tax rates, late 1960s for minimum
wages, and mid-1970s for estate taxes and effective tax rates on the rich.

It is important to note that, like the tax revolts at the state level, all of these preceded the election of Ronald Reagan. One might say that, by analogy with Andrew Jackson riding a wave of democratization to the presidency, Reagan rode a wave of antigovernment sentiment.

Social Security, an extremely important public expenditure, has not suffered the same fate (as of late 2015) as minimum wages for the poor or taxes on the rich. The data are presented in figure 6.4. The Social Security program is financed by a tax that, unlike the estate tax and the income tax, is openly regressive. Earnings above the cap are untaxed. Moreover, the tax is just a payroll tax; income from capital is untaxed. This tax, however, has grown. In an antitax era, as we see in the figure, Congress has supported an increase in the maximum real amount that a wage earner can pay into the system. This increase has been accomplished by raising both the tax rate and the cap (the cap for 2014 was $117,000). At the same time, notwithstanding the perpetual "crisis" in

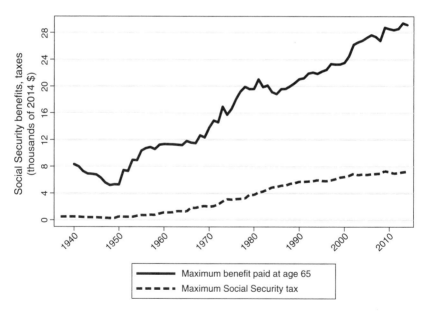

Figure 6.4
Social Security benefits and taxes, 1938–2015. *Note:* In thousands of 2014 dollars. Beginning in 2003, the full retirement age was gradually increased from sixty-five years to seventy years. But benefits are still calculated for someone who retires exactly at sixty-five years. *Source* (except CPI-U): Social Security Administration, Annual Statistical Supplement 2014. Available at http://www.ssa.gov/policy/docs/statcomps/supplement/2014/index.html.

Social Security funding, the maximum real amount a worker gets out of the Social Security program has risen dramatically. In part, the rise reflects a generous indexing of benefits to wages rather than prices, thus promising retirees the living standard of the current working generation rather than their own.

Social Security is formally called Old Age Insurance and was, misleadingly, sold to the public in that guise. Although the payments are mildly redistributive to lower-wage earners, it is largely a middle-class program that is not supported by taxes on high incomes or capital. So far, in distinction to high taxes on the rich, Social Security taxes are being maintained. In a nutshell, Social Security insures old-age consumption via a regressive tax. Barry Goldwater's electoral fiasco in 1964 is likely to have been accentuated by his opposition to the Social Security system. In Ronald Reagan's time, Republicans were still running away from this hot potato. Perhaps the increase in real income since 1980 convinced George W. Bush to take on the traditional program because a large portion of the population can now self-insure for old-age consumption. Nonetheless, Bush had a fiasco when he attempted to "reform" the Social Security system by using the "capital" he claimed to have earned in the 2004 election.

Like the Social Security program, Medicare has grown as inequality has grown. Again, we see demand for a government program that offers broad insurance in old age rather than earlier in the life cycle. Medicare taxes, originally capped at the same earnings level as Social Security taxes, had higher caps instituted in 1991 and became totally uncapped in 1994. Because of the great variance in health care outcomes, health care consumption is far riskier than the rest of old-age consumption. This risk, we argue, makes Medicare taxes far less vulnerable than estate taxes or income taxes. Indeed, although George W. Bush pushed tax cuts, the Medicare tax was not on the table. To the contrary, over the opposition of many House conservatives, Bush pushed through a very expensive prescription drug program. Vice presidential candidate Paul Ryan proposed replacing Medicare with a privatized program; his proposal was a nonstarter for the Romney campaign in 2012.

In summary, we would argue that as polarization increased through the last quarter of the twentieth century, policies moved in a less redistributive way when it was a matter of either taxing the income or the estates of the top brackets or improving the wages of the bottom brackets. In contrast, other policies maintained the status quo on some old-age consumption financed by a regressive tax and expanded, in part by moving from regressive to proportional taxation, insurance for the risky component of old-age consumption represented by health care.[7] All of these changes in policy would appear to meet the demands of middle-income voters with rising real incomes and wealth.

Polarization and Gridlock in Public Policy

Having shown how the time series of polarization tracks policy changes with regard to minimum wages and taxes, we now turn to a more detailed discussion of how polarization might influence policy formation. We can then see how polarization relates to the ability of Congress to pass major legislation. Finally, we return to a specific policy, welfare benefits, to illustrate how polarization produces gridlock.

Theories of Majoritarian and Partisan Politics

Some models in political economy have the feature that polarization should have a limited influence on policymaking. The median voter model, which we used in chapter 4, asserts that two-party competition will always lead to policies that enact the preferences of the median voter. If the median voter's preferences change, there should be a swift policy response and no gridlock.

Similarly, the model of partisan, ideological politics in which the winning party enacts its preferences rather than those of the median voter (Alesina 1988; Calvert 1985; Wittman 1983) leaves no gridlock. Polarization should simply lead to wider policy swings after changes in power. (We implicitly used this model in chapter 3 in modeling the tax policies of the two major parties.)

The formal theory of partisan politics sees policy as flowing directly from elections. As in the median voter model, there is no role for a legislature. Nonetheless, the formal theories resonate with views expressed by legislative scholars.

Many legislative scholars (e.g., Cox and McCubbins 1993, 2005) argue that legislators have strong electoral incentives to delegate substantial powers to partisan leaders to shape the legislative agenda and to discipline wayward members. To the extent that parties can successfully pursue such strategies, policymaking becomes the interaction of parties.

In such a world, polarization becomes something of a mixed bag. American political scientists have long suggested that more cohesive, distinct, and programmatic political parties would offer a corrective to the failures of policymaking in the United States. Enamored of the "party responsibility" model of Westminster-style parliaments, they have argued that a system in which a cohesive majority party governs encumbered only by the need to win elections could provide more accountability and rationality in policymaking. As formulated by the American Political Science Association's Report of the Committee on Political Parties (1950): "An effective party system requires, first, that the parties are able to bring forth programs to which they commit themselves and, second, that the parties possess sufficient internal cohesion to carry out these programs."

Implicit in this statement is that policy will, as in the formal theories, be firmly in the control of one of the two parties. Any benefits of polarization, however, are offset when control of the executive and legislative branches is split between cohesive parties. Unfortunately for the Responsible Party model, political polarization has occurred in an era of increasing frequency of divided government. Before World War II, there was no positive association between divided government and polarization, whereas the two phenomena have frequently occurred together in the postwar period.[8]

In situations of divided government with cohesive parties, party theories predict that policymaking will represent bilateral bargaining between the parties. The moderating elections version of the partisan model (Alesina and Rosenthal 1995) assumes that a bargain is struck, thus eliminating wide policy swings. Indeed, it calls, like the median voter model, for immediate enactment of the preferences of a pivotal, if nonmedian, voter.

Polarization, however, may affect whether a bargain can be struck. Just as a house cannot be sold when the buyer values it at less than the seller's reservation price, increased policy differences shrink the set of compromises that both parties are willing to entertain. The increased policy differences have a second effect on bargaining that endangers even feasible compromises. Returning to the analogy of a home buyer, consider the case of a buyer who is willing to pay only slightly more than the seller is willing to accept. Under such circumstances, the buyer may be more willing to make a "low-ball" offer, as her only risk is losing out on a transaction in which she stands to gain little. Returning to the political context, increased policy differences exacerbate the incentives to engage in brinksmanship so that even feasible policy compromises might not be reached.[9] Thus, this perspective predicts that polarization should lead to more gridlock and less policy innovation during periods of divided government. The prediction for unified government would be a positive effect of polarization attributable to increased party responsibility.

Although theories of majoritarian and partisan politics are important benchmarks for the study of legislative politics, their predictions about the consequences for polarization depend heavily on assumptions that eliminate the frictions inherent in American institutions. A very different picture emerges from a more realistic approach that incorporates the internal procedures of each house of Congress and the interactions of the two houses. It is precisely these features of the American political system that give polarization its bite.

In contrast to majoritarian and partisan models of the political process, pivot theories model the implications of various supermajoritarian institutions such as the presidential veto and the Senate filibuster.[10] In these theories, policymaking is driven directly not by pivotal *voters* but by those elected *politicians* whose support is *pivotal* in overcoming vetoes and filibusters.

A pivot is an agent whose support is necessary for the passage of a new law. The possible pivots are the president and critical members of the House and Senate. Here we may consider as an example the effects of the Senate's rules for debate and cloture. Currently, debate on most legislation cannot be terminated without a vote on cloture, which must be supported by three-fifths of the senators present and voting.[11] It is easy to see the effect of the cloture rule within our unidimensional liberal-conservative perspective. If all one hundred senators vote according to their ideal points, the senators located at the 41st and the 60th most leftward positions must support any new legislation, as no coalition can contain three-fifths of the votes without including these legislators. Therefore any policy located between these pivotal senators cannot be altered, or is *gridlocked*. After Alaska and Hawaii were admitted in 1959 (increasing the number of states to fifty) but before the reforms of 1975, the requirement for cloture was a two-thirds vote, so the *filibuster pivots* were located at either the 34th or 67th positions.

Additionally, pivot models take account of the presidential veto. Either the president must support new legislation or a coalition of two-thirds of each chamber must vote to override. Suppose the president is located toward the left on the policy spectrum. Then if the president does not support the legislation, both the legislator at the 145th (one-third of 435) position in the House and the legislator at the 34th position in the Senate must support any policy change. These legislators are dubbed the *veto pivots*. If the president is on the right, similarly placed legislators on the right become the veto pivots.

If we assume the president is more extreme than the veto pivots, a rough measure of the propensity for legislative gridlock is the preference distance between the 34th senator and the 60th senator when the president is on the left and the distance between the 41st senator and the 67th senator when the president is on the right.[12] When these distances are large, new legislation should be harder to achieve.

We have computed the gridlock interval using the NOMINATE scores. Results from a time-series regression of the size of the interval against polarization and a dummy variable for the 1975 reforms are shown in table 6.1. The width of the gridlock interval and party polarization are conceptually distinct, but we can see empirically that they go hand in hand. These two measures are closely related because the filibuster and veto pivots are almost always members of different parties. As the preferences of the parties diverged, so did those of the pivots. In fact, more than 40 percent of the variation in the width of the gridlock interval in the postwar period is accounted for by polarization and the 1975 cloture reforms. Thus, the pivotal politics approach suggests that polarization will be a serious break on legislative activity.

This perspective also underscores why the Senate's cloture rules have come under scrutiny and have elicited calls for reform. Once an

Table 6.1
Polarization and the gridlock interval, 1946–2014 (standard errors in parentheses)

Variable	Coefficient
Senate polarization	0.497
	(0.134)
1975 reforms	−0.030
	(0.042)
Constant	0.180
	(0.064)
N	33
R^2	0.422

Note: Dependent variable: gridlock interval.

infrequently used tool reserved for the most important legislation, with the rise of polarization the filibuster has become a central feature of American politics. Filibusters, both threatened and realized, have been used to kill a number of important pieces of legislation. They have also been used to force accommodation in the legislation. Of the three major pieces of legislation of the Obama administration, the 2009 stimulus package was cut by $200 billion to accommodate the Senate pivot, the Dodd-Frank bill had a tax on banks removed, and the Affordable Care Act had numerous concessions.

Perhaps even more consequentially, the filibuster has led the Senate to greater reliance on legislative tricks to avoid its effects. One such gimmick is using the budget reconciliation process to pass new legislation because reconciliation bills cannot be filibustered. This procedure was used to pass the large income and estate tax cuts in 2001. To avoid points of order under the so-called Byrd Rule, however, such legislation can have only deficit-increasing fiscal effects for the term of the budget resolution (five to ten years).[13] Many important pieces of fiscal policy have become temporary artifices built on a foundation of budgetary gimmicks.

Strategic Disagreement

Another mechanism that might help transform polarization into legislative paralysis is the increased incentive for politicians to engage in strategic disagreement. Strategic disagreement occurs when a president, party, or other political actor refuses to compromise with the other side in an attempt to gain an electoral advantage by transferring blame for the stalemate to the other side. Classic instances include attempts to bring up controversial legislation near an election in the hopes that a president will cast an unpopular veto, as was done with the Family and Medical Leave Act in 1992 and the partial-birth abortion ban before the 2000 election. Such electoral grandstanding not only lowers legislative capacity by diverting resources into an unproductive endeavor, it also makes both sides less willing to engage in the compromises necessary for successful legislation.[14]

Polarization may exacerbate these incentives. As the parties have become more extreme relative to voters, making the other side appear to be the more extreme becomes more valuable. If a veto of a family leave bill can make the president look like a heartless panderer to the pro-business lobby, why exclude small firms from its provisions to get it passed? If a veto of a partial-birth abortion ban can make the president look like a heartless panderer to NARAL Pro-Choice America, why make an exemption for women's health to get it passed? Strategic disagreement leads to the erosion of the remaining strands of common ground.

Exacerbating such grandstanding is contemporary media coverage of politics. Especially since Watergate and Vietnam, the media cover policymaking much as they would a heavyweight boxing match, scoring the winner and loser round by round. In such an environment, both sides are loath to make any compromises for fear of being scored the round's loser. The result is policy stagnation.

Citizen Trust

Another potential pathway from polarization to gridlock lies in how voters respond to polarized elites. David King (1997) and Marc Hetherington (2004) have separately argued that a primary consequence of polarization is that it undermines citizens' trust in the capacity of government to solve problems. Such claims are bolstered by the fact that the polarization measures in chapter 2 track survey evidence of citizen trust in government fairly closely.[15]

It is not hard to speculate how declining trust can lead to policy stalemate. If the two parties cannot agree how to solve a problem, it is hard to mobilize the public around any policy response. It is even worse when one side says a proposed policy ameliorates the problem while the other says it exacerbates it.

Polarization and Legislative Productivity

As discussed in the last section, many approaches to the study of policymaking predict that polarization should make it more difficult for Congress to pass important new legislation. Despite this prediction, there have been few attempts to document such a relationship. For example, in his seminal analysis of post–World War II lawmaking, David Mayhew (1991) studied whether divided party control of the executive and legislative branches produces legislative gridlock, but he did not consider the effects of polarization and declining bipartisanship. Indeed, he attributed his "negative" findings about divided government to the fact that during the postwar period, bipartisanship was the norm.

Despite Mayhew's neglect of polarization, his data on landmark legislative enactments can be used to assess polarization's effects on the legislative process. Figure 6.5 plots the number of significant legislative enactments by congressional term against the NOMINATE polarization measure.[16] It reveals a striking pattern. In the period before polarization began to surge (1977 and before), Congress enacted just over thirteen significant pieces of legislation per term. Since that point, Congress has produced only around ten and a half. The gap would be even bigger except for the enormous legislative output following the September 11, 2001, terrorist attacks during the polarized 2000s.

To control for other factors that might explain these differences, McCarty (2007) developed a multivariate model of legislative output. Here we report on an update and extension of his model. As he did, we attempt to isolate the effect of polarization by controlling for unified party control of government, split party control of Congress, the election cycle (congressional terms preceding presidential

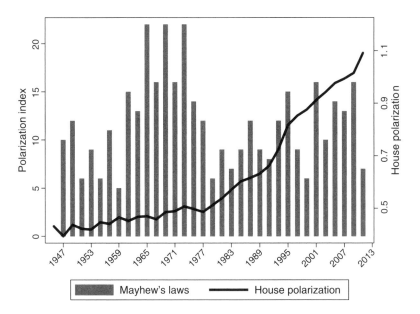

Figure 6.5
Polarization and legislative production, 1947–2012. *Note:* Data on significant legislation are from Mayhew (1991). The figure combines the Sweep I and Sweep II laws from his original analysis, supplemented by his subsequent list of significant laws from 1990 to 2012. *Source:* Available at http://campuspress.yale.edu/davidmayhew/datasets-divided -we-govern.

elections aren't very productive), changes in party control of the presidency and Congress, and secular trends.[17] In the preferred specification, there are substantively large and statistically significant negative effects of polarization. Based on the estimates, the least polarized congressional term produces 111 percent more legislation than the most polarized.[18]

To get at the magnitude of these differences, figure 6.6 presents a counterfactual analysis of Congress's output if polarization had remained at its lowest level, using the estimates of the multivariate model. Even though this figure uses the lowest estimate of the effect of polarization, the effect is substantial. Without polarization, a substantial secular trend in legislative output would likely have continued. Polarization did not just dampen the trend, it reversed it.

One potential objection to these findings is that Mayhew's enactments are only the tip of the legislative iceberg. Perhaps polarization affects the landmark bills but not the merely important ones. McCarty (2007) used data collected by William Howell and his colleagues that can help address this issue (Howell et al. 2000). They coded thousands of postwar statutes according to their "legislative significance,"

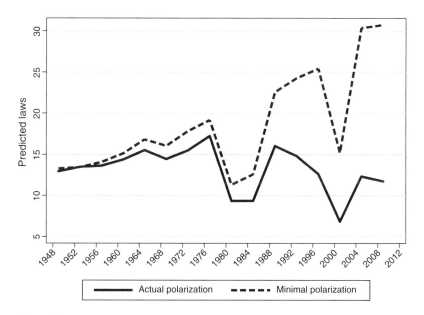

Figure 6.6
What if there were no polarization? The effect of polarization on producing major legislation. *Note:* Based on the estimates of model described in text.

grouping them into four levels. Their A-level statutes roughly correspond to Mayhew's enactments. Their B-level statutes are statutes with
significant policy changes that do not quite reach "landmark" status,
and C-level statutes are the remaining broad and substantive enactments. The lowest level, D, contains the remainder—trivial and narrow
legislation. McCarty estimated a separate multivariate model for each
of these sets of statutes identical to the one run on Mayhew's data. The
results show that polarization has very large effects for the top three
categories of legislation, with the largest effect on B-level statutes.
Polarization appears to reduce output across a broad spectrum of
possible legislation.

One might nonetheless object that the findings reported above are
just for the postwar period and are solely the consequence of the historical coincidence of the Great Society with polarization's nadir. To
alleviate these concerns, McCarty marshaled data collected by a number
of scholars on the legislative output of the late nineteenth and early
twentieth centuries.[19] Estimates based on these data also confirm the
negative effects of polarization on legislative output.

Effects of Polarization on Social Policy

Given the evidence that polarization has reduced Congress's capacity
to legislate, we now ask how this gridlock has affected public policy
outcomes. The most direct effect of polarization-induced gridlock is
that public policy does not adjust to changing economic and demographic circumstances.

There are a number of reasons to believe that these effects would be
most pronounced in the arena of social policy. Insofar as one of the
aims of social policy is to insure citizens against the economic risks
inherent in a market system, it must be responsive to shifts in economic
forces. If polarization inhibits these responses, it may leave citizens
open to the new risks created by economic shifts brought on by dein-
dustrialization and globalization. An example is the political response
in the United States to increasing economic inequality. Inequality can
be attributed to a variety of economic forces, described at the outset
of this chapter. Nevertheless, many West European countries faced
with many of the same forces developed policies to mitigate the consequences so that the level of inequality changed only marginally.[20]
Similarly, Jacob Hacker (2004) has recently argued that polarization

was an important factor in impeding the modernization of many of the policies designed to ameliorate social risks.

A second issue concerns the ways in which social policies in the United States are designed. Many policies, especially those aimed at the poor or near poor, are not indexed with respect to their benefits.[21] Therefore these programs require continuous legislative adjustment to achieve a constant level of social protection. We have seen that the nonindexed minimum wage has withered away in the current era of polarization. We now provide evidence that polarization has had a conservative effect on the creation and implementation of the Affordable Care Act.

Case Studies in Polarized Politics

ACA Implementation

Few issues in American politics have been as polarizing as the role of the federal government in the provision of health care and health insurance. Every Democratic president since Harry Truman has sought major legislation to use the federal government to expand health care coverage to more citizens. Republicans have generally resisted these efforts, arguing for more market-based solutions.

After passage of a stimulus package to deal with the effects of the economic crisis, it is unsurprising that health care reform was the first order of business for the Democrats following their complete takeover of the government in 2009. Although the ultimate legislation was far milder that the single-payer plans proposed by some on the left and was modeled on the Massachusetts program developed by the Republican governor Mitt Romney, the Affordable Care Act (a.k.a. Obamacare) passed by the slimmest of margins, with almost no Republican support. Moreover, the elimination of Obamacare "root and branch" has been the official policy goal of congressional Republicans ever since.

For our purposes, the ACA has two main features. First, it called for the establishment of health care exchanges where consumers could choose between health care plans that met a set of minimum standards. States were encouraged to set up their own exchanges. Citizens in states that chose not to do so would be served on the federal exchange.

The second feature that we focus on is the expansion of Medicaid, the federal-state health insurance program for the poor, to families with an income 133 percent of the poverty level. Originally, the ACA called for penalties for states that failed to expand their Medicaid programs. But in NFIB v. Sebellius, the Supreme Court ruled that the federal government could only withhold new Medicaid funds, not cut existing funding, to those states that chose not to expand their programs. Consequently, states had a lot more latitude over whether to expand their Medicaid programs.

We can use the states' decisions to create and operate their own health care exchanges, as well as their decisions about Medicaid expansion, to illustrate the partisan polarization of social policy. Using data from the Kaiser Foundation, we coded states that had adopted state health insurance exchanges as of November 2014, the start of the second open-enrollment period.[22] Likewise we coded states that had expanded their Medicaid program by March 6, 2015.

In tables 6.2a and 6.2b, the state ACA decisions are broken out by party control in 2013–2014, the period in which most of these legislative decisions were made.[23] Partisan effects are clearly evident in a state's decision related to ACA implementation. All fourteen states under full control of the Democrats created some form of state exchange and expanded their Medicaid program. Conversely, twenty-one out of twenty-three states under full Republican control defaulted to the

Table 6.2a
State decisions on ACA exchanges

Party control	Federal exchange	State exchange
Democratic control	0	14
Divided control	6	7
Republican control	21	2

Table 6.2b
State decisions on Medicaid expansion

Party control	No expansion	Expanded Medicaid
Democratic control	0	14
Divided control	5	8
Republican control	16	7

federal health care exchange. Only one-third of Republican states expanded Medicaid. In states with split control, state exchanges and Medicaid expansion were adopted by just over half.

It is noteworthy that these partisan effects cannot be explained by state-level constituency interests. The simple correlations between the percentage of uninsured in the states and the adoption of exchanges and expanded Medicaid is negative and statistically significant. But in a multivariate model that controls for party control and percent uninsured, the effect of the uninsured on state policies disappears. This pattern arises because states with the highest percentage of uninsured tend to be under Republican control.

In summary, the strong partisan divisions over health care not only delayed a comprehensive response to the uninsured, it helped prevent its full and efficient implementation.

Polarization and Financial Reform

The major push on reforms designed to deal with the problems revealed by the financial crisis and the Great Recession began in June 2009, when the Obama administration released an eighty-nine-page outline of its reform priorities. The administration plan focused on four principal areas: the creation of the Financial Stability Oversight Council, which would help coordinate regulatory agencies and provide oversight; a modest revamping of the structure of banking regulation; enhancement of the government's ability to take over and unwind failed financial firms; and the creation of a new regulatory structure for consumer and investor protection. The proposal was immediately attacked from the left and right ends of the ideological spectrum.

The left felt the bill was little more than weak tea. The administration had not proposed doing enough to rein in executive compensation practices that many felt were responsible for excessive risk taking. Moreover, the administration's proposal was seen as having a light touch in regulating derivative and securitization markets. The proposal also did little to reform credit rating agencies, whose AAA certifications of subprime securitizations helped trigger the crisis. But most important, the bill did nothing to reduce the size and scope of the megabanks.

Conservatives focused on two other aspects. First, there was the typical free market opposition to more regulation, especially in the area of consumer and investor protection. Second, conservatives feared that the creation of a resolution pool for unwinding failed financial firms would perpetuate moral hazard and lead to more government bailouts. This fear was previously manifested in conservative opposition to government bailouts such as the rescue of Bear Stearns, the Troubled Asset Relief Program (TARP), and the auto industry bailout in 2008–2009.

In the fall of 2009, House and Senate committees began work on legislation. Despite concerns that progressives in the House would try to pull the bill to the left, the bill that emerged from the House Financial Services Committee hewed closely to the administration's blueprint. When the bill came to the floor, the two most substantial amendments came from Bart Stupak (D-MI), to tighten rules for central clearing of derivative contracts and for securitization.[24] These amendments were supported overwhelmingly by the left wing of the Democratic Party and allowed those members to go on the record as supporting much more stringent regulation of Wall Street. Ultimately, House Bill 4173 passed on December 11, 2009, by a vote of 223–203. All Republicans voted against the bill, as did twenty-seven Democrats. As would be expected, the Democratic defectors were heavily concentrated in the moderate wing of the party (as measured by NOMINATE scores). Some liberal members did oppose the bill, claiming it did not go far enough.

The main Senate proposal was unveiled in November 2009. Senate Banking Committee chairman Chris Dodd proposed sweeping changes in the power of the Federal Reserve to regulate banks. The changes would have given the Fed little role in consumer protection and systemic risk regulation. Consequently, the Dodd proposal was seen as considerably more ambitious than the administration proposal or the House bill. Dodd and his staff probably felt that the bill would appeal to the populist, anti-Fed Republicans.

But Republican opposition to Dodd's original plan was substantial. Following Scott Brown's victory in the special Senate election in Massachusetts, it became clear that some Republican support would be necessary to secure the sixty votes needed for cloture.

Senator Dodd unveiled his final plan on March 15, 2009. In many ways, the plan moved much closer to the House bill and scaled back many of its earlier provisions. It adopted some Republican demands in the hope of ultimately attracting GOP support, but it did include the so-called Volcker rule banning proprietary trading by deposit-taking banks.[25] Although such a prescription had been pushed by former Fed chair Paul Volcker, it was not endorsed by the administration until early in 2010. This endorsement was at least in part a response to criticism from the left that the administration's proposals were toothless.

The Senate version moved in a considerably pro-regulation direction when a measure backed by Arkansas Democrat Blanche Lincoln was added to the bill. Lincoln's provision called for the largest commercial banks to spin off their lucrative derivatives trading operations.[26] Initially, the proposal engendered opposition not only among Republicans but also within the administration and among Democrats from New York.

The resulting financial reform bill fit into pivotal politics falling along liberal-conservative lines but also in squeaking through with just enough votes on the conference report to beat a Senate filibuster. We return to the Senate's pivotal role after analyzing the liberal-conservative split in the House.

The House agreed to the conference report on June 30, 2010, by a vote of 237–192. There were, in comparison to the stimulus package, more partisan defections in the House, with nineteen Democrats voting against the bill. The number of prediction errors was twenty-one, including three Republicans who voted in favor (see figure 6.7). Two of these were among the most moderate Republicans, Walter Jones of North Carolina and Joseph Cao of Louisiana. The third Yea vote came from Michael Castle of Delaware, the second-ranking Republican on the House Financial Services Committee. Castle was closer to the center of the party. His attempt to move on to the Senate was derailed in the Republican 2010 primary by tea party candidate Christine O'Donnell. Cao had defeated the corruption-tainted William Jefferson in New Orleans. By 2010 Cao's district had returned to normal by electing an African American Democrat. Of the three House Republicans who deviated from free market conservatism and supported Dodd-Frank, Cao and Castle are no longer in Congress. These small changes in representation are part of the larger process of increasing polarization, a process that increased the vulnerability of Dodd-Frank when Republicans took control of the Senate in 2015. Castle's defeat at the hands of the tea party was far from Obama's fantasy of politicians of all stripes engaging in compromise.

The Senate vote on the conference report had four exceptions to a perfect liberal-conservative split. The interesting exception was Russ Feingold of Wisconsin. Feingold's "error" is shown as the leftmost

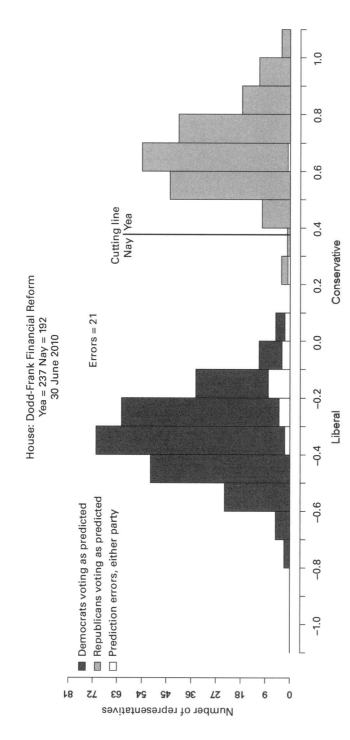

Figure 6.7
The conference report votes on the Dodd-Frank bill. *Note:* For the Senate, the prediction errors shown represent Feingold to the left and Voinovich, Murkowski, and Lugar in the center. The errors in the center are close to the cutting line, indicating that the senators were nearly indifferent on the bill. Feingold's error is far more substantial.

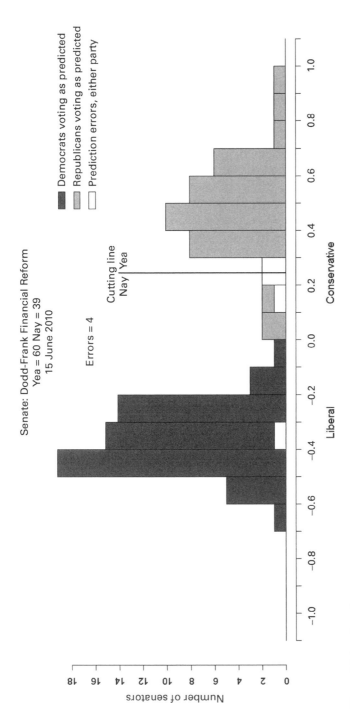

Figure 6.7 (continued)

white block in the Senate histogram in figure 6.7. Feingold, previously one of the most liberal Democrats, decided to stand on principle (if not interest) and refused to vote for cloture. So a third Republican vote, in the person of Scott Brown, was needed.

As it turns out, there were real consequences to Feingold promoting Brown into the pivot position. One of the provisions to come out of the House-Senate conference was a levy on large financial firms to pay for the costs of financial regulation. This provision was quickly dubbed a "bank tax." As a result, Brown, who had supported the earlier Senate version, began to waver. The provision not only ran counter to his ideological opposition to anything resembling a tax increase but would have been costly to large financial firms in Brown's home state.

In the aftermath of Byrd's death, a defection by Brown would have necessitated picking up the two Democrats who had opposed the original Senate bill, Feingold of Wisconsin and Maria Cantwell of Washington. Cantwell did switch her vote, but Feingold did not, necessitating the removal of the bank tax. This shifted $19 billion in costs from the banks to taxpayers. Feingold performed the legislative equivalent of a liberal voting for Ralph Nader in Florida in the 2000 presidential election: standing on principle only to get an outcome he couldn't possibly have wanted.[27]

Given the deep partisan division over financial reform, the passage of Dodd-Frank was hardly the end of the battle. The skirmishes moved to the regulatory agencies where the complexity of Dodd-Frank gave the banks and derivatives dealers the upper hand in their efforts to water down the regulations being promulgated. The banks have a tremendous informational advantage over the regulators and can greatly influence how the regulations are written, largely out of the public eye. As well, they enjoyed the support not only of Republican legislators but also of key players in the Obama administration. In one of the most vivid examples, pressure from the financial sector led to the evisceration of rules designed to require mortgage issuers to have "skin in the game" by retaining an interest in any mortgages used for securitization. But with the Republican takeover of the Senate in 2014, the assault on Dodd-Frank returned to Capitol Hill, and Republicans started to succeed in the legislative rollback. In December 2014, the Republicans inserted a provision into the omnibus appropriations bill that repealed a requirement in Dodd-Frank that forced banks to "push out" some of the riskiest assets from their federally insured banking operations.[28] As of this writing, the House

Republican budget plan takes aim at many far more consequential features of financial reform, such as the resolution authority over failed financial firms and the independence of the Consumer Financial Protection Bureau.[29]

Other Policy Consequences of Polarization

Perhaps one of the most important long-term consequences of the decline in legislative capacity caused by polarization is that Congress's power will decline relative to the other branches of government. Several recent studies have shown that presidents facing strong partisan and ideological opposition from Congress are more likely to take unilateral actions rather than pursuing their goals through legislation.[30] This effect is perhaps best exemplified by the large number of executive orders issued by Bill Clinton at the end of his second term. Many of these had no chance of passage through Congress. The consequence of not getting statutory authorization, however, was that George W. Bush was able to reverse many of Clinton's orders even though the reversals of statutes would have been filibustered in the Senate. President Obama's November 2014 executive order concerning undocumented aliens is similar to the Clinton orders.

Not only are presidents likely to become more powerful, polarization may also increase the opportunities of courts and regulatory agencies to pursue their policy goals since such activism is unlikely to be checked by legislative statute.[31] The courts and regulators have become the dominant arena for a wide swath of policy, from tobacco regulation to firearms to social policy. A much-publicized example is the policy change of the Federal Communications Commission, led by Bush appointee Michael Powell, that banished "racy" material from television and radio broadcasts. Such a policy would have been unlikely to arise via legislation in a polarized Congress. It is also unlikely to be overturned.

We have concentrated on the effects of polarization within the legislative process, but contemporary work in bureaucratic and judicial politics suggests that polarization may also have detrimental effects at the implementation stage. The first effect concerns Congress's willingness to delegate substantial authority to administrative agencies. One of the most systematic studies to date shows that Congress is far less willing to delegate policymaking authority to agencies when there are large ideological disagreements between the president and congressional majorities.[32] Insofar as party polarization has exacerbated these disagreements (especially during divided government), it has caused Congress to rely far less on the expertise of the bureaucracy in the implementation and enforcement of statutes. In many cases, the results are excessive statutory constraints; in others, Congress has chosen to delegate enforcement to private actors and courts rather than agencies (Farhang 2010). This effect further weakens the executive and legislative branches vis-à-vis the judiciary.

The second effect of polarization on policy implementation comes through its distortion of the confirmation process of judges and executive branch officials. In studies of all major executive branch appointments over a century, McCarty and Razaghian (1999) find that increased partisan polarization is a primary culprit in the increasing delays in Senate confirmation. As a consequence, long-term vacancies in the political leadership of many departments and agencies have become the norm. As these problems are exacerbated at the beginning of new administrations, presidential transitions have become considerably less smooth. Polarization has also clearly contributed to the well-documented conflicts over judicial appointments, which have similarly led to an understaffing of the federal bench. These conflicts led to the Democrats changing the cloture rules for appointment in 2013. The flip side is that appointees may be ideologically polarized, with large shifts when control of the presidency and Congress shifts.

Polarization and Policy Paralysis

We have shown that for much of the twentieth century, polarization tracked the evolution of redistribution through taxation and minimum wages. In many respects, this tracking reflects the ability of polarization to paralyze policy formation. Public policies are sticky. The stickiness is exacerbated by polarization.

The pattern of change thus appears to respond to the "pivot" theories we discussed in the second part of this chapter. Real minimum wages have fallen because they are not indexed to inflation. Proposals to lower their nominal value are not even on the table, but proposals for meaningful increases can't pass either. High estate taxes prevailed for the thirty-seven years between 1941 and 1977 largely because, we conjecture, pivots among Democrats blocked change. The adjustments passed under President Ford returned the real value of the minimum taxable estate only to what it had been in the 1960s, and the maximum rates were rolled back only to the levels found in the early Roosevelt administrations. Major changes required the Republican dominance of the 1980s and 2000s. Income taxes began to fall from the levels used to finance World War II only during Kennedy's presidency.

There are many other striking examples of legislative failure to respond to changes in voter preferences or to changes in economic circumstances. Here are three:

1. In the previous period of great polarization at the turn of the twentieth century, presidential vetoes forestalled restrictive immigration legislation until the 1920s, even though congressional majorities had favored it for several decades (Goldin 1994). The restrictive immigration laws of the 1920s remained largely intact for more than forty years, until the reforms enacted in 1965. Although Congress subsequently passed compromise immigration bills, the liberal 1965 policy was extended in 1990 and prevailed for the rest of the century.

2. Economic regulations adopted in the New Deal remained in effect for decades. Transportation and telecommunications were deregulated only in the late 1970s and 1980s. The Public Utilities Holding Company Act of 1935 remained fully in force until 1992 and was repealed only in 2005. The separation of commercial and investment banking and other aspects of the Glass-Steagall Act remained in effect from 1933 until the passage of the Gramm-Leach-Bliley Act in 1999. (At the same time, many changes in financial services were produced by the Treasury and the Federal Reserve. These changes illustrate our point about polarization increasing discretion outside the legislature.)

3. Welfare as an entitlement, in the form of the assistance program known as Aid to Families with Dependent Children (AFDC), was initiated by the Social Security Act of 1935. The basic system remained in place and was extended until more than sixty years later, with the passage of the Personal Responsibility and Work Opportunity Reconciliation Act (PRWORA) of 1996.

Inactivity, we have argued, is more likely to occur in periods of polarization. In addition to its consequences for redistribution, the increasing polarization of the past twenty-five years may have produced a number of less than desirable outcomes. There is considerable evidence that it has weakened the ability of legislatures to engage in policymaking and has reduced their responsiveness to new economic and social problems. At the same time, it has shifted influence to less representative and accountable institutions, such as the president and the courts. In light of the evidence that polarization is a problem, what can be done about it? We turn to this problem in our concluding chapter.

7   Where Have You Gone, Mr. Sam?

Sam Rayburn's third and final term as Speaker of the House of Representatives ran from 1955 to 1961. Mr. Sam ran the House on a relatively genteel and bipartisan basis. While contemporary Americans often wax nostalgic about Rayburn's style of leadership or perhaps that of his fellow Texan Lyndon Johnson, the fact of the matter is that their approach to leadership was better suited for their times than ours. In the Rayburn-Johnson era, congressional polarization was near its perigee. In its economy, the country seemed destined to have but one class, the middle class.

The two decades that ran from the end of World War II until the passage of civil rights and immigration reform in the mid-sixties were not a "golden age" for everyone. There was no equality of opportunity or results for minorities, women, and the LGBTQ community. On the other hand, household income inequality, with minorities included in the computation, was low. Because immigration had been sharply curtailed in the 1920s, those at the lower end of the income distribution outside the South typically had voting rights. Dwight Eisenhower, a Republican not in thrall to corporate and wealthy campaign contributors, could leave office with a famous warning about "the military-industrial complex."

In the time of Obama-Reid-McConnell-Boehner-Pelosi, political elites literally hate each other and CEOs live on a different planet than their lowest-wage employees. Little wonder that we cannot resurrect the Rayburn-Johnson playbook!

We are not so presumptuous as to assert that we can identify any single causal factor that would explain the conjunction of high levels of political polarization and economic inequality. Instead, we have taken a much more modest approach and identified some causal pathways that would explain the strong set of empirical regularities reported in this book. The commonality of these microlevel relationships is that American political institutions are ill-suited to mitigating the economic pressures that lead to greater levels of inequality. Two features of the American system are especially important in this regard. The first is an electoral system that relies on plurality rule to elect senators and representatives. Plurality rule tends toward the development of two major political parties (see Duverger 1954; Fey, 1997; and Palfrey 1989).[1] A two-party system might hold economic inequality in check if the policy positions of the parties converged on the preferences of the median (income) voter, as suggested by Anthony Downs (1957). If convergence were the result of electoral competition, an increase in inequality marked by a fall in median income relative to the average income in the economy would produce a majority in favor of increasing taxes and transfers, resulting in a reduction of inequality.

As we thoroughly documented in chapter 2, however, the Republican and Democratic Parties have diverged, not converged. Political scientists have generated dozens of explanations as to why political parties might not converge. In relation to our arguments, several stand out as especially important. First, if there is sufficient uncertainty about voter preferences, the distinct ideological preferences of politicians and the activist bases of each party will produce divergence in platforms.[2] In such situations, rational parties make trade-offs between satisfying ideological preferences and choosing more moderate policies in order to win elections. Consequently, the position of each party partially reflects the views of its activist base.

The movement of the base has been most profound in the Republican Party, where the modern conservative movement that emerged from Barry Goldwater's wipe-out in 1964 shifted the party sharply to the right (Micklethwait and Wooldridge 2004; Perlstein 2001). Nevertheless, this conservative movement would have failed to obtain power had electoral conditions not moved in its favor; in particular the rising overall affluence produced by the long periods of economic growth after World War II. As we demonstrated in chapter 3, the underlying Democratic advantage in presidential voting and identification began to give way to the Republicans during the 1970s. This increase in the electoral fortunes of the Republican Party allowed it to shift to the right and still win elections because its message of lower taxes and more limited government resonated with the increasing population of affluent voters.[3]

The Democratic Party, while more supportive of progressive taxation than the Republicans, has avoided any advocacy of the high tax rates of the Roosevelt-Truman years. The party has in fact bought into the free market mantra by acquiescing in and even leading substantial market deregulation, particularly in the financial sector.[4] The party has appealed to its base by advocating policies that are targeted to group identities—affirmative action for minorities and women, equal pay for women, reproductive rights for women, hate crimes and sexual abuse legislation, and immigrant rights. These identity-oriented issues may have caused the party to move slightly to the left in the 112th and 113th Congresses. Nonetheless, even with increased salience of identity politics, voting has remained one-dimensional. Hare and Poole (2014) point out that "one of the underappreciated aspects of contemporary political polarization has been how a diverse set of policy conflicts—from abortion to gun control to immigration—have collapsed into the dominant economic liberal-conservative dimension of American politics. That is, not only have the parties moved further apart on this ideological dimension in recent decades, but the meaning of the dimension itself has changed as it now encompasses a wider range of issues. The phenomenon has been termed 'conflict extension' by Geoffrey Layman and Tom Carsey, and its occurrence among party activists and strong partisans in the electorate has been thoroughly documented by Layman, Carsey and colleagues."[5]

The second factor leading to platform divergence is that American political parties are reasonably undisciplined coalitions of politicians who seek to win election among a heterogeneous collection of constituencies. Thus, politicians will have strong incentives to defect from a party platform at the national median toward the position of the district median. In an innovative model, Snyder and Ting (2002) show that this lack of discipline produces polarized parties (in a world where disciplined ones would converge).[6] Thus, during periods of increasing inequality, when the fortunes of different economic groups are diverging, the policies preferred by each will diverge as well. In the current context, the Democratic Party will continue to support policies that redistribute to the poor and collectivize social risks, while the Republican Party will continue to represent the interests of those whose incomes are growing rapidly and hence will support policies to cut taxes and privatize risk. Of course, we do not argue that everyone who votes for the Democratic or Republican Party is in complete sympathy with the respective party's positions on these economic issues. But the essence of a two-party system is that these are the only choices voters have.[7] As a result, electoral behavior is considerably better predicted by a voter's income than before the parties polarized, as we showed in chapter 3.

Another implication of America's electoral system is that it does little to stimulate high voter turnout, especially among lower-income citizens. As we demonstrated in chapter 4, however, the socioeconomic biases in turnout among *citizens* have been relatively constant since 1972. The real economic biases in turnout come from the dramatically increased numbers of resident noncitizens and the decline in the economic status of this group. While overall inequality has increased, the pressure for redistributive policies has been sharply mitigated by the fact that the income inequality of *voters* did not increase until very recently.

Once the voters have spoken, the politicians enact policies in a unique institutional setting. Specifically, the American government is not majoritarian. The separation of powers and bicameralism require that very large majority coalitions, typically bipartisan, must be formed to pass new laws and revise old ones. Thus any policy response to the economic and social factors that lead to inequitable economic growth will be muted by the gridlock of our institutions. Exemplary in this regard is one of the more important policy areas in our story, immigration. Bipartisan majorities passed the Immigration Act of 1965 when polarization was low. An unanticipated consequence of the legislation, however, was a large influx of less-skilled labor. This influx contributed to economic growth (and was driven in part by that growth) but also contributed to competition in low-wage labor markets. Congress has attempted to reform immigration laws several times over the past thirty years, but partisan divisions over the distributive consequences of reform have precluded major reform. As we demonstrated in chapter 6, in addition to immigration policy, social welfare and tax policies have been especially affected by the gridlock produced by polarization.

We should emphasize that America's nonmajoritarian institutions do not in themselves produce either polarization or economic inequality. The institutions are almost immutable, while both polarization and inequality have varied sharply since the end of Reconstruction in 1876. If anything, the institutions have become slightly more majoritarian with the loosening of the Senate cloture rule in 1975 and 2013 and with the ability of the Senate to vote some bills using "reconciliation." What is true is that the nonmajoritarian institutions can block policy change once polarization sets in. If economic inequality rises through changes in the economy, such as innovations in technology and finance, Washington cannot react.

When gridlock can be broken, policy must reflect a bargaining "compromise" within and between the chambers and the president. The nonmajoritarian institutions of policy formation can feed back into polarization in party electoral platforms. The very system of checks and balances, whereby power is shared between the executive branch and the legislature, affords voters an opportunity to "moderate" the parties by splitting their tickets (Alesina and Rosenthal 1995). If the parties know that there is moderation in the policy process, they will "posture" and take more extreme platform positions than would be the case if only the president made policy (Alesina and Rosenthal 2000). More-over, the tendency to polarize will increase as the power of Congress is increased relative to that of the president. Political scientists have argued that Congress became more assertive after Watergate (Sun-dquist 1981) and have documented (Fiorina 1996) that voter ticket splitting has increased. To put the argument slightly differently, the possibility of divided government with increased congressional powers contributes to polarization.

Polarization also contributes to gridlock by enhancing the incentives to engage in strategic disagreement, or "blame game" politics (Gilmour 1995; Groseclose and McCarty 2000). In a world of polarized parties and moderate voters, each party will attempt to portray the other as comprising the real extremists. Such a strategy often involves distor-tions of the other party's proposals and an increased recalcitrance in negotiation.

While the basic electoral system and legislative institutions are an important part of our story, other institutions, although seen by some scholars as sources of polarization, seem in retrospect to not be so important. For example, partisan gerrymandering cannot explain the polarization of the Senate. Consequently, we are reluctant to see ger-rymandering as a major source of the overall polarization of American politics (see McCarty, Poole, and Rosenthal 2009). Furthermore, we find that its effects on polarization in the House of Representatives are likely highly overrated. Polarization does not grow significantly more following reapportionment, and the distribution of partisanship across congressional districts does not differ much from the overall geographic distribution of partisanship. Yes, districting has gotten more sophisticated and politicized, but that seems to be as much a consequence of the current electoral and ideological divides as the cause. Similarly, we are not terribly persuaded that primary elections play a role in our dance either. Primary elections for Congress have been nearly universal for more than half a century, so it is hard to explain a change with a constant. Further, the evidence shows that it is unlikely that opening up primaries to less partisan voters would have much of an effect on who is elected to office. What has happened within the Republican Party since 2010 is that the Tea Party, the Club for Growth, and other far right organizations have turned out their voters, thereby electing more extreme Republicans, especially in 2010 and 2014.

The link between polarization and the American campaign finance system is somewhat more complex. We do not find much evidence that the evolution of campaign finance since the 1970s caused polarization. Giving by interest groups through PACs has not become more polarized. Contributions by individuals, especially soft money, have tilted the scales toward the extremes. The biggest effect, however, seems to have been to increase the reliance of the Democratic Party on very wealthy contributors, and it is this reliance, we conjecture, that has tempered its demands for more redistribution. The money wing of the party, especially donors in Hollywood and Silicon Valley, are largely supportive of the identity issues that appeal to the base and of the party's pro-environment and pro-gun control positions. The move to the left by the Democrats on these issues has offset its moderation on redistribution. The net effect going forward is a likely shift to the left on the part of the Democrats.

Extending Invitations

We conceded at the outset that we were going to focus primarily on the link between political polarization and income distribution. Given the evidence we presented about long-term trends in these variables, we felt that this focus was the most fruitful.

The data used to establish these trends in the first edition ran through the early years of the presidency of George W. Bush. At the end of his presidency, the U.S. economy suffered the financial crisis and the Great Recession. The Bush presidency was followed by the election of the first African American president, Barack Obama. Some of the trends appear to have moderated or vanished in the following years. In particular, the increasing linkage between constituency income and the liberal versus conservative position went away in 2013 (chapter 2). The income effect on partisan identification and presidential voting became smaller after 2008 (chapter 3). (On the other hand, at the county level, median income has become increasingly linked to Republican voting for president, with the strongest effect found for the 2012 elections.) The ratio of median voter income to mean family income had stabilized, even with increasing overall inequality, with the increasing numbers of noncitizens. But by 2012, the ratio had fallen (chapter 4). But we caution against overinterpreting these findings as a harbinger of deep changes to the structure of American politics. Only the future will reveal the extent to which the findings are long-run political shifts or simply short-term consequences of such major events as the financial crisis and the election of an African American president.

These recent changes in trends in income effect, however, lead us to consider other macrosocial trends that have also moved with polarization over the last half century. Perhaps the most prominent of these are trends in social capital (see Putnam 2000, 2015). Many measures of social capital, such as rates of volunteering and membership in organizations, began declining in the 1970s after increases following World War II. These trends in social capital complement our story in a number of ways. The first is that the declines in social capital are clearly related to the changes in income inequality and the increases in ethnic diversity brought about by relaxed immigration policies. Costa and Kahn (2003a, 2003b) find that a very large proportion of the declines in volunteering, membership, and social trust among twenty-five- to fifty-four-year-olds is a result of the increased economic and ethic heterogeneity of metropolitan areas. These results complement the cross-sectional findings of Alesina and La Ferrara (2000, 2002).

Second, declining social capital may have played a role in the declining support for redistribution and the increase in income voting. In theory, both declining trust and cross-class bonds may make higher-income citizens less likely to tax themselves for redistribution to lower-income classes. This disincentive to redistribute may be especially large in diverse communities, where the upper and lower classes may be separated not only by income but also by race or ethnicity (Alesina, Baqir, and Easterly 1999; Luttmer 2001).

While the time-series evidence and the theoretical logic of a social capital story are compelling, the cross-sectional evidence linking social capital to our story is weak. Putnam's state-level social capital index does not correlate with the level of Shor and McCarty's (2011) legislative polarization measure in either levels or changes. To isolate the effects of social capital, we added control variables that might explain polarization, including state median household income, racial and ethnic composition, church attendance, the percentage of noncitizens, and urbanization. Even when these factors were controlled for, however, the effect of social capital on polarization was not statistically significant. Thus, while inequality and perhaps immigration have played very important roles in undermining social capital, there is little evidence of a strong direct link to polarization.

From Bush to Obama

We completed the first draft of the first edition for the Eric M. Mindich Encounter with Authors Symposium at Harvard in January 2005. Thus, the 2004 presidential election had been fully interpreted by the pundits, but the data were not readily available to determine the extent to which our arguments held up in its aftermath.

The headlines on Wednesday, November 3, 2004, told a story very different from ours. The interpretations of the partisans were not terribly surprising. The winning party struck a triumphant pose. Although the election was as close as a 50,000-vote swing in Ohio, Republicans reveled in their new mandate, with George W. Bush proclaiming that he had some political capital and was going to spend it. The losing party was characteristically dejected. The Democrats engaged in the time-worn debate of losing parties over how poor their candidate was, how their message didn't get across, or how the party was too liberal (or moderate or conservative, or something else).

The pundits' approach to the election was also predictable. They needed to find *the* cause of the election outcome. The most prominent explanation in the week following the election was the role of "moral values." Journalists seemed to converge on this explanation when it was revealed that 22 percent of respondents in the national voter exit poll listed "moral values" as their top issue concern, by far the modal response. The power of this explanation, however, was undercut by the fact that the survey listed no other social issues for the voters to select.[8] There were also the "terror" voters. Yes, those who said that fighting international terror was a "very important" foreign policy goal voted disproportionately for Bush (56–44). But those who said that fighting terrorism was important were also whiter, richer, more male, and more

Republican than those who did not. Consequently, some of the difference can be accounted for by the fact that Republican voters were especially attuned to terrorism rather than by the proposition that terrorist fears led voters to Bush.

In contrast to the direction of the leaps of the pundit ballet chorus, the noneconomic issues may well have worked against President Bush. At least this is the view that comes from well-tested and accepted social science models that predict presidential elections based on aggregate economic conditions and incumbent advantage. These models all showed the president winning reelection in a near landslide, with a popular vote share somewhere around 55 percent (see Cuzán and Bundrick 2005).

With some hindsight and the release of systematic data on the election, moreover, this second edition shows that 2004 fit well into the thesis established in the first edition. In the graphs and statistical analyses in the preceding chapters, 2004 is not an exceptional year. It just happens to be one, like 1980, in which the winner was anathema to liberal pundits. Not only did income continue to play a role in the 2004 election, the postelection legislative agenda was much as we would have forecast. While much media attention focused on President Bush returning to Washington from a Texas vacation to sign a congressional intervention in the Terri Schiavo right-to-die case, the more consequent legislative maneuverings concerned highly distributive economic policies. Shortly after the election, President Bush decided to use his new political capital to reform the Social Security system. The centerpiece of his plan was to allow younger workers the opportunity to divert a portion of their payroll taxes into private retirement accounts. The plan had a certain appeal to higher-income voters, who have become much more receptive to the idea of privatizing risk, but was quickly challenged by the Democrats, who felt that the diversion into private accounts would undermine the system's guarantees to lower-income citizens as well as balloon the federal budget deficit. To make sure that his appeal to higher-income voters did not get lost in translation, the president refused to put on the table increases in Social Security taxes by raising either the rate or the income caps. The Democrats, for their part, were unwilling to provide their own plan to restructure the Social Security finance system. Not surprisingly, in light of our discussion in chapter 6, gridlock was the outcome. Nothing has been done to ensure the solvency of Social Security, even though the system has been running a deficit since

2010.[9] To the contrary, there was a temporary reduction in payroll taxes during the Great Recession. Bush lost on Social Security; the status quo won and has persisted at this writing.

In choosing to go first with Social Security, President Bush did not abandon several other controversial economic proposals. First, the president wanted to make the tax cuts of 2001 and 2002 permanent, including the repeal of the estate tax. By pressing for full repeal of the estate tax rather than the much higher exemption offered by Democrats, the Republicans narrowed the debate to the tax liability of only America's richest families.

Because the Bush tax cuts were passed under "reconciliation," they expired in 2011. In principle, the status quo reverted to the taxes in effect in 2000. Obama had campaigned promising to raise taxes only on incomes over $250,000. But during the "fiscal cliff" crisis of late 2012, the Obama administration agreed to extend all of the Bush tax cuts below $450,000 and to generous estate tax exemptions. While Republican conservatives expressed disappointment, the new tax law was a win for the Republicans in comparison to the 2000 rates. On the one hand, the relatively low 2012 rates incorporated an ongoing response to the recession. On the other, it reflected lesser public support for redistribution.

The next pillar of Bush's second-term agenda was tax reform, where he and the Republicans were expected to push for a much flatter tax system with fewer deductions and a much lower top marginal rate. This went nowhere, and despite the Simpson-Bowles Commission under President Obama, tax reform still has not happened. Loopholes, such as the carried interest deduction favored by hedge funds, have not been touched.

Finally, and perhaps most important, given our findings in chapter 4, Bush's immigration proposals, centered on a more extensive guest worker program and limited amnesty, became gridlocked between the Republican paleo-conservatives, who wanted to curtail both legal and illegal immigration, and the Democratic left, which wanted more protections for guest workers as well as more guarantees that guest workers would not compete in the same labor markets as citizens. This gridlock continued into the Obama administration. At least seventy-five members of the Republican House Caucus are extreme no-compromise restrictionists on immigration.[10] Frustrated by Republican inaction, President Obama did substantial immigration reform by executive action in 2014.

While many of Bush's proposals were destined for gridlock's dustbin, it should not be forgotten that the 109th Congress's first important enactment (leaving aside the Terri Schiavo case) was a bankruptcy bill that made it substantially harder for middle-income Americans to obtain the more generous protections of chapter 7 of the bankruptcy code and forces them into chapter 13 filings. Although proponents of the bill point out that it does not affect the lowest-income families, the bill does little to rein in the abuses of the bankruptcy code by high-income earners through sheltering their assets in trusts or in real estate in unlimited household exemption states.[11]

As Bush's presidency tumbled into failure in 2006–2008, the housing boom finally started to sputter and then collapsed, triggering a global recession. Bush essentially became a spectator while his Treasury secretary, Henry Paulson, New York Federal Reserve Bank chairman Timothy Geithner, and Federal Reserve chairman Ben Bernanke took over the handling of the crisis (McCarty, Poole, and Rosenthal 2013).

When Barack Obama became president on January 20, 2009, he was faced with an economic crisis that was the worst since the Great Depression. Extreme polarization largely prevented the parties from cooperating in a response to the crisis. There was no "FDR moment" that resulted in modern-day versions of the Banking and Securities Acts of the 1930s, a government refinancing of indebted mortgagees, public works projects, and high tax rates aimed at reducing economic inequality. Rather than a hundred days, the first two years of the Obama presidency saw relatively quick enactment of an attenuated stimulus package, fourteen months spent passing the Affordable Care Act, which contains numerous concessions to special interests, and finally passage of the Dodd-Frank Act, another Byzantine construction whose provisions have already been breached with respect to disclosure, derivatives, and skin-in-the-game mortgage origination. For example, a provision slipped into the continuing resolution passed in December 2014 relaxed some of the restrictions on derivatives trading by banks.[12] Citicorp, a revolving-door exit for Clinton Treasury secretary Robert Rubin and Obama OMB director Peter Orszag and an entry for Obama Treasury secretary Jacob Lew, was reported to be the prime mover of the legislation. Even when unified government permitted some break in gridlock, institutional and ideological factors—the Senate filibuster, moderate Democrats, and the money wing of the party—prevented decisive action up front and forced retrenchment ex post. And not surprisingly, from the technical end of the Great

Recession in the United States in 2009 until 2012, some 95 percent of the economic gain went to the top 1 percent (Saez 2013). The middle and working classes just continue to tread water.

How Will It End?

In this book, we have outlined a very stable political system, at least through the Great Recession. Partisan polarization and economic inequality have proved to be durable features of our political economy for almost four decades. Thus, it is very doubtful that a simple fine-tuning of institutional arrangements will have much of an effect. We do not doubt that compelling cases could be made for opening up primaries, ending partisan gerrymandering, and making it easier to vote. We feel, however, that the data show that these problems are second- and third-order contributors to our current problems. In any case, partisan polarization is likely to place real limits on how far these reforms will be carried. The movement of the Republicans to the right might be curtailed by serious restrictions on the ability of the rich to make campaign contributions and lobby, but such reforms are hopeless as long as the Supreme Court has a majority of justices appointed by Republican presidents. In addition, the Democrats also get much of their campaign funds from the megarich, so despite the rhetoric about *Citizens United* we are dubious that this flow of money will be seriously curtailed any time soon (Bonica et al. 2013).

A reordering of the current system will require major changes in the loyalties of various groups to the political parties. This dynamic has clearly been important in the fall of prior political regimes. The problems of the Democratic-Whig system resulted in the emergence of slavery as the dominant political cleavage. Slavery temporarily replaced economics as the central issue defining the first NOMINATE dimension. This political realignment led to the complete demise of the Whig Party and, most horrifically, the Civil War. The New Deal realignment replaced a Republican-dominated system following the stock market crash and the Great Depression. Finally, as we have documented, the current system was established only after the rapid economic growth of the postwar period seemed to undermine the logic of the New Deal system.

What factors might lead to a new realignment? In answering this question, it is important to keep in mind the current coalitional structure of the political system we outlined in chapter 3. The Republican

Party, we argued, is primarily supported by high-income secular voters along with middle- and higher-income social conservatives. A number of things could cause such a coalition to unravel. First, Republican actions on social issues might begin to match their rhetoric in such a way that further drives secular voters from the party. As we noted in chapters 2 and 3, there is some evidence that that erosion has become more pronounced in the past few years. While we argue that a religious cleavage has not supplanted the economic one, we do not suggest that it cannot happen.

The second scenario under which the current alignments might change is if the Republicans push so far to the right with libertarian economics that even middle-class social conservatives abandon them. The Republicans seem to be attracting more lower-income whites who were left out of the "recovery" after 2009. However, the Republicans are still stuck promoting the same old policies aimed at Wall Street, the country club Republicans, and small businesses. Everyone seems to agree on the need for tax reform but the Republicans are simply unwilling to raise taxes on the megarich. They could transfer that money to their new supporters in the working class by zeroing out payroll taxes for low-income workers. But such "out-of-the-box" thinking seems to be confined to a small minority in the party.

It also seems plausible that the Democratic Party need not wait for the Republicans to mess up in order to change the alignment of American politics. Beginning in the 1990s, the apparent strategy of the Democratic Party was to expand by appealing to high-income secular and socially liberal voters. As we showed in chapter 5, the party has done quite well indeed in attracting money from this group. Despite the importance of money in American politics, however, money is not the same as votes, and the party needs more votes. Our results suggest that the votes up for grabs are those of socially conservative middle-class voters so long as the party can temper its secular message. According to the 2004 National Election Study, the Republican gains were greatest not among those who attend church every week or almost every week but among those who attend church once a month. One interpretation of this result is that the Democrats do not need to reach out to the most pro-life or antigay segments of the electorate but only to those individuals who are Christian more by culture than by practice and who have moderate views on many social issues. Democratic politicians like Hillary Clinton seem to recognize this possibility, but it is yet to be seen whether the rest of the party will follow.

Finally, though no one wishes for any of these scenarios, the system is still vulnerable to an economic or domestic security calamity. As we write, although deficits are falling from their crisis peaks, the federal debt (as a percentage of GDP) remains at near historic highs, and real estate prices have begun to increase again. Eventually the Federal Reserve is going to have to increase interest rates, which effectively have been near zero percent since 2009. This has helped the owners of stocks and the banks. But when rates finally begin to rise, this will disproportionately hit Republican constituents. We recall that John McCain was in a tight race with Obama until the Lehman Brothers collapse, after which Obama moved decisively ahead. Another terrorist attack on American soil, if it came before the 2016 elections, could badly hurt the Democrats.

Whether a shift from Republican dominance would end polarization depends on whether the Democrats sit on their heels or occupy the middle. When the Great Depression discredited the Republicans, the Democrats adopted policies they had long advocated that moved *away* from a market economy to a highly regulated state. A large part of the ensuing decrease in polarization was the result of Republican moderating and accommodating in an effort to rebuild their electoral fortunes. Moderation was a slow process. The end of polarization and, as well, of economic inequality should be a process measured not in months or years but in decades.

A quite different route to moderation may in fact pass through Republican dominance. Despite the public turnaround on gay marriage, one should not rule out a long-term success of the coalition of the affluent, the "moral," and working-class whites. After all, the Roosevelt coalition of ethnics in the North and racists in the South held for many years. In the absence of a Great Depression–like shock, the Democrats would have to move to acceptance of an economy with highly unequal outcomes. The Great Recession of 2008–2009 turned out not to be nearly as severe as the Great Depression and was followed, paradoxically, by great Republican success in congressional elections.

The reader who has stuck with us to this point may be feeling a bit gloomy. We have painted mostly negative scenarios and have not offered the reader a happy solution to the problem of polarization. Nevertheless, we end on a positive note. Two of us grew up in the 1950s with Depression-era parents.[13] We know all too well from our parents and our extended families how hard things were during the Great

Depression and how surprised people were when the country did not slide back into depression after World War II. The spread of mass affluence beginning in the 1950s is real, even if median income has gone slightly south in the years following the Great Recession. The modern economy is a tremendous achievement of millions of hard-working Americans just like our extended families. Prosperity also reflects seventy years without a major war. Trade has vastly augmented the goods available to American consumers. Young people today simply have no idea how rich and diverse the cornucopia of goods in the big-box stores of today is in comparison with the small-town five-and-dimes of the 1950s. It has been a sea change of unprecedented magnitude.

In addition, just in the past forty years the old fault lines between the white ethnic groups have virtually disappeared. Intermarriage rates between Protestants, Catholics, and Jews have soared. As we pointed out in chapter 1, there is simply no question to us that the United States is a far more tolerant place than it was fifty years ago.

Why, then, in the midst of affluence and much positive social change are we stuck with political leaders who are at dagger's point while the general population is generally not (Fiorina, Abrams, and Pope 2004)? Compared to our political leaders, the public has been relatively moderate, although the politically informed seem to be tracking the political elites (Bonica et al. 2013). We have no easy cure. We wish we did, as we find this trend deeply disturbing. The failure of the two parties to deal with the economic difficulties of the great bulk of Americans is disheartening. While we may wish that polarization could be solved by the return of the Sam Rayburns, John Heinzes, Dan Rostenkowskis, Sam Nunns, and so on, the structural flaws of our current system make that unlikely.

Notes

Chapter 1: The Choreography of American Politics

1. Hulse and Pear (2015).

2. Martin (2015).

3. See http://www.gallup.com/poll/181580/new-congress-slightly-higher-ratings-unpopular.aspx?utm_source=CONGRESS&utm_medium=topic&utm_campaign=tiles.

4. Data available at http://www.census.gov/hhes/www/income/data/historical/inequality/index.html.

5. See http://www.adaction.org/media/2013%20ADA%20Voting%20Record.pdf (accessed March 5, 2015).

6. We used the least squares unfolding procedure of Poole (1984).

7. On this point, see Snyder (1992).

8. The Census Bureau series does not cover earlier years.

9. A number of commentators date the conservative Republican movement from organizational initiatives, including the formation of the think tanks that arose in the early 1970s following the Goldwater candidacy in the 1964 election. See Perlstein (2001) and a *New York Times* opinion article by former New Jersey senator Bill Bradley at http://www.nytimes.com/2005/03/30/opinion/30bradley.html (accessed April 3, 2005).

10. Updates are available at http://topincomes.parisschoolofeconomics.eu.

11. These results are echoed when we use higher quantiles from the Piketty and Saez data such as the top 0.1 and the top 0.01 percentiles. In each case, there is strong evidence that polarization leads inequality. Generally, the highest correlations between the series come when polarization is lagged eight to twelve years. The largest of these lagged correlations are 0.92 for the top 0.1 percentile with polarization lagged twelve years, and 0.94 for the top 0.01 percentile with polarization lagged eight years. See also Duca and Saving (2015) on the lead-lag structure of polarization and income inequality.

12. It is difficult to pinpoint the switch from stable levels of polarization to an upward surge. The turning point occurred somewhere between the late 1960s (following the passage of the Great Society program of the Johnson administration and the Immigration and Nationality Act amendments of 1965) and the mid- to late 1970s. The statistical

correlations between polarization, income inequality, and immigration are all slightly sensitive to measurement. The polarization measure will change if the sample period used for DW-NOMINATE changes (by ending the series in 2000 or 2014), if Senate rather than House polarization is used, if a two-dimensional rather than one-dimensional measure is used, and so on. Similarly, income inequality will change if one switches from the Gini index to various income shares or other measure, and the immigration measure will change if one uses percentage noncitizens (chapter 4) rather than percentage foreign-born. The substantive tenor of our results is quite robust to these variations.

13. See http://www.ama-assn.org/ama/upload/mm/372/a01report8.rtf (accessed December 12, 2004).

14. See www.migrationpolicy.org/pubs/eight_health.pdf (accessed March 5, 2015).

15. The Personal Responsibility and Work Opportunity Reconciliation Act of 1996 (PRWORA) restricted Medicaid to permanent residents and a few other special immigration categories. It also delayed eligibility for five years for new permanent residents. For the details of these changes, see http://www.cms.hhs.gov/immigrants/default.asp.

16. The formal argument has been laid out by Krehbiel (1998) and developed in a policy context by Brady and Volden (1998).

Chapter 2: Polarized Politicians

1. See Kabaservice (2012) for a history of the decline of the moderate wing of the Republican Party.

2. Political polarization has not prevented the political system from remaining competitive. Poole and Rosenthal (1984) noted the dramatic increase in the number of Senate delegations that were split between the two parties. This number grew from fewer than ten in the 1950s to twenty-six in 1978. This number has fallen back to slightly less than twenty over the past decade—well above its average in the 1950s and 1960s (see Brunell and Grofman 1998).

3. For more detailed discussion of the methodological problems of interest group ratings, see Snyder (1992), Groseclose, Levitt, and Snyder (1999), and Poole (2005).

4. See Ellenberg (2001) for an elegant, nontechnical discussion of these methods.

5. The most widely used procedures include NOMINATE (Poole 2005), which we use throughout this book; optimal classification (Poole 2000); the factor analytic method of Heckman and Snyder (1997); and Bayesian Markov Chain Monte Carlo (MCMC) techniques (Clinton, Jackman, and Rivers 2004).

6. If we were to maximize classification, as Poole (2000) did, the second dimension would always improve classification. By using maximum likelihood techniques as we do in this book, however, classification is not guaranteed to improve as dimensions are added.

7. For each roll call, the Yea vote also has a position on the dimension, as does the Nay vote. (If there were more than one dimension, the legislators and the votes would have positions on each dimension.) See Poole (2005) for a comprehensive exposition of roll call scaling methods. See also Carroll et al. (2013).

8. For simplicity, we use classification in our discussion rather than, say, the geometric mean probability of the observed choices. The results are similar (see Poole and

Rosenthal 1997). Using three or more dimensions adds little to the substantive story. Moreover, improvements to classification for three dimensions or more are very small. Of course, with the large number of observations available to us, these dimensions would be viewed as statistically significant. But they are truly dimensions that only a chi-square can see.

9. There was a conservative GOP uptick, more pronounced in the Senate than in the House, during the New Deal. The few seats in Congress that the Republicans managed to retain represented the most conservative parts of the country at that time.

10. Figure 2.9 differs somewhat from the corresponding figure in the first edition. That figure went through the 108th Congress (2001–2002). The current figure goes through the 113th Congress (2013–2014). Voting in the past five congresses is almost entirely along the first dimension. Because DW-NOMINATE uses a weighted Euclidean metric, the weight of the second dimension can change when many more congresses are added. This has the effect of changing the two-dimension party means. This is why the figures look different. However, the coordinates on the two dimensions do not change very much. The Pearson r^2 values are about 0.98 for both dimensions. See http://voteview.com/dwnomin_comparison.htm.

11. The only member in the chasm is North Carolina's heterodox Republican Walter Jones, who was notable as the first Republican House member to oppose the Iraq War. His DW-NOMINATE score has trended leftward over the past several years. The far right member is Wisconsin's James Sensenbrenner. As a thirty-five-year member of the House, he is an exception to the rule that more junior members are the most extreme.

12. In his speech to the electors of Bristol, British statesman Edmund Burke distinguished between representatives who act as "delegates" by acting only on the expressed wishes of constituents and those who act as trustees, pursuing their own conception of the constituency's interests.

13. In the economic literature on "shirking" politicians, ideology is often measured as the residual from a regression of legislative behavior on district economic interests (e.g., Kalt and Zupan 1984). Of course, such an interpretation could be valid only if all of the relevant economic interests are included in the model and measured correctly.

14. Let NOM denote a NOMINATE score. This interpretation is valid when is a consistent estimate of $E(NOM \mid R_i = 1, C_i) - E(NOM \mid R_i = 0, C_i)$. Some readers will observe that $E(NOM \mid R_i = 1, C_i) - E(NOM \mid R_i = 0, C_i)$ is the "treatment" effect of assigning a Republican (instead of a Democrat) to represent a district with characteristics C_i. For to be a consistent estimate of the treatment effect, we must assume that the treatment is ignorable (Wooldridge 2001). Let NOM_0 be the NOMINATE score if the district is represented by a Republican and NOM_1 the score if it is represented by a Democrat. The assumption of ignorability of treatment requires that $E(NOM_0 \mid R, C_i) = E(NOM_0 \mid C_i)$ and $E(NOM_1 \mid R, C_i) = E(NOM_1 \mid C_i)$. Wooldridge suggests estimating using a "saturated" model that includes R, C, and interactions of R and C (in sample mean deviations). The saturated models produced almost identical estimates with the $\gamma = 0$ restricted model, so we do not report them. Another approach to estimating the within-district polarization is the regression discontinuity method proposed by Lee, Moretti, and Butler (2005). This approach compares the ideal point estimates of winners of extremely close elections under the premise that those outcomes reflect almost random selection of the representative's party. This approach produces estimates of within-district polarization slightly smaller than those reported in model B. But like estimates reported with model B, these estimates have grown substantially over time.

15. Because each term directly follows reapportionment, constituency measures derived from the decennial census are more accurate reflections of current conditions in the district. A different selection of congressional terms would not affect our results.

16. The results are essentially unaffected by averaging the NOMINATE scores for districts with more than one representative in a congressional term.

17. For the 2000 and 2010 censuses, we compute the percentage of African Americans by adding the number who identified solely as African American and those who chose any multiracial category that included African American.

18. Following the standard designation of the political South by *Congressional Quarterly*, the states are the eleven states of the Confederacy plus Oklahoma and Kentucky. We use this designation throughout the book.

19. In the next chapter, we will see that this nonmonotonic effect of education is apparent in voter choices and partisan identification.

20. In his study of Senate voting, Levitt (1996) finds that constituency plus national party can explain only 50 percent of the variance.

21. It is plausible that this null finding is due to the linear specification of the African American percentage. Perhaps there is a threshold effect beyond which the percentage of African Americans moves the representative to the left. Insofar as majority African American districts are all represented by African Americans, it would be hard to identify such a threshold with the available data. Nevertheless, it is worth noting that higher percentages of African Americans have no effect on the NOMINATE scores of African American representatives.

22. Caution is in order. The overall increase in fit when we move from model B to model C is small. This reflects the congruence of personal characteristics of the representative and the characteristics of the constituency. Moreover, we have only proxies to measure personal ideology and constituency preferences. Consequently, it is not possible to get completely satisfying measures of the relative effect of personal ideology.

23. There is one African American Republican in our regressions, Gary Franks (CT) in the 103rd House. The coefficient on African American becomes slightly more negative (−0.189 vs. −0.202) when Franks is dropped from the sample.

24. Of the thirty-eight members of the Congressional Black Caucus in the 108th House, only eight had NOMINATE scores to the right of the median Democrat. By the 113th House, this number had grown to eleven of forty-one. Almost all are southern, are young, or have relatively small minority populations in their district. But the net effect has been for the Congressional Black Caucus to become less ideologically distinct from the Democratic Caucus.

25. Of course, the absolute size of the income gap would increase because of average income growth across all districts even if there were no change in the distribution of income across Republican and Democratic districts. But this effect accounts for only a quarter of the increased gap.

26. The APRE is simply the proportional reduction in error, as defined above, applied to all roll calls on a given issue.

27. The fact that these reforms also decentralized power by strengthening subcommittees is not stressed in these accounts.

28. See Poole (2005) for a comprehensive discussion of this experiment for Houses 1 to 108.

29. Note that this method, in contrast to regression methods such as Snyder and Groseclose's (2000), does not require a uniform adjustment in the ideal points of all members of a party. Only moderates would need to be disciplined. All that is required is a displacement of the cutpoint.

30. We also find that for many of the estimated cut-point pairs, the Democratic cutting line is to the left of the Republican cutting line, seemingly inconsistent with party pressure. There is some debate, even among ourselves (see Cox and Poole 2002), about how to interpret this result.

31. Indeed, the 1982 and 1992 (but not the 2002) post-apportionment elections still produce larger than average increases in polarization.

32. With respect to this question, our results are somewhat at odds with Cameron, Epstein, and O'Halloran (1996). Those authors argue that white representatives are sufficiently responsive to the size of their African American constituencies to make the creation of majority-minority districts counterproductive from the perspective of black interests.

33. See Poole (2007).

34. The following table difference-in-difference between the parties and winning and losing states (Republicans in winning states – Democrats in winning states – Republicans in losing states + Democrats in losing states) for the last five reapportionments.

Decade	Difference-in-difference between parties across winning and losing states
1970	–0.026
1980	0.074
1990	0.095
2000	0.116
2010	0.035

35. Carson et al. (2003) find that members representing newly created districts have NOMINATE scores that are more extreme than those of members from established districts. They did not distinguish between the effects of interregional seat reallocations and the effects of party gerrymandering.

36. These estimates of the distribution are kernel densities that are essentially smoothed histograms. The bandwidth for these estimates is 0.025. Counties are weighted by population size so that the figures are not distorted by the Republican advantage in small counties.

37. The results following the 2010 election are notable, however, in that they appear to reflect a Republican bias where the modal congressional district is majority Republican and the modal (population weighted) county is majority Democrat. Such a pattern is consistent with partisan gerrymandering (although it may arise for other reasons as well; see Chen and Rodden 2013). It is not consistent, however, with the incumbency-protecting gerrymander that would exacerbate polarization.

38. It is appropriate to look at changes in polarization rather than levels, because of the trends in both polarization series.

39. Recently, Hall (2015) has provided compelling evidence that this strategy can be counterproductive as extremists who defeat moderates in primaries fare much worse in the general election.

Chapter 3: Income Polarization and the Electorate

1. That 22 percent was lower than in recent elections and that Bush obtained no measurable gain from the marriage initiatives did little to slow this storyline.

2. Fiorina (2004) argues that the increased partisan differences are as likely to arise as a consequence of elite polarization (as voters better sort themselves into parties) than it is to arise from polarization among the voters.

3. Computed from Green, Palmquist, and Schickler (2002), table 2.3, p. 31. The percentage differences for presidential and midterm election years running from 1972 to 1996 are 25, 30, 32, 36, 34, 35, 36, 34, 36, 29, 38, 48, and 50.

4. Frank (2004).

5. For example, from comparative political economy, see Acemoglu and Robinson (2005), Alesina and Perotti (1995), Alesina and Rodrick (1993), Benabou (2000), Londregan and Poole (1990), Perotti (1996), and Persson and Tabellini (1994).

6. But see Bhatti and Erikson (2011) and Tausanovitch (2014) for contrasting results.

7. American Political Science Association (2004).

8. The focus of their work is the stability of individual partisan self-identification, whereas we focus on changes in the demographic correlates of partisan identification. Our main concern is income, but we also find, in addition to the changes in the South, an important shift with regard to gender.

9. In a study using a more extended set of occupational class categories, however, Manza and Brooks (1999) find that the class cleavage was stable from 1952 to 1996. Manza and Brooks also provide a nice review of the previous findings.

10. Since the publication of the first edition of this book, the relationship between income and partisanship has received substantially more attention. See Gelman et al. (2008). Their findings broadly support our analysis. They further report that the response of partisan identification and voting to income is stronger in states with low average income than in states with high average income.

11. Party identification is measured on a seven-point scale in which the categories are Strong Democrat, Weak Democrat, Lean Democrat, Independent, Lean Republican, Weak Republican, Strong Republican. This measure is constructed from several questions. Respondents are first asked to choose between Democrat, independent, and Republican. "Democrats" are then asked if they are "strong" or "weak." Ditto for "Republicans." "Independents" are asked if they "lean" toward one of the parties. In our analysis of stratification in figure 3.2, we combine the strong and weak Republican categories. In our ordered probit analysis we use all seven categories. We divide the respondents into income quintiles using the Census Bureau's series on the distribution of household income. The details of the computation of our stratification measure are relegated to the appendix.

12. The dramatic increase in the stratification measure in 2008 is substantially larger using the NES than it is in other surveys, but we are mostly focused on the overall trend.

13. See Romer (1975), Roberts (1977), Meltzer and Richard (1981), Perotti (1996), and Roemer (1999).

14. Romer (1975, 1977), Roberts (1977), and Meltzer and Richard (1981) studied tax preferences when labor supply is considered.

15. In the first edition, we normalized income by dividing by average income in the utility functions. Such a normalization is inconsistent with the underlying model, so we now use the level of real income, rather than relative income, in our statistical models.

16. Perhaps only gender and age are truly exogenous variables. Having a Republican identity may facilitate networking that increases income. As part of the networking process, Republican identifiers may strategically attend church or change opinions, as evident in George H. W. Bush's shifting from pro-choice to pro-life. Bishop (2004) has recently argued that residence, hence region, is influenced by political beliefs. Proto-Democrats may find it easier to get high grades from liberal high school teachers. Even race may reflect political preferences, as it is self-identified.

17. The 2012 NES supplemented its standard face-to-face interviews with an Internet survey. For consistency in the time series, we drop the Internet sample and include only the in-person interviews. Of particular concern is that there are substantial differences in the distribution of income within the two samples.

18. Because of the coding of the 1962 NES, the District of Columbia and West Virginia are treated as southern for that year only.

19. Note that the average relative income almost never equals exactly one. This is because the real average household income reported by the Census Bureau is used to compute the relative values. The deviations from unity are therefore a consequence of sampling variation within the NES. Figures in table 3.1 for females and blacks are also skewed by response and sampling issues.

20. We also estimated the model both with income effects "dummied" for each year and with each year estimated separately. The separate estimations allow all the coefficients and thresholds to vary over time. The results were substantively identical.

21. The NES asks respondents about family income. However, even apart from measurement issues, the NES distributions will not exactly match the Census Bureau's family income measures as they exclude single-person households. In the first edition, we overcompensated for this problem by calibrating against the CPS's household income series. But the results do not depend qualitatively on which series is used.

22. The shift to households headed by a single unmarried, separated, or divorced female is extensively documented in Ellwood and Jencks (2004).

23. For a study that links changes in the income distribution across genders to increased divorce rates and changes in the partisanship of women, see Edlund and Pande (2002). Because the NES income variable for female respondents records family income for a respondent from a family and individual income for a respondent from a single-person household, the fall in female income undoubtedly reflects the increased number of females now living in single households.

24. The results are substantively similar when we use other comparison years, such as 1956 and 1996.

25. These are derived from a model where the coefficients of demographic characteristics have linear time trends. Similar results are obtained if each year is estimated separately.

26. Glaeser, Ponzetto, and Shapiro (2005) present results that suggest that religion and moral factors were not the source of elite polarization elaborated in our chapter 2. They show in their figure 4 that the marginal effect of church attendance was higher in the 1968 and 1972 elections than in those of 1976, 1980, and 1984. Church attendance effects surpass their 1968 levels only in 1988 and 1992. (The figure has no results for 1996 and later.) The onset of polarization, shown in chapter 2, is well before 1988. The source of this polarization is clearly economic rather than religious. While it may be true that a polarized Republican elite succeeded in priming voters to vote more on the basis of religion, the work we report in this chapter shows that the effect of income on voting has increased as well. Moreover, Bartels (2008) and Ansolabehere, Rodden, and Snyder (2006) argue that economic issues carry more weight with voters than do social ones.

27. It reads, "Would you call yourself a born-again Christian; that is, have you personally had a conversion experience related to Jesus Christ?"

28. Even this difference is somewhat exaggerated after we take into account that the born-again Christians live disproportionately in regions where the cost of living is low.

29. The *age* variable is the median age of residents in the county. The education variables *some college* and *college degree* are computed from the proportion of county residents over twenty-four in those categories. *African American* is the percentage of self-reported African Americans in the county. Following the 2000 census, we combined all multirace categories that included an African American designation. The number of religious congregations is preferable to the number of members and adherents. There is significant variation as to how related membership and adherence are to actual observance and support of religious institutions. The number of congregations better reflected aggregate observance and support. The sample size is smaller when the number of congregations is included because of missing data.

30. Each observation is weighted by county population, and we cluster across counties over time in estimating the standard errors.

31. The full set of results is available at http://www.voteview.com. The sample size is smaller when demographics are included because of missing data on the number of congregations.

32. See http://www.census.gov/housing/hvs/data/histtabs.html, table 14 (accessed July 5, 2015).

33. We use a similar approach with data from the Current Population Survey in chapter 4.

34. We thank Christine Eibner for sharing these data with us.

Chapter 4: Immigration, Income, and the Voters' Incentive to Redistribute

1. Our computations are from the Census Bureau's November Current Population Survey. The November CPS family income series includes single adult households but does not combine the incomes of unmarried individuals with the same residence.

2. A Migration Policy Institute report indicates that in 2012, 18.7 million individuals, representing 46 percent of the immigrant population, were naturalized citizens. See http://www.migrationpolicy.org/article/frequently-requested-statistics-immigrants -and-immigration-united-states (accessed February 23, 2015). For historical data on naturalizations, see James Lee and Katie Foreman, "U.S. Naturalizations: 2013" (U.S. Department of Homeland Security, 2014).

3. Welch (1999) finds that inequality has increased much less when one looks within the population that remains in the labor force in two periods or within age cohorts. This also reinforces the main claim of this chapter—that the median voter's incentive to redistribute has not increased. Voters may take into account where they stand in the life cycle when making voting decisions.

4. But see the discussion in Bonica et al. (2013).

5. See chapter 6 for a discussion of these changes in public policy.

6. See http://www.insee.fr/fr/ffc/chifcle_fiche.asp?ref_id=NATTEF02131&tab_id=339 (accessed December 7, 2004). We equate "*étrangers*" to noncitizens. Immigrants, comprising both noncitizens and naturalized ("*acquisition*") citizens, rose slightly from 9.1 percent to 9.6 percent. We should point out that France counts citizens of other EU nations as noncitizens even though there is free mobility of labor within the EU. The EU "noncitizens" would have had, until the recent admission of former Soviet bloc nations, a very different skill mix from that of the largely unskilled Latin American, Caribbean, and Asian immigrants who have come to the United States.

7. Source of 2013 data, Eurostat.

8. See Chico Harlan, "Strict Immigration Rules May Threaten Japan's Future," http:// www.washingtonpost.com/wp-dyn/content/article/2010/07/27/AR2010072706053 .html (accessed July 1, 2015).

9. We thank Patrick Bolton for suggesting this decomposition. The disenfranchisement and sharing effects will be present even if, as in chapter 3, altruism is added to the basic model. The altruism effect, which we do not consider directly, would have an additional negative impact on support for redistribution (see McCarty 2013).

10. See https://docs.google.com/spreadsheets/d/1or-N33CpOZYQ1UfZo0h8yGPSyz0Db -xjmZOXg3VJi-Q/edit#gid=1670431880 (accessed March 3, 2015).

11. From 1972 to 1976, the CPS did not ask directly about citizenship status. These surveys, however, ask respondents who are not registered "why not?" One of the possible responses is "not a citizen." We make the assumption that all noncitizens are captured by this registration question in this period. This assumption may be reasonably solid, as the percentage of noncitizens grew slowly but steadily from 1972 on.

12. In some NES surveys, reported turnout was validated by checking to see whether the respondent had actually voted. Palfrey and Poole (1987) compared results using reported and validated turnout in models of the effect of information on vote choice. Their results were not highly sensitive to the reported-validated distinction.

13. For 2004–2012 the top coding was at $150,000. For 1974–1980 the top coding was at $50,000. In 1972 the top coding was at $25,000.

14. CPS respondents are interviewed once a month for four months, dropped for eight months, and then reinterviewed once a month for an additional four months. In general it is possible to link information on individuals across months. Because March and

November do not fall within a four-month period, we cannot supplement our data with information from the March survey.

15. We used both linear and logarithmic interpolation. The results are highly similar.

16. A linear regression of the ratio on trend shows an estimated yearly decrease of 0.0022 ($t = 9.4$, $R^2 = 0.82$, one-tailed p-value < 0.000).

17. The linear regression shows an estimated yearly decrease of only 0.0016 ($t = 5.9$, $R^2 = 0.63$, p-value< 0.000), less than three-fourths of the decrease that occurred in the entire population.

18. In particular, the log-normal estimates of the median fall outside the boundary of the category that must (except for sampling error) contain the median, as follows: noncitizens, 1976 and 1990; nonvoters, 1978 and 1986; voters, 1972, 1974, 1996, and 2012; all families, 1974, 1984, 1988, 2006, and 2012.

19. Results using linear interpolation are highly similar. For a detailed comparison of estimates of the median from the log-normal approximation, linear interpolation, and geometric interpolations, see Rosenthal and Eibner (2005). However, because of the computational errors discussed in the next footnote, those comparisons are valid only for the years 1974 through 1986.

20. There are only four years, 1988, 1996, 2008, and 2012, in which the percentage of noncitizens decreased from what it was two years earlier. The year 1996, however, was one of record naturalizations, presumably undertaken to benefit the Clinton administration in the 1996 elections. See U.S. Department of Homeland Security (2004, 137). The 2012 decline, like the 2008 decline, may reflect a weaker labor market and, as well, stricter enforcement and greater deportations by the Obama administration.

21. Freeman (2004, 709) reports a regression similar (but with the dependent variable in log form) to ours, obtaining a positive but insignificant trend and a highly significant presidential election year effect. He then claims that turnout has declined by running a regression where the dependent variable is the natural logarithm of voters as a *proportion of the voting-age population* and the independent variables are trend, presidential election year, and the log of the eligible as a proportion of the voting-age population. He views this procedure as a way of dealing with measurement error in the number of eligible voters. But the log of the eligible has a t-statistic less than 1.0 in magnitude, which means that the adjusted R^2 does not increase from a regression without this variable. It is thus difficult to use this specification to arrive at a firm conclusion of how turnout as a *proportion of the eligible electorate* is changing.

22. Replicating the analysis using the log-normal estimates of the median gives results that are somewhat more favorable to our argument.

23. The self-reports of noncitizenship and ethnicity or race match up quite well with the official yearly statistics on immigrants admitted and naturalizations. See U.S. Department of Homeland Security (2004).

24. We begin this analysis with 1974 data rather than 1972 data because the November 1972 CPS did not ask about Hispanic ethnicity.

25. A private exchange with an academic demographer suggests that overreporting is largely a matter of citizenship claims by unauthorized Mexicans residents in the United States for less than ten years. The overreport rate is "guesstimated" to be about 20 percent.

Chapter 5: Campaign Finance and Polarization

1. A super-PAC may raise unlimited amounts of money and make expenditures that expressly advocate support for an individual candidate. Unlike traditional PACs (see below), they may not contribute directly to an individual campaign.

2. Insofar as the average household net worth is $35,000, these investments in electoral politics are the equivalent of the typical American spending $525.

3. Steve Forbes is not on his own list. Other *Forbes* 400 members who leveraged their personal fortunes to run for office are John Castimatidis, Thomas Golisano, Craig Benson, Meg Whitman, Winthrop Rockefeller, and Al Checchi. John Kerry's wife, Teresa Heinz Kerry, edged onto the list at $750 million, but her wealth was not a resource for his presidential campaign. Consequently, Kerry had to rely on contributors and his personal fortune of more than $160 million. Mitt Romney spent $17.5 million of his estimated $250 million to fund his presidential campaign in 2008 but opted instead to rely on the largesse of others during his 2012 presidential campaign. Maria Cantwell similarly declined to spend her much-reduced personal fortune on her reelection campaigns in 2006 or 2012.

4. Corzine dipped further into his fortune to run for governor of New Jersey. Cantwell's story is more cautionary. After spending $10 million to win her seat, she saw her wealth evaporate as the tech bubble popped. See Shaid (2001).

5. See https://www.opensecrets.org/overview/topself.php?Cycle=2014&Display=S&Type=A2 (accessed March 17, 2015).

6. See http://www.opensecrets.org/pfds/overview.php?type=W&year=2013&filter=H (accessed March 17, 2015). Because congressional financial disclosure forms omit the value of primary residences, this estimate is conservative. See Loughlin and Yoon (2003). By comparison, about 1 percent of the U.S. population has assets exceeding $5 million; see http://spectrem.com/Content/market-size-pre-recession-levels.aspx (accessed March 17, 2015).

7. Section 527 of the Internal Revenue Code provides for organizations that may raise and disburse funds to influence elections. These groups are regulated by and report to the IRS rather than to the Federal Election Commission. They may not engage in "express advocacy" for the election or defeat of any federal candidate. Many 527 organizations are affiliated with PACs.

8. See http://www.opensecrets.org/527s/527indivs.asp?cycle=2004.

9. See Coral Davenport "Meager Returns for the Democrats' Biggest Donor," *New York Times*, November 6, 2014.

10. Of the members of the *Forbes* lists, only Steven Bing comes close to contributing 2 percent of his wealth to 527s in an election cycle as he spent $13 million out of $750 million in 2004.

11. See http://www.opensecrets.org/bigpicture/topindivs.asp?cycle=2002.

12. These figures include only expenditures made by the candidates themselves and do not include independent expenditures made by groups and parties on their behalf.

13. The implications of the increase in real campaign expenditures are open to some dispute. Ansolabehere, de Figueredo, and Snyder (2003) point out that campaign

expenditures have not grown as fast as GDP, so campaign expenditures were a falling share of national income. The number of elected offices, however, has not grown on the federal level and is falling at the state and local level, so real spending rather than percentage of GDP seems to be the more appropriate metric. In any event, in the last ten years, GDP growth has been below 2 percent per year, while campaign expenditures have grown much faster.

14. Until the Bipartisan Campaign Reform Act (BCRA) of 2002 (McCain-Feingold), individuals could contribute $1,000 to each PAC, and PACs could contribute $5,000 per candidate per election (primary and general).

15. Political spending by 501(c) corporations is reported to the IRS.

16. Individual contributions are reported to the FEC only if they exceed $200. Therefore the individual contribution totals used in the index are the sum of contributions exceeding $200. The truncation at $200 and the omission of the hundreds of millions of Americans who make zero contributions bias the indices downward. We calculated the total contribution amounts for individuals using the Database on Ideology, Money in Politics, and Elections (DIME), which includes unique identifiers for all itemized individual donors (Bonica, 2013a). The database can be accessed at http://data.stanford.edu/dime.

17. Other measures of inequality, such as the percentage of contributions made by the top one thousand contributors, show essentially the same pattern.

18. Kroszner and Stratmann (1998) present a particularly insightful discussion of how contributions should flow from interest groups to members.

19. For other approaches to estimating the ideological behavior of contributors, see Poole and Romer (1985) and McCarty and Poole (1999).

20. The "unclassified" groups are those for which no interest group designation appears in the FEC master committee file.

21. Including less active political action committees would not alter the basic message of figure 5.4: the inverted U-shaped relationship holds for PACs making as few as eight contributions per cycle.

22. Lowess curves are generated by estimating the relationship between the variables for each narrow band of values in the domain. These local estimates are smoothed by fitting them to a high-order polynomial. These estimates are particularly useful in detecting nonlinearities.

23. Obtaining a value of $S > 0.577$ is consistent with concentrating contributions on both extremes.

24. Restricting the sample to incumbent legislators helps control for variation in nonspatial candidate characteristics associated with incumbency.

25. One reason why there may be so many individuals with values of S exceeding 0.577 might be that extremists are more likely to build seniority and power. This scenario would produce bimodal access contributions generating values of S exceeding the random contribution benchmark.

26. This finding is not surprising, however, given S's close relationship to F^2.

27. The results from a Tobit model are very similar. The Heckman model cannot be used because the selection and outcome equations have the same regressors.

28. See McCarty and Rothenberg (2002) for a formal model of these trade-offs.

29. See Noah (2004). According to opensecrets.org, the Club for Growth spent more than $13 million, making it the ninth largest 527 group. This money does not include the more than $4 million raised and spent by its Internet fundraising arm, ClubForGrowth.org.

30. See http://www.nytimes.com/2015/01/27/us/politics/kochs-plan-to-spend-900 -million-on-2016-campaign.html?_r=0 (accessed March 17, 2015).

Chapter 6: Polarization and Public Policy

1. Kopczuk and Saez (2004), table 1, pp. 450–451.

2. Poole and Rosenthal (1991) provide a more extensive discussion of congressional action on minimum wages through the 1980s.

3. Information may be found in the Voteview database, available at voteview.com.

4. As of 2013, 4.3 percent of workers age sixteen and older worked at or below the federal minimum wage. This compares to more than 15 percent in 1980. See http://www.bls.gov/ cps/minwage2013.pdf.

5. State minimum wage data are from the National Council of State Legislatures. See http://www.ncsl.org/research/labor-and-employment/state-minimum-wage-chart .aspx (accessed March 21, 2015).

6. See http://www.treasury.gov/resource-center/tax-policy/tax-analysis/Documents/ ota80.pdf(accessed July 2, 2015).

7. The Affordable Care Act passed in 2009 added a 0.9% Medicare surtax that applies to high-income earners. Thus, the Medicare tax is now progressive.

8. The average level of polarization during postwar divided governments is 0.64, while the average for unified governments is 0.59. Such a correlation is predicted by "party balancing" models of voter behavior (e.g., Alesina and Rosenthal 1995; Fiorina 1996; Mebane 2000; Mebane and Sekhon 2002). These theories argue that moderate voters have incentives to split their tickets as a way of forcing polarized parties to bargain toward moderate policies. The difference was statistically significant in the first edition, but it is now not significant owing to the number of years with unified governments in the 2000s. The p-value for the difference is 0.222 (one-tailed).

9. See Cameron (2000) for the application of bargaining theory to policymaking.

10. See Krehbiel (1998) and Brady and Volden (1998).

11. The most prominent exceptions are budget reconciliation bills, which require only a majority vote. This topic is discussed in greater detail later in the chapter.

12. This formulation embeds the additional assumptions that the preferences in the U.S. House are similar enough to those of the Senate that obtaining cloture or an override in the Senate is sufficient to ensure a majority in the House. These are all reasonable approximations.

13. The Byrd Rule, named for Senator Robert Byrd (D-WV), specifies that a point of order may be called on any provision in a reconciliation bill that authorizes discretionary appropriations and provisions increasing entitlement spending or that cuts taxes beyond the five (or more)-year window provided for in the reconciliation directive. Because it takes sixty votes to waive the rule, failure to abide by its terms essentially removes the parliamentary protections otherwise afforded reconciliation bills.

14. See Gilmour (1995) and Groseclose and McCarty (2000).

15. The lack of data on trust before the 1970s makes it difficult to evaluate the ability of this hypothesis to explain longer-term trends in polarization.

16. See Mayhew (1991) for the details of his compilation of significant statutes. Figure 6.5 uses both the data published in his original study and his subsequent updates. It also combines Mayhew's series on contemporary judgments with his series based on retrospective judgments.

17. The difference between our models and McCarty is that we control for split party control of Congress as distinct from divided government. Such a specification was facilitated by new observations of that pattern of control. We also deal with the substantial outlier of 9/11 by eliminating the legislation that was a direct response to the terrorist attacks. When that legislation is included, the estimates of the effect of polarization are attenuated and imprecise, but there is still a substantial negative effect.

18. A second model interacts polarization with unified government. The results suggest that the difference between unified government and divided government gets larger as polarization increases. From this model the output gap between the least polarized divided government and the most polarized government is 175 percent.

19. These data are from Petersen (2001) and Clinton and Lapinski (2007).

20. Many political economy models of redistribution predict that there will be more redistribution following increases in pretax and transfer income inequality (e.g., Meltzer and Richard 1981; Romer 1975). Our arguments about polarization and gridlock may explain why this redistribution did not happen in the United States. See also Bonica et al. (2013).

21. Programs with large middle-class constituencies, such as Social Security and Medicare, are generally indexed. There are some tax policies, however, such as the alternative minimum tax, where the lack of indexing had negative effects on portions of the upper middle class. Indexing the AMT was finally achieved as part of the "fiscal cliff" bill passed on January 1, 2013.

22. See http://kff.org/health-reform/state-indicator/state-decisions-for-creating-health -insurance-exchanges-and-expanding-medicaid. We code states with "Federally-supported State-based Marketplace" and "State-partnership Marketplaces" as having state exchanges.

23. In forty-nine of the fifty states, party control was the same in 2014 as it was in 2013. In the 2013 elections, Virginia went from split control of the legislature to Republican control and from a Republican governor to a Democratic governor. We use the 2014 composition for Virginia. Nebraska's nonpartisan legislature is coded as Republican-controlled.

24. Central clearing refers to a requirement that derivatives counterparties engage a clearing house that would guarantee each party's performance on the contract.

25. See Applebaum (2010b), Chan (2010), and Dennis (2010b).

26. See Applebaum (2010a), Dennis (2010a), and Wyatt (2010).

27. The Feingold story is elaborated by McCarty et al. (2010).

28. See Eavis (2014.).

29. See Lynch (2015).

30. Howell (2003) documents such an effect with respect to the overall issuance of executive orders, and Lewis (2003) finds that presidents are more likely to create agencies by executive order rather than by statute when there is interbranch policy conflict. Moreover, Lewis finds that agencies created by presidential order are often short-lived and underfunded.

31. Such arguments are consistent with the "separation of powers" model of judicial decision making. See Ferejohn and Shipan (1990) and Spiller and Gely (1992) for the theory and evidence.

32. See Epstein and O'Halloran (1999).

Chapter 7: Where Have You Gone, Mr. Sam?

1. The president is also, for all intents and purposes, chosen by plurality rule. Although the Electoral College can give a result that differs from the popular vote plurality, as was the case in 2000, the presidential election is—barring the knife-edge case that would send the election to the House—a mechanism for aggregating individual votes to choose just one elected individual.

2. See Wittman (1977, 1983) and Calvert (1985).

3. Our argument is consistent with that of Wittman (1983). Such logic is formalized in Groseclose's (2001) extension of Wittman's model.

4. See McCarty, Poole, and Rosenthal (2013).

5. See Layman and Carsey (2002a, 2002b), Carsey and Layman (2006), and Layman and co-workers (2010).

6. See McCarty (2015) for an argument and evidence that weak party organizations contribute to polarization.

7. In a proportional representation system, extreme parties that diverge lose votes to moderate parties. As these centrist parties are often pivotal in government formation, the effects of polarization are also lessened. Austen-Smith (2000) presents a model of redistributive politics under proportional representation. The model, however, has no obvious analogue under plurality rule. Therefore, he compares his results to the median voter theorem.

8. When all responses listing a social issue (abortion, gay rights, and so on) as the number one issue in previous exit polls were added up, the number of "morals" voters was actually down a bit in 2004.

9. See table histz1 at http://www.whitehouse.gov/omb/budget/Historicals (accessed March 6, 2015).

10. See the vote on the "clean" funding bill for the Department of Homeland Security on our blog, *VoteView* (https://voteviewblog.wordpress.com/2015/03/06/hello-world). The extreme conservatives objected to the passage of the funding of DHS because a provision that would have blocked President Obama's executive order partially legalizing many undocumented immigrants had been removed.

11. Although families with incomes lower than the median for their state can still use chapter 7, they are subject to "credit counseling" and other measures that raise the cost of bankruptcy.

12. See http://www.thefiscaltimes.com/2014/12/14/CRomnibus-Swaps-Provision-Some -Real-Problems-Some-Imaginary-Ones (accessed March 7, 2015).

13. The third member of the trio grew up in the 1970s, with gasoline lines and a general sense of malaise.

References

Acemoglu, Daron, and James A. Robinson. 2005. *Economic Origins of Dictatorship and Democracy: Economic and Political Origins*. New York: Cambridge University Press.

Alesina, Alberto. 1988. Credibility and Policy Convergence in a Two-Party System with Rational Voters. *American Economic Review* 78 (4): 796–805.

Alesina, Alberto, Reza Baqir, and William Easterly. 1999. Public Goods and Ethnic Divisions. *Quarterly Journal of Economics* 114 (4): 1243–1284.

Alesina, Alberto, and Edward L. Glaeser. 2004. *Fighting Poverty in the U.S. and Europe*. New York: Oxford University Press.

Alesina, Alberto, and Eliana La Ferrara. 2000. Participation in Heterogeneous Communities. *Quarterly Journal of Economics* 115 (3): 847–904.

Alesina, Alberto, and Eliana La Ferrara. 2002. Who Trusts Others? *Journal of Public Economics* 85 (2): 207–234.

Alesina, Alberto, and Roberto Perotti. 1995. Income Distribution, Political Instability, and Investment. *European Economic Review* 40 (6): 1203–1228.

Alesina, Alberto, and Dani Rodrick. 1993. Income Distribution and Economic Growth: A Simple Theory and Some Empirical Evidence. In *The Political Economy of Business Cycles and Growth*, ed. Alex Cukierman, Zvi Herscovitz, and Leonardo Leiderman. Cambridge, MA: MIT Press.

Alesina, Alberto, and Howard Rosenthal. 1995. *Partisan Politics, Divided Government, and the Economy*. New York: Cambridge University Press.

Alesina, Alberto, and Howard Rosenthal. 2000. Polarized Platforms and Moderate Policies with Checks and Balances. *Journal of Public Economics* 75 (1): 1–20.

Altonji, Joseph, and David Card. 1989. The Effects of Immigration on the Labor Market Outcomes of Natives. National Bureau of Economic Research Working Paper 3123. Cambridge, MA: National Bureau of Economic Research.

Alvaredo, Facundo, Anthony B. Atkinson, Thomas Piketty, and Emmanuel Saez. 2015. The World Top Incomes Database, January. http://topincomes.g-mond.parisschoolofeconomics.eu.

American Political Science Association. 1950. Toward a More Responsible Two-Party System: A Report of the Committee on Political Parties. *American Political Science Review* 44 (3): Pt. 2, Suppl.

American Political Science Association. 2004. *Inequality and American Democracy: What We Know and What We Need To Learn.* New York: Russell Sage Press.

Ansolabehere, Stephen, John de Figueredo, and James Snyder. 2003. Why Is There So Little Money in Politics? *Journal of Economic Perspectives* 17 (1): 105–130.

Ansolabehere, Stephen, Jonathan Rodden, and James M. Snyder. 2006. Purple America. *Journal of Economic Perspectives* 20 (2): 97–118.

Applebaum, Binyamin. 2010a. Six Key Points of the Financial Regulation Legislation. *Washington Post*, March 16.

Applebaum, Binyamin. 2010b. Lawmakers at Impasse on Trading. *New York Times*, June 23.

Atkinson, A. B. 1997. Bringing Income Distribution in From the Cold. *Economic Journal* 107 (441): 297–321.

Austen-Smith, David. 2000. Redistributing Income under Proportional Representation. *Journal of Political Economy* 108 (6): 1235–1269.

Bartels, Larry M. 2008. *Unequal Democracy: The Political Economy of the New Gilded Age.* Princeton, NJ: Princeton University Press.

Bean, Frank D., and Stephanie Bell-Rose. 1999. Introduction. In *Immigration and Opportunity: Race, Ethnicity, and Employment in the United States*, ed. Frank D. Bean and Stephanie Bell-Rose, 1–28. New York: Russell Sage Foundation.

Bell, Daniel. 1960. *The End of Ideology: On the Exhaustion of Political Ideas in the Fifties.* Cambridge, MA: Harvard University Press.

Benabou, Roland. 2000. Unequal Societies: Income Distribution and the Social Contract. *American Economic Review* 90 (1): 96–129.

Bhatti, Yosef, and Robert S. Erikson. 2011. How Poorly Are the Poor Represented in the US Senate? In *Who Gets Represented*, ed. Peter K. Enns and Christopher Wlezien, 223–246. New York: Russell Sage Press.

Bishop, Bill. 2004. The Schism in U.S. Politics Begins at Home. *Austin American Statesman*, April 4.

Bolton, Patrick, and Gerard Roland. 1997. The Breakup of Nations. *Quarterly Journal of Economics* 112 (4): 1057–1090.

Bonica, Adam, Nolan McCarty, Keith T. Poole, and Howard Rosenthal. 2013. Why Hasn't Democracy Slowed Rising Inequality? *Journal of Economic Perspectives* 27 (3): 103–123.

Bonica, Adam. 2013a. Database on Ideology, Money in Politics, and Elections: Public version 1.0. http://data.stanford.edu/dime.

Bonica, Adam. 2013b. Ideology and Interests in the Political Marketplace. *American Journal of Political Science* 57 (2): 294–311.

Bonica, Adam. 2014. Mapping the Ideological Marketplace. *American Journal of Political Science* 58 (2): 367–386.

Borjas, George J. 1987. Immigrants, Minorities, and Labor Market Competition. *Industrial & Labor Relations Review* 40 (3): 382–392.

Borjas, George J. 1999. *Heaven's Door: Immigration Policy and the American Economy.* Princeton, NJ: Princeton University Press.

Borjas, George J. 2003. The Labor Demand Curve Is Downward Sloping: Reexamining the Impact of Immigration on the Labor Market. *Quarterly Journal of Economics* 118 (4): 1335–1376.

Borjas, George J., Richard B. Freeman, and Lawrence F. Katz. 1997. How Much Do Immigration and Trade Affect Labor Market Outcomes? *Brookings Papers on Economic Activity* 1997 (1): 1–67.

Brady, David W., Hahrie Han, and Jeremy C. Pope. 2007. Primary Elections and Candidate Ideology: Out of Step with the Primary Electorate? *Legislative Studies Quarterly* 32 (1): 79–105.

Brady, David W., and Craig Volden. 1998. *Revolving Gridlock: Politics and Policy from Carter to Clinton.* Boulder, CO: Westview Press.

Brady, Henry. 2004. An Analytical Perspective on Participatory Inequality and Income Inequality. In *Social Inequality*, ed. Kathy Neckerman. New York: Russell Sage Foundation.

Brunell, Thomas L., and Bernard Grofman. 1998. Explaining Divided Senate Delegations: A Realignment Approach. *American Political Science Review* 92 (2): 391–399.

Bullock, Will, and Joshua D. Clinton. 2011. More a Molehill Than a Mountain: The Effects of the Blanket Primary on Elected Officials' Behavior from California. *Journal of Politics* 73 (3): 915–930.

Calvert, Randall L. 1985. Robustness of the Multidimensional Voting Model: Candidate Motivations, Uncertainty, and Convergence. *American Journal of Political Science* 29 (1): 69–95.

Cameron, Charles. 2000. *Veto Bargaining: Presidents and the Politics of Negative Power.* New York: Cambridge University Press.

Cameron, Charles, David Epstein, and Sharyn O'Halloran. 1996. Do Majority-Minority Districts Maximize Black Substantive Representation in Congress? *American Political Science Review* 90 (4): 794–812.

Carmines, Edward G., and James Stimson. 1989. *Issue Evolution: Race and the Transformation of American Politics.* Princeton, NJ: Princeton University Press.

Carroll, Christopher D. 2002. Portfolios of the Rich. In *Household Portfolios*, ed. Luigi Guiso, M. Haliassos, and Tullio Jappelli. Cambridge, MA: MIT Press.

Carroll, Royce, Jeffrey B. Lewis, James Lo, Keith T. Poole, and Howard Rosenthal. 2013. The Structure of Utility in Spatial Models of Voting. *American Journal of Political Science* 57 (4): 1008–1028.

Carson, Jamie L., Michael H. Crespin, Charles J. Finocchiaro, and David Rohde. 2003. Linking Congressional Districts across Time: Redistricting and Party Polarization in Congress. Paper presented at the 2003 Midwest Political Science Association Meetings, Chicago, April 3–6.

Carsey, Thomas M., and Geoffrey C. Layman. 2006. Changing Sides or Changing Minds? Party Identification and Policy Preferences in the American Electorate. *American Journal of Political Science* 50 (April): 464–477.

Chan, Sewall. 2010. Democrats Are at Odds on Relevance of Keynes. *New York Times*, October 18.

Chen, Jowei, and Jonathan Rodden. 2013. Unintentional Gerrymandering: Political Geography and Electoral Bias in Legislatures. *Quarterly Journal of Political Science* 8 (3): 239–269.

Clausen, Aage R. 1973. *How Congressmen Decide: A Policy Focus*. New York: St. Martin's Press.

Clinton, Joshua, Simon Jackman, and Douglas Rivers. 2004. The Statistical Analysis of Roll Call Data. *American Political Science Review* 98 (2): 355–370.

Clinton, Joshua, and John Lapinski. 2007. Measuring Significant Legislation, 1877–1948. In *Process, Party, and Policymaking: Further New Perspectives on the History of Congress*, ed. David Brady and Matthew McCubbins. Palo Alto, CA: Stanford University Press.

Costa, Dora L., and Matthew E. Kahn. 2003a. Civic Engagement and Community Heterogeneity: An Economist's Perspective. *Perspectives on Politics* 1 (1): 103–111.

Costa, Dora L., and Matthew E. Kahn. 2003b. Understanding the American Decline in Social Capital, 1952–1998. *Kyklos* 56 (1): 17–46.

Cox, Gary W., and Jonathan N. Katz. 2002. *Elbridge Gerry's Salamander: The Electoral Consequences of the Reapportionment Revolution*. New York: Cambridge University Press.

Cox, Gary W., and Mathew D. McCubbins. 1993. *Legislative Leviathan: Party Government in the House*. Berkeley: University of California Press.

Cox, Gary W., and Mathew D. McCubbins. 2005. *Setting the Agenda: Responsible Party Government in the U.S. House of Representatives*. New York: Cambridge University Press.

Cox, Gary W., and Keith T. Poole. 2002. On Measuring Partisanship in Roll-Call Voting: The U.S. House of Representatives, 1877–1999. *American Journal of Political Science* 46 (3): 477–489.

Cuzán, Alfred G., and Charles M. Bundrick. 2005. Deconstructing the 2004 presidential election forecasts: the fiscal model and the Campbell collection compared. *Political Science and Politics* 38 (2): 255–262.

Dahl, Robert A. 1961. *Who Governs: Democracy and Power in an American City*. New Haven, CT: Yale University Press.

Dennis, Brady. 2010a. Sen. Dodd to Introduce Plan to Overhaul Financial Regulatory System. *Washington Post*, March 15.

Dennis, Brady. 2010b. Sen. Blanche Lincoln's Derivatives-Spinoff Plan Gains Support in Congress. *Washington Post*, June 15.

DiMaggio, Paul, John Evans, and Bethany Bryson. 1996. Have Americans' Social Attitudes Become More Polarized? *American Journal of Sociology* 102 (3): 690–755.

Downs, Anthony. 1957. *An Economic Theory of Democracy*. New York: Harper and Row.

Duca, John V., and Jason L. Saving. 2008. The Political Economy of the Mutual Fund Revolution: How Rising Stock-Ownership Rates Affect Congressional Elections. *Economic Inquiry* 46: 454–479.

Duca, John V., and Jason L. Saving. 2015. Income Inequality and Political Polarization: Time Series Evidence over Nine Decades. *Review of Income and Wealth* 61 (forthcoming).

Duverger, Maurice. 1954. *Political Parties*. New York: Wiley.

Eavis, Peter. 2014. Wall St. Wins a Round in a Dodd-Frank Fight. *New York Times*, December 12 http://dealbook.nytimes.com/2014/12/12/wall-st-wins-a-round-in-a-dodd-frank-fight.

Edlund, Lena, and Rohini Pande. 2002. Why Have Women Become Left-Wing? The Political Gender Gap and the Decline of Marriage. *Quarterly Journal of Economics* 117 (3): 917–962.

Ellenberg, Jordan. 2001. Growing Apart: The Mathematical Evidence for Congress' Growing Polarization. Slate, December 26. http://www.slate.com/articles/life/do_the_math/2001/12/growing_apart.html.

Ellwood, David T., and Christopher Jencks. 2004. The Uneven Spread of Single-Parent Families: What Do We Know? Where Do We Look for Answers? In *Social Inequality,* ed. Kathryn Neckerman, 3–79. New York: Russell Sage Foundation.

Epstein, David, and Sharyn O'Halloran. 1999. *Delegating Powers: A Transaction Cost Politics Approach to Policy Making under Separate Powers*. New York: Cambridge University Press.

Evans, John H. 2003. Have Americans' Attitudes Become More Polarized? An Update. *Social Science Quarterly* 84 (1): 71–90.

Farhang, Sean. 2010. *The Litigation State: Public Regulation and Private Lawsuits in the United States*. Princeton, NJ: Princeton University Press.

Ferejohn, John, and Charles Shipan. 1990. Congressional Influence on Bureaucracy. *Journal of Law Economics and Organization* 6 (1): 1–21.

Fey, Mark. 1997. Stability and Coordination in Duverger's Law: A Formal Model of Preelection Polls and Strategic Voting. *American Political Science Review* 91 (1): 135–147.

Fiorina, Morris. 1978. *Congress: Keystone of the Washington Establishment*. New Haven, CT: Yale University Press.

Fiorina, Morris. 1996. *Divided Government*. 2nd ed. Boston: Allyn and Bacon.

Fiorina, Morris, with Samuel J. Abrams and Jeremy C. Pope. 2004. *Culture War? The Myth of a Polarized America*. New York: Longman.

Foley, Duncan K. 1967. Resource Allocation and the Public Sector. *Yale Economic Essays* 7:45–98.

Fowler, Linda L. 1982. How Interest Groups Select Issues for Rating Voting Records of Members of the U.S. Congress. *Legislative Studies Quarterly* 7 (3): 401–413.

Frank, Thomas. 2004. American Psyche. *New York Times Book Review*, November 28.

Freeman, Richard B. 2004. What, Me Vote? In *Social Inequality*, ed. Kathryn E. Neckerman, 667–702. New York: Russell Sage Foundation.

Gelman, Andrew, with David Park et al. 2009. *Red State, Blue State, Rich State, Poor State: Why Americans Vote the Way They Do*. Princeton, NJ: Princeton University Press.

Gerber, Elisabeth R., and Rebecca B. Morton. 1998. Primary Election Systems and Representation. *Journal of Law Economics and Organization* 14 (2): 304–324.

Gerring, John. 1998. *Party Ideologies in America, 1828–1996*. New York: Cambridge University Press.

Gilens, Martin. 1999. *Why Americans Hate Welfare: Race, Media, and the Politics of Antipoverty Policy*. Chicago: University of Chicago Press.

Gilens, Martin. 2012. *Affluence and Influence: Economic Inequality and Political Power in America*. Princeton, NJ: Princeton University Press.

Gilmour, John. 1995. *Strategic Disagreement: Stalemate in American Politics*. Pittsburgh: University of Pittsburgh Press.

Glaeser, Edward L., Giacomo A. M. Ponzetto, and Jesse M. Shapiro. 2005. Strategic Extremism: Why Republicans and Democrats Divide on Religious Values. *Quarterly Journal of Economics* 120 (1): 1283–1330.

Glenmary Research Center. 2010. Religious Congregations and Membership in the United States. http://www.rcms2010.org/index.php (accessed July 5, 2015).

Goldin, Claudia. 1994. The Political Economy of Immigration Restriction: The United States, 1890–1921. In *The Regulated Economy: A Historical Approach to Political Economy*, ed. Claudia Goldin and Gary Libecap. Chicago: University of Chicago Press.

Green, Donald, Bradley Palmquist, and Eric Schickler. 2002. *Partisan Hearts and Minds: Political Parties and the Social Identities of Voters*. New Haven, CT: Yale University Press.

Groseclose, Tim. 2001. A Model of Candidate Location When One Candidate Has a Valence Advantage. *American Journal of Political Science* 45 (4): 862–886.

Groseclose, Tim, Steven D. Levitt, and James M. Snyder, Jr. 1999. Comparing Interest Group Scores across Time and Chambers: Adjusted ADA Scores for the U.S. Congress. *American Political Science Review* 93 (1): 33–50.

Groseclose, Timothy, and Nolan McCarty. 2000. The Politics of Blame: Bargaining before an Audience. *American Journal of Political Science* 45 (1): 100–119.

Guiso, Luigi. Michael Haliassos, and Tullio Jappelli, eds. 2002. *Household Portfolios*. Cambridge, MA: MIT Press.

Hacker, Jacob S. 2004. Privatizing Risk without Privatizing the Welfare State: The Hidden Politics of Social Policy Retrenchment in the United States. *American Political Science Review* 98 (2): 243–260.

Hall, Andrew B. 2015. What Happens When Extremists Win Primaries? *American Political Science Review* 109 (1): 18–42.

Hare, Christopher, and Keith T. Poole. 2014. The Polarization of Contemporary American Politics. *Polity* 46: 411–429.

Heckman, James, and James Snyder. 1997. Linear Probability Models of the Demand for Attributes with an Empirical Application to Estimating the Preferences of Legislators. *RAND Journal of Economics* 28:S142–S189.

Hetherington, Marc J. 2004. *Why Trust Matters: Declining Political Trust and the Demise of American Liberalism*. Princeton, NJ: Princeton University Press.

Hirano, Shigeo, James M. Snyder, Jr., Stephen Ansolabehere, and John Mark Hansen. 2010. Primary Elections and Partisan Polarization in U.S. Congressional Elections. *Quarterly Journal of Political Science* 5 (2): 169–191.

Howell, William. 2003. *Power without Persuasion: The Politics of Direct Presidential Action*. Princeton, NJ: Princeton University Press.

Howell, William, Scott Adler, Charles Cameron, and Charles Riemann. 2000. Divided Government and the Legislative Productivity of Congress, 1945–1994. *Legislative Studies Quarterly* 25 (2): 285–312.

Hulse, Carl, and Robert Pear. 2015. Departing Lawmakers Bemoan the Lack of Compromise. *New York Times*, January 3. http://www.nytimes.com/2015/01/03/us/politics/departing-lawmakers-lament-capitols-partisanship.html.

Jacobs, Lawrence R., and Benjamin I. Page. 2005. Who Influences U.S. Foreign Policy? *American Political Science Review* 99 (1): 107–123.

Kabaservice, Geoffrey. 2012. *Rule and Ruin: The Downfall of Moderation and the Destruction of the Republican Party, from Eisenhower to the Tea Party*. New York: Oxford University Press.

Kalt, Joseph P., and Mark A. Zupan. 1984. Capture and Ideology in Politics. *American Economic Review* 74 (3): 279–300.

Kaufmann, Karen M., James G. Gimpel, and Adam H. Hoffman. 2003. A Promise Fulfilled? Open Primaries and Representation. *Journal of Politics* 65 (2): 457–476.

Key, V. O. 1949. *Southern Politics in State and Nation*. New York: A. A. Knopf.

King, David C. 1997. The Polarization of American Political Parties and Mistrust of Government. In *Why People Don't Trust Government*, ed. Joseph S. Nye, Philip Zelikow and David C. King. Cambridge, MA: Harvard University Press.

Kopczuk, Wojciech, and Emmanuel Saez. 2004. Top Wealth Shares in the United States, 1916–2000: Evidence from Estate Tax Returns. *National Tax Journal* 67 (2): 445–487.

Krehbiel, Keith. 1998. *Pivotal Politics: A Theory of U.S. Lawmaking*. Chicago: University of Chicago Press.

Kroszner, Randall S., and Thomas Stratmann. 1998. Interest-Group Competition and the Organization of Congress: Theory and Evidence from Financial Services' Political Action Committees. *American Economic Review* 88 (5): 1163–1187.

Lalonde, Robert J., and Robert W. Topel. 1989. Labor Market Adjustments to Increased Immigration. In *Immigration, Trade, and the Labor Market*, ed. Richard B. Freeman. Chicago: University of Chicago Press; Cambridge, MA: National Bureau of Economic Research.

Layman, Geoffrey C., and Thomas M. Carsey. 2002a. Party Polarization and "Conflict Extension" in the American Electorate. *American Journal of Political Science* 46 (October): 786–802.

Layman, Geoffrey C., and Thomas M. Carsey. 2002b. Party Polarization and Party Structuring of Policy Attitudes: A Comparison of Three NES Panel Studies. *Political Behavior* 24 (September): 199–236.

Layman, Geoffrey C., Thomas M. Carsey, John C. Green, Richard Herrera, and Rosalyn Cooperman. 2010. Activists and Conflict Extension in American Party Politics. *American Political Science Review* 104 (May): 324–346.

Lee, David S. 1999. Wage Inequality in the United States during the 1980s: Rising Dispersion or Falling Minimum Wage? *Quarterly Journal of Economics* 114 (3): 977–1023.

Lee, David S., Enrico Moretti, and Matthew J. Butler. 2005. Do Voters Affect or Elect Policies? Evidence from the U.S. House. *Quarterly Journal of Economics* 119 (3): 807–859.

Lerman, Robert. 1999. U.S. Wage Inequality Trends and Recent Immigration. *American Economic Review* 89 (2): 23–28.

Levitt, Steven D. 1996. How Do Senators Vote? Disentangling the Role of Voter Preferences, Party Affiliation, and Senator Ideology. *American Economic Review* 86 (3): 425–441.

Lewis, David E. 2003. *Presidents and the Politics of Agency Design.* Stanford, CA: Stanford University Press.

Lijphart, Arend. 1997. Unequal Participation: Democracy's Unresolved Dilemma. *American Political Science Review* 91 (1): 1–14.

Londregan, John, and Keith T. Poole. 1990. Poverty, the Coup Trap, and the Seizure of Executive Power. *World Politics* 62 (2): 151–183.

Loughlin, Sean, and Robert Yoon. 2003. Millionaires Populate U.S. Senate. http://www.cnn.com/2003/ALLPOLITICS/06/13/senators.finances.

Luttmer, Erzo. 2001. Group Loyalty and the Taste for Redistribution. *Journal of Political Economy* 109 (3): 500–528.

Lynch, Sarah N. 2015. Republicans Attack Wall Street Reform in Budget Plan. Reuters, March 17. http://www.huffingtonpost.com/2015/03/17/republicans-wall-street-reform-budget-dodd-frank_n_6886308.html.

Manza, Jeff, and Clem Brooks. 1999. *Social Cleavages and Political Change: Voter Alignments and U.S. Party Coalitions.* New York: Oxford University Press.

Martin, Douglas. 2015. Edward W. Brooke III, 95, Senate Pioneer, Is Dead. *New York Times,* January 5. http://www.nytimes.com/2015/01/04/us/edward-brooke-pioneering-us-senator-in-massachusetts-dies-at-95.html.

Mayhew, David R. 1991. *Divided We Govern: Party Control, Lawmaking, and Investigations, 1946–1990.* New Haven, CT: Yale University Press.

McCarty, Nolan. 2007. The Policy Consequences of Political Polarization. In *The Transformation of American Politics: Activist Government and the Rise of Conservatism,* ed. Paul Pierson and Theda Skocpol. Princeton, NJ: Princeton University Press.

McCarty, Nolan. 2013. The Political Economy of Immigrant Incorporation into the Welfare State. In *Outsiders No More: Models of Immigrant Political Incorporation,* ed. Jennifer Hochschild, Jacqueline Chattopadhyay, Claudine Gay, and Michael Jones-Correa. New York: Oxford University Press.

McCarty, Nolan. 2015. *Reducing Polarization by Making Parties Stronger. In Solutions to Polarization in America*, ed. Nathaniel Persily. New York: Cambridge University Press.

McCarty, Nolan, and Keith T. Poole. 1999. An Empirical Spatial Model of Congressional Campaigns. *Political Analysis* 7 (1): 1–30.

McCarty, Nolan, Keith T. Poole, Thomas Romer and Howard Rosenthal. 2010. The Price of Principle. *Huffington Post*, July 20.

McCarty, Nolan, Keith T. Poole, and Howard Rosenthal. 1997. *Income Redistribution and the Realignment of American Politics*. Washington, DC: American Enterprise Institute.

McCarty, Nolan, Keith T. Poole, and Howard Rosenthal. 2001. The Hunt for Party Discipline in Congress. *American Political Science Review* 95 (3): 673–687.

McCarty, Nolan, Keith T. Poole, and Howard Rosenthal. 2009. Does Gerrymandering Cause Polarization? *American Journal of Political Science* 53 (July):666–680.

McCarty, Nolan, Keith T. Poole, and Howard Rosenthal. 2013. *Political Bubbles: Financial Crises and the Failure of American Democracy*. Princeton, NJ: Princeton University Press.

McCarty, Nolan, and Rose Razaghian. 1999. Advice and Consent: Senate Response to Executive Branch Nominations, 1885–1996. *American Journal of Political Science* 43 (3): 1122–1143.

McCarty, Nolan, and Lawrence Rothenberg. 2002. A Positive Theory of Group-Politician Alliances: The Logic of Coopertation. Paper presented at the Public Choice Society, San Diego, CA, March 14.

McDonald, Michael P., and Samuel Popkin. 2001. The Myth of the Vanishing Voter. *American Political Science Review* 95 (4): 963–974.

McGhee, Eric, Seth Masket, Boris Shor, Steven Rogers, and Nolan McCarty. 2014. A Primary Cause of Partisanship? Nomination Systems and Legislator Ideology. *American Journal of Political Science* 58 (2): 337–351.

McKelvey, Richard D., and William Zavoina. 1975. A Statistical Model for the Analysis of Ordinal Level Dependent Variables. *Journal of Mathematical Sociology* 4:103–120.

Mebane, Walter R. 2000. Coordination, Moderation, and Institutional Balancing in American Presidential and House Elections. *American Political Science Review* 94 (1): 37–57.

Mebane, Walter R., and Jasjeet S. Sekhon. 2002. Coordination and Policy Moderation at Midterm. *American Political Science Review* 96 (1): 141–157.

Meltzer, Allan H., and Scott F. Richard. 1981. A Rational Theory of the Size of Government. *Journal of Political Economy* 89 (5): 914–927.

Merrill Lynch/Cap Gemini Ernst & Young. 2004. World Wealth Report 2004. http://www.ml.com/index.asp?id=7695_7696_8149_6261_14832_14938.

Micklethwait, John, and Adrian Wooldridge. 2004. *The Right Nation: Conservative Power in America*. New York: Penguin Books.

Myrdal, Gunnar. 1960. *Beyond the Welfare State: Economic Planning and its International Implications*. New Haven, CT: Yale University Press.

Noah, Tim. 2004. Who's Afraid of the Club for Growth? *Slate*, November 16.

Palfrey, Thomas R. 1989. A Mathematical Proof of Duverger's Law. In *Models of Strategic Choice in Politics*, ed. Peter Ordeshook. Ann Arbor: University of Michigan Press.

Palfrey, Thomas R., and Keith T. Poole. 1987. The Relationship between Information, Ideology, and Voting Behavior. *American Journal of Political Science* 31 (3): 511–530.

Perlstein, Rick. 2001. *Before the Storm: Barry Goldwater and the Unmaking of the American Consensus*. New York: Hill and Wang.

Perotti, Roberto. 1996. Political Equilibrium, Income Distribution, and Growth. *Review of Economic Studies* 60 (4): 755–776.

Persson, Torsten, and Guido Tabellini. 1994. Is Inequality Harmful for Growth? Theory and Evidence. *American Economic Review* 84 (3): 600–621.

Petersen, R. Eric. 2001. Is It Science Yet? Replicating and Validating the Divided We Govern List of Important Statutes. Presented at the Annual Meeting of the Midwest Political Science Association, Chicago, April 19–22.

Phillips, Kevin. 2002. *Wealth and Democracy: A Political History of the American Rich*. New York: Broadway Books.

Piketty, Thomas, and Emmanuel Saez. 2003. Income Inequality in the United States, 1913–1998. *Quarterly Journal of Economics* 118 (1): 1–39.

Poole, Keith T. 1984. Least Squares Metric, Unidimensional Unfolding. *Psychometrica* 49:311–323.

Poole, Keith T. 1998. Recovering a Basic Space from a Set of Issue Scales. *American Journal of Political Science* 42 (3): 954–993.

Poole, Keith T. 2000. Non-Parametric Unfolding of Binary Choice Data. *Political Analysis* 8 (3): 211–237.

Poole, Keith T. 2005. *Spatial Models of Parliamentary Voting*. New York: Cambridge University Press.

Poole, Keith T. 2007. Changing Minds, Not in Congress! *Public Choice* 131:435–451.

Poole, Keith T., and R. Steven Daniels. 1985. Ideology, Party, and Voting in the U.S. Congress, 1959–1980. *American Political Science Review* 79 (2): 373–399.

Poole, Keith T., and Thomas Romer. 1985. Patterns of Political Action Committee Contributions to the 1980 Campaigns for the U.S. House of Representatives. *Public Choice* 47 (1): 63–111.

Poole, Keith T., and Thomas Romer. 1993. Ideology, Shirking, and Representation. *Public Choice* 77 (1): 185–196.

Poole, Keith T., and Howard Rosenthal. 1984. The Polarization of American Politics. *Journal of Politics* 46 (4): 1061–1079.

Poole, Keith T., and Howard Rosenthal. 1991. The Spatial Mapping of Minimum Wage Legislation. In *Politics and Economics in the 1980s*, ed. Alberto Alesina and Geoffrey Carliner. Chicago: University of Chicago Press.

Poole, Keith T., and Howard Rosenthal. 1997. *Congress: A Political-Economic History of Roll Call Voting*. New York: Oxford University Press.

Putnam, Robert. 2000. *Bowling Alone: The Collapse and Revival of American Community*. New York: Simon and Schuster.

Putnam, Robert. 2015. *Our Kids: The American Dream in Crisis*. New York: Simon and Schuster.

Quadagno, Jill S. 1994. *The Color of Welfare: How Racism Undermined the War on Poverty*. Oxford: Oxford University Press.

Roberts, Kevin W. S. 1977. Voting over Income Tax Schedules. *Journal of Public Economics* 8 (3): 329–340.

Roemer, John. 1999. The Democratic Political Economy of Progressive Income Taxation. *Econometrica* 67 (1): 1–19.

Rohde, David W. 1991. *Parties and Leaders in the Post-Reform House*. Chicago: University of Chicago Press.

Romer, Thomas. 1975. Individual Welfare, Majority Voting, and the Properties of a Linear Income Tax. *Journal of Public Economics* 4 (2): 163–185.

Romer, Thomas. 1977. Majority Voting on Tax Parameters: Some Further Results. *Journal of Public Economics* 7 (1): 127–133.

Rosenthal, Howard, and Christine Eibner. 2005. Immigration and the Median Voter's Incentive to Redistribute Income in the United States. Paper presented at the ASCE meetings, Budapest, Hungary, June 29–July 2.

Saez, Emmanuel. 2013. Striking It Richer: The Evolution of Top Incomes in the United States (updated with 2012 preliminary estimates). Working Paper, UC Berkeley.

Saez, Emmanuel. 2015. Income and Wealth Inequality: Evidence and Policy Implications. Neubauer Collegium Lecture, University of Chicago, March 3. http://eml.berkeley.edu/~saez.

Shaid, Anthony. 2001. Sen. Dot-Com. Boston Globe, May 21.

Shor, Boris, and Nolan McCarty. 2011. The Ideological Mapping of American Legislatures. *American Political Science Review* 105 (03): 530–551.

Snyder, James. 1992. Artificial Extremism in Interest Group Ratings. *Legislative Studies Quarterly* 17 (3): 319–345.

Snyder, James, and Tim Groseclose. 2000. Estimating Party Influence in Congressional Roll-Call Voting. *American Journal of Political Science* 44 (2): 193–211.

Snyder, James M., and Michael M. Ting. 2002. An Informational Rationale for Political Parties. *American Journal of Political Science* 46 (1): 90–110.

Sorauf, Frank J. 1992. *Inside Campaign Finance: Myths and Realities*. New Haven, CT: Yale University Press.

Spiller, Pablo, and Raphael Gely. 1992. Congressional Control or Judicial Independence: The Determinants of U.S. Supreme Court Labor-Relations Decisions, 1949–1988. *Rand Journal of Economics* 23 (4): 463–492.

Sundquist, James L. 1981. *The Decline and Resurgence of Congress*. Washington, DC: Brookings Institution.

Tausanovitch, Chris. 2014. Income, Ideology, and Representation. Paper presented at for the Russell Sage Foundation Journal of the Social Sciences, Conference on Big Data in Political Economy. Russell Sage Foundation, New York City, October 8–9.

Uggen, Christopher, and Jeff Manza. 2002. Democratic Contraction? Political Consequences of Felon Disenfranchisement in the United States. *American Sociological Review* 67 (6): 777–803.

U.S. Census Bureau. 2014. Gini Ratios for Families, by Race and Hispanic Origin of Householder (table F 4). http://www.census.gov/hhes/www/income/data/historical/inequality/index.html (accessed July 5, 2015).

U.S. Department of Homeland Security. 2004. Yearbook of Immigration Statistics. Washington, DC: U.S. Department of Homeland Security, Office of Immigration Statistics. http://www.dhs.gov/yearbook-immigration-statistics-2004-0.

Weingast, Barry R., Kenneth A. Shepsle, and Christopher Johnsen. 1981. The Political Economy of Benefits and Costs: A Neoclassical Approach to Distributive Politics. *Journal of Political Economy* 89 (4): 642–664.

Wallace, Steven P., Jacqueline Torres, Tabashir Sadegh-Nobari, Nadereh Pourat, and E. Richard Brown. 2012. Undocumented Immigrants and Health Care Reform, Los Angeles, CA, UCLA Center for Health Policy Research. http://healthpolicy.ucla.edu/publications/Documents/PDF/undocumentedreport-aug2013.pdf (accessed July 7, 2015).

Welch, Finnis. 1999. In Defense of Inequality. *American Economic Review* 89 (2): 1–17.

Wittman, Donald. 1983. Candidate Motivation: A Synthesis of Alternatives. *American Political Science Review* 77 (1): 142–157.

Wolff, Edward N. 2002. Recent Trends in Living Standards in the United States. Typescript, Department of Economics, New York University.

Wolfinger, Raymond E., and Steven J. Rosenstone. 1980. *Who Votes?* New Haven, CT: Yale University Press.

Woodward, C. Vann. 1951. *Reunion and Reaction: The Compromise of 1877 and the End of Reconstruction*. Boston: Little, Brown.

Wooldridge, Jeffrey M. 2001. *Econometric Analysis of Cross Section and Panel Data.* Cambridge, MA: MIT Press.

Wyatt, Edward. 2010. Veto Threat Raised over Derivatives. *New York Times*, April 16.

Index